STUDIES IN HINDU RELIGION

Studies in Hindu Religion

U.S. SHAJI

2008

CYBER TECH PUBLICATIONS
4264/3, Ansari Road, Daryaganj, New Delhi-110002 (India)
Ph.: 011-23244078. Fax: 011-23280028
E-Mail: cyberpublicationsdelhi@yahoo.com

Studies in Hindu Religion

First Edition 2008

Published by G.S. Rawat
For Cyber Tech Publications
4264/3, Ansari Road, Daryaganj, New Delhi - 110 002
E-mail : cyberpublicationsdelhi@yahoo.com
Phone : 011-23244078,
Fax : 011-23280028

Printed at
Amit Enterprises, Moujpur, Delhi. Ph. - 9810878184

Preface

India has a rich and unique cultural heritage, and has managed to preserve its established traditions throughout history. It has always absorbed customs, traditions and ideas from both invaders and immigrants. Many cultural practices, languages, customs and even monuments are examples of this co-mingling over centuries.

Indian society is largely pluralist, multilingual and multicultural. Diversity is a part of Indian way of life. From region to region, diversity in the social structure is prominently seen. The diversity factor notwithstanding, there is a common thread running through the Indians. Unity in diversity is best seen in India in a maze of seemingly disparate peoples.

In the long-drawn process of civilization in our sub-continent the trio-phenomenon of Culture, Religion and Traditions had complex innings which had deep bearing on numerous castes, races and creeds. In fact the societal existence depended upon a routine-like following on varied rituals of Hinduism, Buddhism, Jainism, Brahmanism and Islam. For several centuries these have been practised in one form or the other in the regions of India. Other factors which cemented the bonds of unity and discipline were the status of women and their role in domestic and non-domestic affairs, celebration of festivals, the mode of living and the over-all behaviour in society.

This book attempts to present exhaustive and elaborate details about Indian society and culture. It provides comprehensive information on the roots of Indian civilistion, the caste system, religion and faith, social relations, education, languages, arts and crafts, dance, music, fairs and festivals, status of women and so on. This work will be a valuable reference tool for teachers, students and researchers of social sciences and all who are interested in Indian society and culture.

—*Author*

Contents

1

INDIAN SOCIETY

India is justly famous for its complex social systems. Indian society is multifaceted to an extent perhaps unknown in any other of the world's great civilizations. Virtually no generalization made about Indian society is valid for all of the nation's multifarious groups. Comprehending the complexities of Indian social structure has challenged scholars and other observers over many decades.

The ethnic and linguistic diversity of Indian civilization is more like the diversity of an area as variable as Europe than like that of any other single nation-state. Living within the embrace of the Indian nation are vast numbers of different regional, social, and economic groups, each with different cultural practices. Particularly noteworthy are differences between social structures in the north and the south, especially in the realm of kinship systems. Throughout the country, religious differences can be significant, especially between the Hindu majority and the large Muslim minority; and other Indian groups--Buddhists, Christians, Jains, Jews, Parsis, Sikhs, and practitioners of tribal religions--all pride themselves on being unlike members of other faiths.

Access to wealth and power varies considerably, and vast differences in socioeconomic status are evident everywhere. The poor and the wealthy live side by side in urban and rural areas. It is common in city life to see a prosperous, well-fed man or woman chauffeured in a fine car pass gaunt street dwellers huddled beneath burlap shelters along the roadway. In many villages, solid cement houses of landowners rise not far from the flimsy thatched shacks of landless labourers. Even when not so obvious, distinctions of class are found in almost every settlement in India.

Urban-rural differences can be immense. Nearly 74 percent of India's population dwells in villages, with agriculture providing support for most of these rural residents. In villages, mud-plastered walls ornamented with traditional designs, dusty lanes, herds of grazing cattle, and the songs of birds at sunset provide typical settings for the social lives of most Indians. In India's great cities, however, millions of people live amidst cacophony--roaring vehicles, surging crowds, jammed apartment buildings, busy commercial establishments, loudspeakers blaring movie tunes--while breathing the poisons of industrial and automotive pollution.

Gender distinctions are pronounced. The behaviour expected of men and women can be quite different, especially in villages, but also in urban centres. Prescribed ideal gender roles help shape the actions of both sexes as they move between family and the world outside the home.

Crosscutting and pervading all of these differences of region, language, wealth, status, religion, urbanity, and gender is the special feature of Indian society that has received most attention from observers: caste. The people of India belong to thousands of castes and castelike groups--hierarchically ordered, named groups into which members are born. Caste members are expected to marry within the group and follow caste rules pertaining to diet, avoidance of ritual pollution, and many other aspects of life. Given the vast diversity of Indian society, any observation must be tempered with the understanding that it cannot apply to all Indians. Still, certain themes or underlying principles of life are widely accepted in India.

THE VILLAGE COMMUNITY

Scattered throughout India are approximately 500,000 villages. The Census of India regards most settlements of fewer than 5,000 as a village. These settlements range from tiny hamlets of thatched huts to larger settlements of tile-roofed stone and brick houses. Most villages are small; nearly 80 percent have fewer than 1,000 inhabitants, according to the 1991 census. Most are nucleated settlements, while others are more dispersed. It is in villages that India's most basic business--agriculture--takes place. Here, in the face of vicissitudes of all kinds, farmers follow time-tested as well as innovative methods of growing wheat, rice, lentils, vegetables, fruits, and many other crops in order to accomplish the challenging task of feeding themselves and the nation. Here, too, flourish many of India's most valued cultural forms.

Viewed from a distance, an Indian village may appear deceptively simple. A cluster of mud-plastered walls shaded by a few trees, set among a stretch of green or dun-coloured fields, with a few people slowly coming or going, oxcarts creaking, cattle lowing, and birds singing--all present an image of harmonious simplicity. Indian city dwellers often refer nostalgically to "simple village life." City artists portray colourfully garbed village women gracefully carrying water pots on their heads, and writers describe isolated rural settlements unsullied by the complexities of modern urban civilization. Social scientists of the past wrote of Indian villages as virtually self-sufficient communities with few ties to the outside world.

In actuality, Indian village life is far from simple. Each village is connected through a variety of crucial horizontal linkages with other villages and with urban areas both near and far. Most villages are characterized by a multiplicity of economic, caste, kinship, occupational, and even religious groups linked vertically within each settlement. Factionalism is a typical feature of village politics. In one of the first of the modern anthropological studies of Indian village life, anthropologist Oscar Lewis called this complexity "rural cosmopolitanism."

Throughout most of India, village dwellings are built very close to one another in a nucleated settlement, with small lanes for passage of people and sometimes carts. Village fields surround the settlement and are generally within easy walking distance. In hilly tracts of central, eastern, and far northern India, dwellings are more spread out, reflecting the nature of the topography. In the wet states of West Bengal and Kerala, houses are more dispersed; in some parts of Kerala, they are constructed in continuous lines, with divisions between villages not obvious to visitors.

In northern and central India, neighbourhood boundaries can be vague. The houses of Dalits are generally located in separate neighbourhoods or on the outskirts of the nucleated settlement, but there are seldom distinct Dalit hamlets. By contrast, in the south, where socioeconomic contrasts and caste pollution observances tend to be stronger than in the north, Brahman homes may be set apart from those of non-Brahmans, and Dalit hamlets are set at a little distance from the homes of other castes.

The number of castes resident in a single village can vary widely, from one to more than forty. Typically, a village is dominated by one or a very few castes that essentially control the village land and on whose patronage members of weaker groups must rely. In the village of about 1,100 population near Delhi studied by Lewis in the 1950s, the Jat caste (the largest cultivating caste in northwestern India) comprised 60 percent of the residents and owned all of the village land, including the house sites. In Nimkhera, Madhya Pradesh, Hindu Thakurs and Brahmans, and Muslim Pathans own substantial land, while lower-ranking Weaver (Koli) and Barber (Khawas) caste members and others own smaller farms. In many areas of the south, Brahmans are major landowners, along with some other relatively high-ranking castes. Generally, land, prosperity, and power go together.

In some regions, landowners refrain from using plows themselves but hire tenant farmers and labourers to do this work. In other regions, landowners till the soil with the aid of labourers, usually resident in the same village. Fellow villagers typically include representatives of various service and artisan castes to supply the needs of the villagers--priests, carpenters, blacksmiths, barbers, weavers, potters, oilpressers, leather-workers, sweepers, water-bearers, toddy-tappers, and so on. Artisanry in pottery, wood, cloth, metal, and leather, although diminishing, continues in many contemporary Indian villages as it did in centuries past. Village religious observances and weddings are occasions for members of various castes to provide customary ritual goods and services in order for the events to proceed according to proper tradition.

Aside from caste-associated occupations, villages often include people who practice nontraditional occupations. For example, Brahmans or Thakurs may be shopkeepers, teachers, truckers, or clerks, in addition to their caste-associated occupations of priest and farmer. In villages near urban areas, an increasing number of people commute to the cities to take up jobs, and many migrate. Some migrants leave their families in the village and go to the cities to work for months at a time. Many people from Kerala, as well as other regions, have temporarily migrated to the Persian Gulf states for employment and send remittances back to their village families, to which they will eventually return.

At slack seasons, village life can appear to be sleepy, but usually villages are humming with activity. The work ethic is strong, with little time out for relaxation, except for numerous divinely sanctioned festivals and rite-of-passage celebrations. Residents are quick to judge each other, and improper work or social habits receive strong criticism. Villagers feel a sense of village pride and honour, and the reputation of a village depends upon the behaviour of all of its residents.

URBAN AREAS

Accelerating urbanization is powerfully affecting the transformation of Indian society. Slightly more than 26 percent of the country's population is urban, and in 1991 more than half of urban dwellers lived in 299 urban agglomerates or cities of more than 100,000 people. By 1991 India had twenty-four cities with populations of at least 1 million. By that year, among cities of the world, Bombay (or Mumbai, in Marathi), in Maharashtra, ranked seventh in the world at 12.6 million, and Calcutta, in West Bengal, ranked eighth at almost 11 million. In the 1990s, India's larger cities have been growing at twice the rate of smaller towns and villages. Between the 1960s and 1991, the population of the Union Territory of Delhi quadrupled, to 8.4 million, and Madras, in Tamil Nadu, grew to 5.4 million. Bangalore, in Karnataka; Hyderabad, in Andhra Pradesh; and many other cities are expanding rapidly. About half of these increases are the result of rural-urban migration, as villagers seek better lives for themselves in the cities.

Most Indian cities are very densely populated. New Delhi, for example, had 6,352 people per square kilometre in 1991. Congestion, noise, traffic jams, air pollution, and major shortages of key necessities characterize urban life. Every major city of India faces the same proliferating problems of grossly inadequate housing, transportation, sewerage, electric power, water supplies, schools, and hospitals. Slums and jumbles of pavement dwellers' lean-tos constantly multiply. An increasing number of trucks, buses, cars, three-wheel autorickshaws, motorcycles, and motorscooters, all spewing uncontrolled fumes, surge in sometimes haphazard patterns over city streets jammed with jaywalking pedestrians, cattle, and goats. Accident rates are high (India's fatality rate from road accidents, the most common cause of accidental death, is said to be twenty times higher than United States rates), and it is a daily occurrence for a city dweller to witness a crash or the running down of a pedestrian. In 1984 the citizens of Bhopal suffered the nightmare of India's largest industrial accident, when poisonous gas leaking from a Union Carbide plant killed and injured thousands of city dwellers. Less spectacularly, on a daily basis, uncontrolled pollutants from factories all over India damage the urban environments in which millions live.

THE DECLINE OF FEUDALISM

Feudalism's decline in India may be said to date from the inability of Indian feudalism to defend the country against British penetration. To be sure, the British conquered and held the country by means of an Indian army, paid from India's resources and under British discipline; though in this respect the feudal powers of the day were not so different as might at first appear, since their own armies, also maintained at Indian expense, were often staffed by European drill sergeants and artillery experts. The difference-and it was a crucial difference-was that the British paid all their soldiers regularly in cash every month, in war or peace, paying also for supplies acquired during the march or for the barracks. The contrast is pointed up by the opposing Indian factions that fought the Battle of Panipat (A.D. 1761). Ahmad Shah Durrani's soldiers mutinied after winning the battle because they had not been paid for years; while their opponents, the Marathas, maintained themselves by looting the countryside. Faced with opposition of this kind, British-led arms were bound to triumph. (The same contrast-again involving the spoils of India, though indirectly-could be observed a few years later when the British defeated Napoleon in Spain; the French army lived off the countryside while the British used their superior wealth, much of it extracted from India, to pay the very Spaniards they were defending for all supplies.)

Indian feudalism tried its strength against the British bourgeoisie for the last time in the unsuccessful rebellion of 1857. Soon thereafter, the British abandoned their long-standing policy of liquidating feudal principalities and instead began to bolster up remaining regimes of this kind-provided they were weak enough to be dependent and hence compliant. Marx noted that the very same people who fought in the British Parliament against aristocratic privilege at home voted to maintain far worse rajahs and nabobs in India-as a matter of policy, for profit.

Despite British support, and in a sense because of it, Indian feudalism no longer had any independent strength and vitality of its own. Its economic basis had been ruined by the construction of railroads, the decay of village industry, the establishment of a system of fixed assessment of land values and payment of taxes in cash rather than in kind, the importation of commodities from England, and the introduction of mechanised production in Indian cities. The role of the village usurer changed. Previously he had been an integral part of the village economy, but he had been legally obliged to cancel a debt on which total repayment amounted to double the original loan: there was no redress against default since land could not be alienated nor could a feudal lord be brought to court. With British rule came survey and registry of land plots, cash taxes, cash crops for large-scale export to a world market (indigo, cotton, jute, tea, tobacco, opium), registration of debts and mortgages, alienability of the peasants' land-in a word, the framework within which land could gradually be converted into capitalist private property which the former usurer could acquire and rent out and exploit.

How thoroughly British rule undermined Indian feudalism has been dramatically demonstrated by events of recent years. The police action undertaken in 1948 by India's central government against Hyderabad, the largest and most powerful remaining feudal state, was over in two days. Political action in Travancore and Mysore, direct intervention in Junagadh and Kashmir, indirect intervention in Nepal, the absorption of Sikkim, the jailing of Saurashtra barons as common criminals-all these events showed that feudal privilege meant nothing before the new paramount power, the Indian bourgeoisie.

It should not be overlooked, however, that the decline of Indian feudalism had another side to it-the partial amalgamation of the old ruling class into the new. Just as the rise of factories and mechanised production converted primitive barter into commodity production and the usurer's hoard into capital, so too it opened a way for the feudal lord to join the capitalist class by turning his jewellery and his hoarded wealth into landed or productive capital. What the feudal lord could not do was to claim additional privileges not available to the ordinary investor, or any rights that would impede the free movement of Indian industrial or financial capital. This process of converting feudal lords into capitalists began relatively early: even before World War I, the Gaekwar of Baroda became one of the world's richest men by investing his large feudal revenues in factories, railways, and company shares.

Another process involving the liquidation of feudalism is exemplified by what has been happening since independence in the Gangetic basin. There the East India Company had created the class of Zamindars, tax collectors whose function was to extract tribute in kind from the peasants and convert it into cash payments to the company. As time went on, the Zamindars acquired the status and privileges of landholders and in return provided valuable political support for British rule. In recent years, a new class of capitalist landlords and well-to-do peasants of the kulak variety has been substituted for the zamindars by legislative action (the zamindars, of course, receiving compensation for their expropriated holdings).

Everywhere in India, by one means or another, feudal wealth has already become or is rapidly becoming capital, either of the owner or of his creditors. [Every feudalism known to history rested, in the final analysis, upon primitive handicraft production, and upon a special type of land ownership. The former of these is no longer basic in India, and the latter does not exist.] Talk of fighting feudalism today is on a level with talk of fighting dinosaurs. No part of the mechanism of coercion is now in feudal hands. The legislature is bourgeois (and petty bourgeois) in composition. The armed forces, the police, the judiciary are all directly under bourgeois control, where these functions would formerly have been carried out by feudal levies, retainers, or the feudal lords themselves. Even the beginnings of capitalist production in agriculture may be seen, notably the introduction of tractor cultivation in Uttar Pradesh and Gujarat, but with smaller manifestations all over the country, especially where industrial crops like cotton are grown and where transport conditions are exceptionally favourable.

The liquidation of Indian feudalism, then, is general and complete. But it is necessary to guard against drawing unwarranted conclusions from this undoubted fact. The older privilege is being replaced or expropriated only with the due compensation. No basic improvement has been effected in the condition of the rural population, still the overwhelming majority of the Indian nation. All agrarian reforms-community schemes, voluntary (bhoodan) redistribution of land, scaling-down of peasant indebtedness, counter-erosion measures, afforestation, and so forth-have turned out to be piddling. Hunger, unemployment, epidemic disease remain the permanent and massive features of Indian society. The sole achievements have been the elimination of older property forms (with recruitment of most former owners into the bourgeoisie) and the creation of a vast class of workers with no land and no prospect of absorption into industry as long as the social structure of India remains what it is.

BOURGEOISIE AND PETTY BOURGEOISIE

Except possibly in a few negligible corners of recently integrated backward areas, Indian production today is bourgeois 'in the sense that commodity production is prevalent and even a small plot of land is valued and taxed in rupees. But it is still petty production, consisting for the most part of the growing of foodstuffs from small holdings by primitive, inefficient methods; the produce is still largely consumed by the producer or in the locality of production.

Nevertheless, the petty bourgeoisie, inhomogeneous as it is in all but its greed, completely dominates food production and, through middlemen, controls the supply to towns and cities. Though roads and other means of communication have increased, still the density of the transportation network i$ very low by American, British, or Japanese standards. The present national Five Year Plan estimates the annual national income at 90 billion rupees (one rupee equals 21 cents), which it proposes to increase to 100 billion by 1956.

But the total value of all productive assets in private hands (excluding fields and houses for rent, but including plantations) is estimated at no more than 15 billion rupees, while the central and local governments' own facilities are worth more than 13 billion rupees in the field of transport, electricity, broadcasting and other means of communication, and so on. These figures prove conclusively the petty-bourgeois nature of the economy as a whole and indicate clearly that the industrialisation of India under bourgeois management can proceed only through tight cooperation between government and private capital.

Therefore, the fact that the government is the biggest capitalist, the main banker, the greatest employer, and the ultimate refuge or ineffable solace of the bootlicking intelligentsia makes for only a formal, superficial, difference. The main question to ask is: what special class-interest does this government serve? Whenever it seems to rise above the classes, or act against the bourgeois interests, does it go beyond regulating individual greed, or at most holding the balance between the petty and the big bourgeoisie? Do the government's ineffective food regulations and costly food imports mean anything beyond assuring the petty-bourgeois food-producer his pound of vital flesh while the cities are supplied with food cheap enough for the industrial labourer to maintain himself at subsistence level on the wages the factory owners are willing to pay?

The government today is undoubtedly in the hands of the bigger bourgeoisie, a fact which is shown no less by its personnel than by its policies which favour Big Business and impose only such restraints as serve the interests of the subclass as a whole and prevent any single capitalist group from dominating the rest. Moreover, there is no question that the big bourgeoisie wants industrialisation. In this connection, it is interesting to recall the economic plan hopefully drawn up (with the aid of tame economists) by the biggest capitalists and promulgated in 1944 (published at that time as a Penguin Special, No. S148). The scheme, to be financed from unspecified sources, called for a 500 per cent increase in industry, a 130 per cent increase in agriculture, and a 200 per cent increase in "services" within 15 years.

The basic figures used by planners, however, related to the year 1932 and were hence way out of date. Not only did wartime inflation and its aftermath balloon the national income beyond the dreams of the capitalist planners, but the planned agricultural output would not have sufficed to feed the population even at starvation levels (for some years after the war, India was obliged to import a billion rupees worth of food annually and the imports still continue irregularly).

To a far greater extent than is generally realised, the big Indian bourgeoisie owes its present position to two war periods of heavy profit making. World War I gave Indian capital its first great impetus and initiated the process of Indianising the bureaucracy. World War II vastly expanded the army and Indianised the officer corps; further, it swelled the tide of Indian accumulation and enabled the capitalists, by rallying the masses behind the Congress Party, to complete the process of pushing the British out of the country. How great the accumulation was during the most recent war and postwar period of inflation is indicated by changes in the relative importance of different taxes as sources of revenue: the agricultural (land) tax now accounts for less than eight per cent of total state revenue as compared to 25 per cent in 1939, while taxes on what by Indian standards may be called luxury goods (including automobiles) rose from negligible importance to 17 per cent of the total in the same period. [The government asked in 1957 for appropriations about 100 times the central budget at the beginning of World War II. The other side of the coin as always in periods of marked inflation, has been a decline in the real income of workers and other low-income groups. It is interesting to note that the current national Five Year Plan aims to restore the general living standard of 1939-then universally recognised as totally inadequate-without, of course curtailing the immense new power and wealth that have accrued to the bourgeoisie in the intervening years.

We encounter here one of the basic contradictions of the Indian economy, the decisive roadblock to rapid development under present conditions. The civilised money-makers of advanced capitalist countries are accustomed to looking on a five percent return as something akin to a law of nature, but not so their Indian counterparts. The usual rate of return on black-market operations in recent years is 150 percent, and even the most respectable capitalist's idea of a "reasonable" profit is anywhere from 9 to 20 percent. [The very same capitalists who ask for and obtain tariff protection for their manufactures even before beginning to produce them for the market do not hesitate to hoard smuggled gold and jewellery to the tune of (a reasonably estimated) 100 million rupees per year. This not only shows their contempt for their own government, its laws, and its plans for industrialisation in the 'private sector', but further illustrates the petty bourgeois mentality even in the wealthiest Indians.]

This kind of profiteering, however, is incompatible with the balanced development of India's economy as a whole. Seventy percent of the population still works on the land or lives off it, holdings being mostly less than two acres per family and cultivated by primitive methods. Wages are low and prevented from rising by the relative surplus population which is always pressing for available jobs. In the countryside, at least 50 percent of the population is made up of landless labourers. These conditions spell low mass purchasing power and restricted markets. When even these restricted markets are ruthlessly exploited by a capitalist class snatching at immediate maximum profits, the result can only be industrial stagnation and growing poverty.

And indeed this is precisely what we observe in fact. Idle plant is widespread; night shifts have disappeared in most textile mills; other industries show machinery and equipment used to 50 percent of capacity or even less. It is the familiar capitalist dilemma, but in a peculiarly acute form: increase of poverty and idle resources but with no adequate incentives to invest in the expanded production which is so desperately needed.

This is the pass to which bourgeois rule has brought India. There is no apparent escape within the framework of the bourgeois mode of production. [The situation was changed for a while by the "pump-priming" of the First Five-Year plan-a curious jump from a colonial to a pseudo-New-Deal economy; but future prospects are decidedly gloomier.]

COLONIALISM AND FOREIGN DOMINATION

In a sense the tragedy of the Indian bourgeoisie is that it came of age too late, at a time when the whole capitalist world was in a state of incurable crisis and when one-third of the globe had already abandoned capitalism forever.

In fact, the Five Year Plans mentioned above are self-contradictory in that they are obviously inspired by the great successes of Soviet planning without, however, taking any account of the necessity of socialism to the achievement of these successes: effective planning cannot leave the private investor free to invest when and where he likes, as is done in India, nor can its main purpose be to assure him of profitable opportunities for the investment of his capital. The Indian bourgeoisie cannot be compared to that of England at the time of the Industrial Revolution, nor to that of Japan during the late 19th and early 20th centuries, nor again to that of Germany from the time of Bismarck. There are no great advances in science that can be taken advantage of by a country with preponderant illiteracy and no colonies to exploit. Under the circumstances, as we have already seen, rapid industrialisation runs into the insuperable obstacle of a narrowly restricted domestic market.

Do all these unfavourable facts mean that capitalist India must inevitably fall under the domination of foreign industrialists and financiers with their control over the shrinking capitalist world market? Must we see signs of such a relapse into colonial status when, for example, the Indian government invites powerful foreign capitalist groups to invest in oil refineries on terms apparently more favourable than those granted to Indian capital, including guarantees against nationalisation?

The bogey of a new economic colonialism can be quickly disposed of. For one thing, the Indian bourgeoisie is no longer bound to deal with one particular foreign capitalist power, and the answer to stiff terms from the United States and Britain has already been found in the drive to recovery of Germany and Japan. The Indian government has invited Krupp-Demag to set up a steel plant; the Tata combine comes to quite reasonable terms with Krauss. Maffei for locomotive works and foundries, and with Daimler-Benz for equipment to manufacture diesel-engine transport.

The more advanced capitalist powers, in short, can be played off against each other (and even better against the USSR), as they could not be in the days of British rule. And for another thing, the guarantees against nationalisation granted to the great British and American oil monopolies are really no more than Indian Big Business itself enjoys. The only industries that have been nationalised in India are those which, in private hands, hinder the development of larger capital (for example, road transport in Bombay State, taken over without compensation) or those in which there was danger of big investors losing money (for example, the nationalisation of civil aviation, with heavy compensation to the former owners).

The Indian bourgeoisie has taken its own precautions against genuine nationalisation and hardly needs to give itself the formal guarantees demanded by foreign capitalists. [Perhaps, the strongest of these, and the most crippling to the supposedly planned advance towards socialism, is the systematic creation of revenue deficits. The first deliberate step in this direction, taken as a sweeping measure in Bombay state (where the bourgeoisie is at its strongest) was the costly, wasteful, and palpably inefficient prohibition policy. Now, deficit state budgets seem quite the normal fashion, while parallel outcries against the Five Year Plan become louder].

No, the invitation to foreign capital does not mean sudden, unaccountable lunacy on the part of those now in power, those who fought so desperately only a few years ago to remove foreign capitalist control from India. Entry is not permitted in fields where Indians have investments and mastery of technique, as for example in textiles. Even in the new fields opened up to the foreigners-fields in which Indians lack both know-how and the assurance of sufficiently large and quick returns to justify heavy investment-a "patriotic" strike or two could ruin the foreign enterprises should they ever become a threat or a nuisance to the Indian bourgeoisie. Fissionable materials (uranium, monazite, ilmenite) which foreign interests wanted to buy at the price of dirt are being processed by a company financed by the government and directed by Tatas. (On the other hand, high-grade Indian manganese ore is still being exported unrefined for lack of a sufficiently strong profit incentive to Indian capital).

THE ALTERNATIVE

Invitations to foreign capital, however, do have one function in addition to that of giving a fillip to industrialisation (which could have been secured by inviting much more technical aid from the USSR and the People's Democracies). That additional function is to provide a measure of insurance against popular revolt.

The Indian bourgeoisie shows unmistakable signs of fearing its own masses. The leading bourgeois party (the Congress) has not yet exhausted the reservoir of prestige built up during the period of its leadership in the struggle for national independence.

In addition, the bourgeoisie controls the bureaucracy, the army, the police, the educational system, and the larger part of the press. And there are the opposition bourgeois parties, like the Praja-Socialists, which can be relied upon to talk Left and act Right, to win election on an anti-Congress platform and then turn around immediately after to a policy of cooperation with Congress politicians, as they did after the Travancore-Cochin elections last spring.

Nevertheless, "defence" expenditures continue to take about two billion rupees a year, about half the central budget (and a half that the Five Year Plans do not even mention); and police expenditures mount strangely and rapidly under the direction of those who took power in the name of Gandhian nonviolence. Extra-legal ordinances, (against which the bourgeoisie protested so vigorously when the British first applied them to suppressing Indian nationalism), are actually strengthened now for use against the working class; the Press Acts remain in force; and on the very eve of the first general election, important civil liberties were removed from a constitution on which the ink was scarcely dry.

All these factors together, however, will not prevent rapid disillusionment at promises unfulfilled, nor the inevitable mass protest against hunger, the ultimate Indian reality. There may come a time when the Indian army, officered by Indian bourgeois and aided by a transport system designed for an army of occupation, may not suffice. The Indian capitalists calculate, quite understandably, that it is safer to have foreigners interested so that they could be called upon to intervene with armed force in case of necessity.

But note that neither special political rights, nor monopolies, nor military bases have been given to any foreign power, and that even those (France and Portugal, backed by the United States and Britain) which still have pockets on Indian soil are being vigorously pushed out, by popular action as well as by politico-diplomatic demands. Colonial status would mean foreign control of Indian raw materials and domination of the Indian market, both today unmistakably at the hands of the Indian capitalists themselves. And there is always the hope that a third world war will lead to even more fantastic profits for a neutral India-as the ruling class dreams of neutrality.

The solution for India, of course, would, be socialism, which alone can create a demand rising with the supply, a solution which can be utilised not only by advanced countries but by backward countries (as China is demonstrating), and without which planning is futile. But just as the Indian bourgeoisie imports the latest foreign machinery for production, so, when all else fails, the latest capitalist developments in politics will also be imported. And this means fascism, in the long run the only possible alternative to socialism. Already the talk in circles that count is of the need for a "strong man." And models are at hand, from nearby Thailand to faraway Egypt and Guatemala.

Monthly Review (New York), vol. 6, 1954, pp. 205-213. Nationalism, and its logical extension provincialism, are manifestations of the bourgeoisie. In the feudal period, the Peshwas defeated the Nizam more than once, but saw nothing wrong in leaving Marathi-speaking regions in the Nizam's possession. The political reorganisation of India on a linguistic basis into new states was thus an index of bourgeoisie development and competition.

The in-violability of private property as guaranteed by the Constitution no longer suffices. Each local bourgeoisie wants full political control over its own hinterland to safeguard investments and to exclude powerful competitors. This was seen in the bitter strife over the creation-not even by pretence of freely expressed public opinion, but by police action--of the new, enlarged, hybrid, anomalous, bi-lingual state of Bombay. The quarrel passed off as one between Gujarathi and Maharashtrian. The real fight, however, was between the veteran, entrenched capital of Bombay city, and the newer money of Ahmedabad. The Maharashtra petty-bourgeoisie remained characteristically helpless in disunity, to the end. Those who doubt that the big bourgeoisie can do what it likes with the government might give some thought to the TELCO affairs being discussed publicly (for the first time) since September 5, 1957.

The chances of fascism have not been diminished by the 1957 election. These showed that the only state government able to show an honest, incorruptible, bourgeois administration, able to raise funds without deficit finance for an honest attempt to carry out the Nehru policy was led by the communists in Kerala. In addition, this regime had at least made a start towards dealing with the most serious fundamental questions: food, agrarian production, re-division of land, employment, education, yet within the bourgeoisie framework, without touching bourgeois property relations. The dangers of this example cannot have escaped the brighter minds of the ruling class, whose cleverness far outstrips their honesty.

2

DEMOGRAPHICS OF INDIA

This population is remarkably diverse; it has more than two thousand ethnic groups, and every major religion is represented, as are four major families of languages (Indo-European, Dravidian, Austro-Asiatic and Tibeto-Burman languages) as well as two language isolates (Nihali and the Burushaski language spoken in disputed parts of Jammu & Kashmir).

Further complexity is lent by the great variation that occurs across this population on social parameters such as income and education. These factors render the task of comprehensively detailing the Demographics of India prohibitive; some important indices are available, nevertheless.

SALIENT FEATURES

Although India occupies only 2.4% of the world's land area, it supports over 16% of the world's population. Currently it is the second most populous nation on Earth, though if current trends persist, India will replace China as the most populous nation in less than 40 years.

Almost 40% of Indians are younger than 15 years of age. More than 70% of the people live in more than 550,000 villages, and the remainder in more than 200 towns and cities.

Over thousands of years of its history, India has had invasions and migrations from the Middle East, Central Asia and the West, as well as migrations from Tibet and southern China; Indian people and culture have absorbed and changed these influences to produce a remarkable racial and cultural synthesis.

Religion, caste, and language are major determinants of social and political organization in India today. The government has recognized 22 languages as official; Hindi is the most widely spoken. India also has the second largest number of English speakers in the world, after the US, with over 60 million people speaking English in India. Many millions more have a rudimentary knowledge of English.

Although 82.0% of the people are Hindus, India is also home to the second-largest Muslim population in the world (13.1%). India also contains the majority of the world's Zoroastrians (0.01%), Sikhs (1.94%) and Jains (0.40%). Other religious groups include Christians (2.3%), Buddhists (0.76%), Jews and Bahais.

The caste system reflects Indian occupational and socio-religiously defined hierarchies. Traditionally, there are four broad categories of castes (varnas), including a category of outcastes, earlier called "untouchables" but now commonly referred to as "dalits." Within these broad categories there are thousands of castes and subcastes, called jatis, whose relative status varies from region to region.

Despite economic modernization and laws countering discrimination against the lower end of the class structure, the caste system remains an important source of social identification for most Hindus and many non-Hindus as well, thus making it a potent factor in the political life of the country.

CENSUS

The most recent census of India was performed in 2001. It was the 14th census in an unbroken series, and the 6th after independence in 1947 (except for Assam which did not figure in the 1981 census). Eight censuses were performed under the British Raj, the first one was carried out throughout the 1860s and completed in 1871. After this, there has been one census every decade.

The 2001 census was conducted in two phases, the first being Housenumbering and Houselisting operations, carried out in May 2000, and the second being population enumeration, carried out from February 9 to 28, 2001.

The reference time for the census is 1 March, 2001. The houseless population was enumerated on 28 February. A revisional round was undertaken 1 to 5 March 2001 to account for mutations between the time of visit in February and 1 March.

The total population calculated for 1 March 2001 was 1,027,015,247, making the 2001 census the first to count more than a billion Indians.

The population had risen by 21.34% compared to the 1991 total. The female population had increased by 0.3 percentage points to 48.4%.

Maharashtra has the largest urban agglomeration while Delhi is the most urbanised market at over 93%.

KEY DATA

Population: 1,128,000,000 (July 2006 est.); 1,027,000,000 (2001 Census)

Rural Population: 742,617,747 (72.2%)

Male: 381,668,992,

Female: 360,948,755 (2001 Census)

Table: Population History

Year	*Total Population*
1960	443,000,000
1970	553,000,000
1980	684,000,000
1990	838,141,000
2000	1,004,591,054
2005	1,095,054,669
2007	1,129,866,154
2010	1,184,000,000
2020	1,364,000,000
2030	1,532,000,000
2040	1,684,000,000
2050	1,807,000,000

Table: Population Projections (in millions)

Year	*Under 15*	*15-64*	*65+*	*Total*
2000	361	604	45	1010
2005	368	673	51	1093
2010	370	747	58	1175
2015	372	819	65	1256
2020	373	882	76	1331

Source: Based on P.N. Mari Bhat, "Indian Demographic Scenarion 2025", Institute of Economic Growth, New Delhi, Discussion Paper No. 27/2001.

Urban: Age structure:

0-14 years: 30.8% (male 173,478,760/female 163,852,827)

15-64 years: 64.3% (male 363,876,219/female 340,181,764)

65 years and over: 4.9% (male 27,258,020/female 26,704,405) (2006 est.)

The average age of Indians is 26 years.

Population Growth Rate: 1.38% (2006 est.)

Birth Rate: 22.01 births/1,000 population (2006 est.)

Death Rate: 8.18 deaths/1,000 population (2006 est.)

Literacy Rate: 79.9%

Percent of the population under the poverty line: 22% (2006 est.)

Unemployment Rate: 9.2%

Sex Ratio:

At Birth: 1.05 male(s)/female

Under 15 Years: 1.06 male(s)/female

15-64 Years: 1.07 male(s)/female

65 Years and Over: 1.02 male(s)/female

Total Population: 1.06 male(s)/female (2006 est.)

Infant Mortality Rate:

Total: 54.63 deaths/1,000 live births female: 55.18 deaths/1,000 live births (2006 est.) male: 54.05 deaths/ 1,000 live births

Life Expectancy at Birth:

***Total Population*:** 64.71 years

***Male*:** 63.9 years

***Female*:** 65.57 years (2006 est.)

Total Fertility Rate: 2.73 children born/woman (2006 est.) The TFR (Totalnumber of children born per women) according to Religion in 2001 was:

Hindus-2.27, Muslims-3.06, Sikhs-1.86, X'ians-2.06, Budhists-2.29, Jains-1.50, Animists and Others-2.99, Tribals-3.16, Scheduled Castes-2.89.

Nationality:

Noun: Indian(s)

Adjective: Indian

Religions:

Hindu 82%, Muslim 12.20%, Christian 2.31%, Sikh 2.00%, Buddhists 0.77%, Jains 0.41 %,

Others or not stated 0.76% (2001 Census)

Scheduled Castes and Tribes: Scheduled Castes: 16.2% (2001 Census) Scheduled Tribes: 8.2% (2001 Census)

Languages: There are 216 languages with more than 10,000 native speakers in India. The largest of these by far is Hindi with some 337 million (the second largest being Telugu with some 80 million). 22 languages are recognized as "official languages". In India, there are 1,652 languages and dialects in total.

RELIGIOUS BREAKDOWN

Censuses were conducted in India in ancient times with examples such as Kautilya's Arthashastra which describes the collection of population statistics for taxation.

The British census in 1871 was the first conducted in modern times in India.

1. All figures in %.
2. Gender Ratio*: no of females/1000 males
3. Others includes Jews, Parsis and Bahais
4. Tribal Animists (and non religious) are grouped under Others after 1926 (1931 census onwards)

Table: Census Information for 2006

Composition	Hindus	Muslims	Christians	Sikhs	Buddhists	Jains	Others
% total of population 2001	81.50	12.70	2.31	2.00	0.77	0.41	0.76
10-Yr Growth % (est '91-'01)	20.3	36.0	22.6	18.2	24.5	26	NA
Gender ratio* (avg. 944)	935	936	1009	893	953	950	992
Literacy rate (avg. 79.9)	75.1	69.1	90.3	79.4	82.7	100.0	49.6
Work Participation Rate	40	31.3	40	37.7	40	32.9	NA
Rural gender ratio	944	953	1001	895	958	937	995
Urban gender ratio	894	907	1026	886	944	941	966
Child gender ratio (0-6 yrs)	925	950	964	786	942	870	927

However, some unofficial estimates claim a higher figure of Muslim population supposedly discounted in Censuses. For instance, in an interview with a well circulated newspaper of India The Hindu Justice K.M. Yusuf, a retired Judge from Calcutta High Court and Chairman of West Bengal Minority Commission, says that the real percentage of Muslims in India is at least 20%. On the other hand, some believe that Muslim population figures are exaggerated due to various reasons. For instance, As per Syed Shahabuddin, a diplomat-turned-politician, a Muslim scholar and one of the members in the All India Muslim Personal Law Board, both Hindu and Muslim 'spokesmen', speaking for their respective communities amplify and exaggerate the Muslim population in India, the first, to convince their followers about the rising 'Islamic menace', a threat to the country and at least to its Hindu character, the second, to raise the morale of a politically deprived, educationally backward, economically poor and socially vilified, frustrated community.

3

ETHNIC GROUPS

Unlike the USA, UK, and Australian Censuses, the national Census of India does not recognize racial or ethnic groups within India but recognizes many of the tribal groups as Scheduled Castes and Tribes. Organizations and individuals not affiliated with India's national census have classified India into racial/ethnic groups. These racial and ethnic groups are debated. According to the Joshua Project, there are 2,334 ethnic groups in India. The Indian people are descended from more or less all of the peoples that historically settled the subcontinent, including the Caucasiod groups of Dravidians, Indo-Aryans, Iranians, Bactrians, Europeans, Greeks, Hepthalites, Arabs, the Australoid Austro-Asiatics, the Mongoloid Tibeto-Burmans, Kushans, Turks, Mughals, and a few African Siddis exist as well.

It should be noted that Dravidian, Indo-Aryan, Austro-Asiatic and Tibeto-Burman are linguistic terms and cannot be directly taken as ethnic terms. It simply means a speaker of a language belonging to a particular linguistic family. The speakers of these languages descend from a plethora of different ethnic groups that eventually adopted one or more set of languages. The imprint of each of these groups can be found in at least some small segments of the population, but at the same time over a long period of time these superficial differences in appearances have blurred to a great extent. The framework of the culture of the Indian people comes from these various peoples who contributed to Indian civilization as it is today.

RACIAL GROUPS IN INDIA

This article presents some historical definitions of race in India. Most of these theories are pre-1940 and only of historical interest now. The scientific support for terms such as Caucasoid, Negroid, Mongoloid used widely in these theories has fallen steadily. Where 78 percent of the articles in the 1931 Journal of Physical Anthropology employed these or similar synonymous terms reflecting a bio-race paradigm, only 36 percent did so in 1965, and just 28 percent did in 1996.

Since the 1940s, the evolutionary scientists have rejected the view of race. Also, it should be noted that the national Census of India does not recognize any racial groups in India. In India, the Dravidian, Indo-Aryans and similar words are generally considered as linguistic terms, rather than ethnic terms. Pre-colonial Indian literature and traditions make no such racial classifications. Throughout most anthropological research, the so-called "Indo-Aryan" and "Dravidian" groups are identified as members of the same race (but perhaps of different subraces.)

IDEA THAT MANY MORE RACIAL GROUPS EXIST

Richard McCulloch: Richard McCulloch (born 1949) is an author, who proposes racial separatism. He divides Indian people into three races.

- Indic race, North India
- Dravidic race, Central India
- Veddoid race, South India

Risley (1881): British anthropologist Sir Herbert Hope Risley's Racial Classification of India (1881) is as follows.

- Mongoloid
- Dravidian
- Indo-Aryans
- Turko-Iranian
- Mongolo-Dravidian
- Aryo-Dravidian
- Scytho-Dravidian

Hodson and Wyse: In Analysis of the 1931 Census of India (Government of India Press, 1937), Prof. Thomas Callan Hodson (1871-1953) and William Wyse (Professor of Social Anthropology, Fellow, St. Catharine's College, Cambridge), analysed the physical types in India, in great detail. This analysis was independent of the castes, and Brahmins and Dalits were classified in the same racial groups. For example, Telugu Brahmins and Chamars were classified as Racial Element A.

Hodson and Wyse believed that the earliest occupants of India were probably of the Negrito race, followed by the proto-Australoids. Later, an early stock probably of the Mediterranean race, came to India and mingled with the proto-australoids. These people spoke an agglutinative tongue from which the present Austro-Asiatic languages are derived. They had a rudimentary knowledge of agriculture, building stone monuments, and primitive navigation. This migration was followed by an immigration of civilised Mediterraneans from the Persian Gulf (ultimately from Eastern Europe). These people had the knowledge of the metals, but not of iron. They were followed by later waves of immigrants who developed the Indus valley civilization. All these immigrants were of the dolichocephalic type, but the Indus valley people had a mixed brachycephalic element coming from the Anatolian plateau, in the form of the Armenoid branch of the Alpine race. These people probably spoke the Dravidian languages. Later, a brachycephalic race speaking perhaps an Indo-European language of the "Pisacha or Dardic family", migrated to India from the Iranian plateau and the Pamirs. During about 1500 B.C., the Indo-Aryans migrated into Northern India.

Hudson and Wyse stated that, broadly, seven racial elements are present in Indian people:

Racial Element A: Characterized by short-stature, long-head with high cranial vault but faintly marked supra-orbital ridges and broad, short but ortho-gnathous face, with medium lips. The nose is prominent and long but the alae moderately spread out, giving a mesorrhine index. The skin colour varies from light brown to dark tawny brown. The eye colour is dark brown, and the hair colour is usually black. The authors stated the Telugu Brahmins, "Kallas of Southern Tamil country" and the "Illuvas of Cochin" (Ezhava) as examples. They said that this element is predominant in the lower stratum of the population of Northern India, including to some extent the Punjab (for example, Chubra and Chamar, which appear to be closely related to the Mediterranean stock of Europe)

Racial Element B: A Brachycephalic element of medium stature with flattened occiput but having also high head and not infrequently receding forehead. Characterized by short and orthognathous, but somewhat broader face. "The nose is long and quite often arched and convex".

The skin colour varies from a pale white to light brown. The eye colour is usually dark brown, but a small per cent shows light eyes. The hair colour is black with a small proportion showing a dark brown tint. The hair is generally straight and the pilous system well developed. The examples given by the authors included the Nagar Brahmins of Gujarat, the Kayastha of Bengal and the Kannada non-Brahmins.

Racial Element C: A long-headed strain with comparatively lower but longer head and tall stature and possessing a long face and prominent narrow long nose. The skin colour varies from a rosy white tint to light transparent brown. The eye colour is usually grey-blue, and the hair colour is chestnut. A small proportion of people have light eyes and brownish hair. Among this type also the hair is usually straight and the pilous system well developed. The examples stated by the authors included the "Northwest Himalayan tribes like the Kaffirs and the Pathans", the Sikhs of the Punjab, and the Brahmins of U. P.

Racial Element D: A short and moderately high-headed strain with very often strongly marked brow ridges, broad short face, the mouth slightly inclined forwards and small flat nose with the alae extended. The hair varies from wavy to curliness and the skin is of a shade of dark chocolate brown approaching black.

The examples given were the aboriginal tribes of Central and Southern India, including Bhils and the Chenchus. The authors also stated that this strain seems to have entered in a considerable degree in the lower stratum of the Indian population. The authors also believed that this type is closely related to the Veddas of Ceylon, the Toalas of Celebes, and the Sakais of the Malay Peninsula. The Aborigines of Australia were considered a primitive form of this type by the authors.

Racial Element E: A dark Pygmy strain having spirally curved hair. The examples given were the Kadars, the Pulayans, and the Angairti Nagas. The authors stated that the Andamanese are racially homogeneous and of distinct type, characterised by a dwarfish stature, black complexion and woolly hair.

Racial Element F: A brachycephalic Mongoloid type, having. The authors stated that the Mongoloid racial strain does not appear to have entered in any considerable extent in mainland Indians. It is found along the sub-Himalayan region of North-Eastern Kashmir to Bhutan. The type that forms the dominant element in Burma (which was then a part of British India) is also brachycephalic but somewhat shorter in stature and having a short flat nose and a tendency to alveolar prognathism. It appears to exhibit certain affinities with the Siamese, the Malay and the Cochin Chinese.

Racial Element G: A second Mongoloid strain characterised by medium stature, longish head and medium nose, but exhibiting like the typical Mongoloid characteristics of the face and eye. Examples given were people of Assam and Northern Burma, including the Angami Nagas and the Mikir-Bodo people.

Dr. B. S. Guha's Classification: Dr. Biraja Sankar Guha (1894-1961), an eminent Indian anthropologist, believed that the population of India is derived from six main ethnic groups.

Negritos: Guha stated that the Negritos or the Brachycephalic (broad headed) people from Africa were the earliest inhabitants of India. They have survived in their original habitation in Andaman and Nicobar Islands. The Jarawa, Onge, Sentinelese, and the Great Andamanese are some examples. Some hill tribes such as the Irulas, Kodars, Paniyans, and Kurumbas are found in some places in the southern part of mainland India. Siddis are tribes found in Gujarat.

Pro-Australoids or Austrics: According to Guha, Austrics were the next to come to India after the Negritos. He believed that the Austrics were the main builders of the Indus Valley Civilization. The people that Guha classified as Austrics are now found in some parts of India, in Myanmar and on the islands of South-East Asia. Their languages have survived in Central and Eastern India and are said to "form the bedrock of the people".

Mongoloids: These people are found in northeastern India in the states of Assam, Nagaland, Mizoram, Meghalaya, Arunachal Pradesh, Manipur, and Tripura. They also are found in northern regions of West Bengal, Sikkim, and Laddakh.

Dravidians: Guha stated that this group came to India from the Southwest Asia. These people built up the city civilization of the Indus Valley and comprised of three types: Paleo-Mediterranean, the true Mediterranean and Oriental Mediterranean.

Western Bracycephals: These include the Alpinoids, Dinarics and Armenoids. The Parsis, who arrived long after the Indo-Aryans, and the Kodavas (Coorgis) were also classified in this category by Guha.

Indo-Aryans: According to Guha, this group arrived between 2000 and 1500 B.C, and is now mainly found in the northern and central parts of India.

INDIAN CASTE SYSTEM

Although many other nations are characterized by social inequality, perhaps nowhere else in the world has inequality been so elaborately constructed as in the Indian institution of caste. Caste has long existed in India, but in the modern period it has been severely criticized by both Indian and foreign observers. Although some educated Indians tell non-Indians that caste has been abolished or that "no one pays attention to caste anymore," such statements do not reflect reality. Caste has undergone significant change since independence, but it still involves hundreds of millions of people. In its preamble, India's constitution forbids negative public discrimination on the basis of caste.

However, caste ranking and caste-based interaction have occurred for centuries and will continue to do so well into the foreseeable future, more in the countryside than in urban settings and more in the realms of kinship and marriage than in less personal interactions.

Castes are ranked, named, endogamous (in-marrying) groups, membership in which is achieved by birth. There are thousands of castes and subcastes in India, and these large kinship-based groups are fundamental to South Asian social structure. Each caste is part of a locally based system of interdependence with other groups, involving occupational specialization, and is linked in complex ways with networks that stretch across regions and throughout the nation.

The word caste derives from the Portuguese casta, meaning breed, race, or kind. Among the Indian terms that are sometimes translated as caste are varna, jati, jat, biradri, and samaj. All of these terms refer to ranked groups of various sizes and breadth. Varna, or colour, actually refers to large divisions that include various castes; the other terms include castes and subdivisions of castes sometimes called subcastes. Many castes are traditionally associated with an occupation, such as high-ranking Brahmans; middle-ranking farmer and artisan groups, such as potters, barbers, and carpenters; and very low-ranking "Untouchable" leatherworkers, butchers, launderers, and latrine cleaners. There is some correlation between ritual rank on the caste hierarchy and economic prosperity. Members of higher-ranking castes tend, on the whole, to be more prosperous than members of lower-ranking castes. Many lower-caste people live in conditions of great poverty and social disadvantage.

According to the Rig Veda, sacred texts that date back to oral traditions of more than 3,000 years ago, progenitors of the four ranked varna groups sprang from various parts of the body of the primordial man, which Brahma created from clay (see The Vedas and Polytheism, ch. 3). Each group had a function in sustaining the life of society—the social body. Brahmans, or priests, were created from the mouth. They were to provide for the intellectual and spiritual needs of the community. Kshatriyas, warriors and rulers, were derived from the arms. Their role was to rule and to protect others. Vaishyas—landowners and merchants—sprang from the thighs, and were entrusted with the care of commerce and agriculture. Shudras—artisans and servants—came from the feet. Their task was to perform all manual labour.

Later conceptualized was a fifth category, "Untouchable" menials, relegated to carrying out very menial and polluting work related to bodily decay and dirt. Since 1935 "Untouchables" have been known as Scheduled Castes, referring to their listing on government rosters, or schedules. They are also often called by Mohandas Karamchand (Mahatma) Gandhi's term Harijans, or "Children of God." Although the term Untouchable appears in literature produced by these low-ranking castes, in the 1990s, many politically conscious members of these groups prefer to refer to themselves as Dalit, a Hindi word meaning oppressed or downtrodden. According to the 1991 census, there were 138 million Scheduled Caste members in India, approximately 16 percent of the total population.

The first four varnas apparently existed in the ancient Aryan society of northern India. Some historians say that these categories were originally somewhat fluid functional groups, not castes. A greater degree of fixity gradually developed, resulting in the complex ranking systems of medieval India that essentially continue in the late twentieth century.

Although a varna is not a caste, when directly asked for their caste affiliation, particularly when the questioner is a Westerner, many Indians will reply with a varna name. Pressed further, they may respond with a much more specific name of a caste, or jati, which falls within that varna. For example, a Brahman may specify that he is a member of a named caste group, such as a Jijotiya Brahman, or a Smartha Brahman, and so on. Within such castes, people may further belong to smaller subcaste categories and to specific clans and lineages. These finer designations are particularly relevant when marriages are being arranged and often appear in newspaper matrimonial advertisements.

Members of a caste are typically spread out over a region, with representatives living in hundreds of settlements. In any small village, there may be representatives of a few or even a score or more castes.

Numerous groups usually called tribes (often referred to as Scheduled Tribes) are also integrated into the caste system to varying degrees. Some tribes live separately from others--particularly in the far northeast and in the forested centre of the country, where tribes are more like ethnic groups than castes. Some tribes are themselves divided into groups similar to subcastes. In regions where members of tribes live in peasant villages with nontribal peoples, they are usually considered members of separate castes ranking low on the hierarchical scale.

Inequalities among castes are considered by the Hindu faithful to be part of the divinely ordained natural order and are expressed in terms of purity and pollution. Within a village, relative rank is most graphically expressed at a wedding or death feast, when all residents of the village are invited. At the home of a high-ranking caste member, food is prepared by a member of a caste from whom all can accept cooked food (usually by a Brahman). Diners are seated in lines; members of a single caste sit next to each other in a row, and members of other castes sit in perpendicular or parallel rows at some distance. Members of Dalit castes, such as Leatherworkers and Sweepers, may be seated far from the other diners--even out in an alley. Farther away, at the edge of the feeding area, a Sweeper may wait with a large basket to receive discarded leavings tossed in by other diners. Eating food contaminated by contact with the saliva of others not of the same family is considered far too polluting to be practiced by members of any other castes. Generally, feasts and ceremonies given by Dalits are not attended by higher-ranking castes.

Among Muslims, although status differences prevail, brotherhood may be stressed. A Muslim feast usually includes a cloth laid either on clean ground or on a table, with all Muslims, rich and poor, dining from plates placed on the same cloth. Muslims who wish to provide hospitality to observant Hindus, however, must make separate arrangements for a high-caste Hindu cook and ritually pure foods and dining area.

Castes that fall within the top four ranked varnas are sometimes referred to as the "clean castes," with Dalits considered "unclean." Castes of the top three ranked varnas are often designated "twice-born," in reference to the ritual initiation undergone by male members, in which investiture with the Hindu sacred thread constitutes a kind of ritual rebirth. Non-Hindu castelike groups generally fall outside these designations.

Each caste is believed by devout Hindus to have its own dharma, or divinely ordained code of proper conduct. Accordingly, there is often a high degree of tolerance for divergent lifestyles among different castes. Brahmans are usually expected to be nonviolent and spiritual, according with their traditional roles as vegetarian teetotaler priests. Kshatriyas are supposed to be strong, as fighters and rulers should be, with a taste for aggression, eating meat, and drinking alcohol. Vaishyas are stereotyped as adept businessmen, in accord with their traditional activities in commerce. Shudras are often described by others as tolerably pleasant but expectably somewhat base in behaviour, whereas Dalits--especially Sweepers--are often regarded by others as followers of vulgar life-styles. Conversely, lower-caste people often view people of high rank as haughty and unfeeling.

The chastity of women is strongly related to caste status. Generally, the higher ranking the caste, the more sexual control its women are expected to exhibit. Brahman brides should be virginal, faithful to one husband, and celibate in widowhood. By contrast, a Sweeper bride may or may not be a virgin, extramarital affairs may be tolerated, and, if widowed or divorced, the woman is encouraged to remarry. For the higher castes, such control of female sexuality helps ensure purity of lineage--of crucial importance to maintenance of high status. Among Muslims, too, high status is strongly correlated with female chastity.

Within castes explicit standards are maintained. Transgressions may be dealt with by a caste council, meeting periodically to adjudicate issues relevant to the caste. Such councils are usually formed of groups of elders, almost always males. Punishments such as fines and outcasting, either temporary or permanent, can be enforced. In rare cases, a person is excommunicated from the caste for gross infractions of caste rules. An example of such an infraction might be marrying or openly cohabiting with a mate of a caste lower than one's own; such behaviour would usually result in the higher-caste person dropping to the status of the lower-caste person.

Activities such as farming or trading can be carried out by anyone, but usually only members of the appropriate castes act as priests, barbers, potters, weavers, and other skilled artisans, whose occupational skills are handed down in families from one generation to another. As with other key features of Indian social structure, occupational specialization is believed to be in accord with the divinely ordained order of the universe.

The existence of rigid ranking is supernaturally validated through the idea of rebirth according to a person's karma, the sum of an individual's deeds in this life and in past lives. After death, a person's life is judged by divine forces, and rebirth is assigned in a high or a low place, depending upon what is deserved. This supernatural sanction can never be neglected, because it brings a person to his or her position in the caste hierarchy, relevant to every transaction involving food or drink, speaking, or touching.

In past decades, Dalits in certain areas (especially in parts of the south) had to display extreme deference to high-status people, physically keeping their distance--lest their touch or even their shadow pollute others--wearing neither shoes nor any upper body covering (even for women) in the presence of the upper castes. The lowest-ranking had to jingle a little bell in warning of their polluting approach. In much of India, Dalits were prohibited from entering temples, using wells from which the "clean" castes drew their water, or even attending schools. In past centuries, dire punishments were prescribed for Dalits who read or even heard sacred texts.

Such degrading discrimination was made illegal under legislation passed during British rule and was protested against by preindependence reform movements led by Mahatma Gandhi and Bhimrao Ramji (B.R.) Ambedkar, a Dalit leader. Dalits agitated for the right to enter Hindu temples and to use village wells and effectively pressed for the enactment of stronger laws opposing disabilities imposed on them. After independence, Ambedkar almost single-handedly wrote India's constitution, including key provisions barring caste-based discrimination. Nonetheless, discriminatory treatment of Dalits remains a factor in daily life, especially in villages, as the end of the twentieth century approaches.

In modern times, as in the past, it is virtually impossible for an individual to raise his own status by falsely claiming to be a member of a higher-ranked caste. Such a ruse might work for a time in a place where the person is unknown, but no one would dine with or intermarry with such a person or his offspring until the claim was validated through kinship networks. Rising on the ritual hierarchy can only be achieved by a caste as a group, over a long period of time, principally by adopting behaviour patterns of higher-ranked groups. This process, known as Sanskritization, has been described by M.N. Srinivas and others. An example of such behaviour is that of some Leatherworker castes adopting a policy of not eating beef, in the hope that abstaining from the defiling practice of consuming the flesh of sacred bovines would enhance their castes' status. Increased economic prosperity for much of a caste greatly aids in the process of improving rank.-1995 data. India's caste system. Courtesy Library of Congress.

SOCIAL SYSTEMS

Indian society is multifaceted to an extent perhaps unknown in any other of the world's great civilizations. Virtually no generalization made about Indian society is valid for all of the nation's multifarious groups. Comprehending the complexities of Indian social structure has challenged scholars and other observers over many decades.

The ethnic and linguistic diversity of Indian civilization is more like the diversity of an area as variable as Europe than like that of any other single nation-state. Living within the embrace of the Indian nation are vast numbers of different regional, social, and economic groups, each with different cultural practices. Particularly noteworthy are differences between social structures in the north and the south, especially in the realm of kinship systems. Throughout the country, religious differences can be significant, especially between the Hindu majority and the large Muslim minority; and other Indian groups--Buddhists, Christians, Jains, Jews, Parsis, Sikhs, and practitioners of tribal religions--all pride themselves on being unlike members of other faiths.

Access to wealth and power varies considerably, and vast differences in socioeconomic status are evident everywhere. The poor and the wealthy live side by side in urban and rural areas. It is common in city life to see a prosperous, well-fed man or woman chauffeured in a fine car pass gaunt street dwellers huddled beneath burlap shelters along the roadway. In many villages, solid cement houses of landowners rise not far from the flimsy thatched shacks of landless labourers. Even when not so obvious, distinctions of class are found in almost every settlement in India.

Urban-rural differences can be immense in the Indian Society. Nearly 74 percent of India's population dwells in villages, with agriculture providing support for most of these rural residents. In villages, mud-plastered walls ornamented with traditional designs, dusty lanes, herds of grazing cattle, and the songs of birds at sunset provide typical settings for the social lives of most Indians. In India's great cities, however, millions of people live amidst cacophony--roaring vehicles, surging crowds, jammed apartment buildings, busy commercial establishments, loudspeakers blaring movie tunes--while breathing the poisons of industrial and automotive pollution.

Gender distinctions are pronounced. The behaviour expected of men and women can be quite different, especially in villages, but also in urban centres. Prescribed ideal gender roles help shape the actions of both sexes as they move between family and the world outside the home. Crosscutting and pervading all of these differences of region, language, wealth, status, religion, urbanity, and gender is the special feature of Indian society that has received most attention from observers: caste. The people of India belong to thousands of castes and castelike groups--hierarchically ordered, named groups into which members are born. Caste members are expected to marry within the group and follow caste rules pertaining to diet, avoidance of ritual pollution, and many other aspects of life.

Given the vast diversity of Indian society, any observation must be tempered with the understanding that it cannot apply to all Indians. Still, certain themes or underlying principles of life are widely accepted in India.

4

ANCIENT INDIAN RITUALS

THE QUEEN-HORSE COPULATION RITUAL OF THE ASVAMEDHA YAJNA

The *asvamedha yajna* was the grand horse sacrifice which Aryan (Hindu) kings conducted to celebrate their supremacy and for the prosperity & fertility of their kingdoms. The queen-horse copulation ritual was sometimes conducted during this sacred rite; the relevant Hindu scriptural quotes are presented below.

I. The sexual ritual of the *asvamedha yajna* quoted from the Vedas (*Satapatha Brahmana*).

II. Lord Rama's mom & co-moms participate in the queen-horse sexual ritual of the *asvamedha* in the Valmiki Ramayana.

The Sexual Ritual of the Asvamedha Yajna Quoted from the Vedas

The priests supervising the *asvamedha*: the efficient (*adhvaryu*), overseer (*brahman*), cantor (*udgatri*) and the invoker (*hotri*). The king's wives which participate in the queen-horse copulation ceremony of the *asvamedha*: the chief wife (*mahishi*), favourite wife, rejected wife and the fourth wife. The *Satapatha Brahmana*, quoted below, offers clear instructions on how the queen-horse copulation ritual of the *asvamedha* is to be conducted; the king's chief wife (the *mahishi*) is to copulate with the carcass of the horse while the priests and all the participants curse each other in degenerate language:

> *"A cloth, an upper cloth, and gold is what they spread out for the horse, and on that they 'quiet' him. When the sacrificial animals have been 'quieted', the (king's) wives come up with water for washing the feet—four wives, and a maiden as the fifth, and four hundred women attendants. When the water for washing the feet is ready, they make the chief queen (Mahishi) lie down next to the horse, and they cover the two of them up with the upper cloth as they say the verse, 'Let the two of us cover ourselves in the world of heaven', for the world of heaven is where they 'quiet' the sacrificial animal. Then they draw out the penis of the horse and place it in the vagina of the chief queen, while she says, 'May the vigorous virile male, the layer of seed, lay the seed'; this she says for sexual intercourse. While they are lying there, the sacrificer insults the horse by saying, 'Lift up her thighs and put it in her rectum.' No one insults (the sacrificer) back, lest there should be someone to act as a rival against the sacrificer.*
>
> *The efficient (Adhvaryu) then insults the maiden: 'Hey, maiden, hey, maiden, the little female bird...' and she insults him back: 'Hey, efficient, hey, efficient, that little bird....' And then the overseer (Brahman) insults the chief queen: 'Hey, chief queen, hey, chief queen, your mother and father climb to the top of a tree....' She has as her attendants a hundred daughters of kings; they insult the overseer in return: 'Hey, overseer, hey, overseer, your mother and your father play in the top of a tree....' Then*

the cantor (Udgatri) insults the king's favourite wife: 'Hey, favourite, hey, favourite wife, raise her up erect....' She has as her attendants a hundred royal women; they insult the cantor in return: 'Hey, cantor, hey, cantor, raise him *up erect....' Then the invoker (Hotri) insults the rejected wife: 'Hey, rejected wife, hey, rejected wife, when inside her tight crack....' She has as her attendants a hundred daughters of bards and village headmen; they insult the invoker in return: 'Hey, invoker, hey, invoker, when the gods see that miserable penis....'*

Then the carver (Kshatri) insults the fourth wife: 'Hey, fourth wife, hey, fourth wife, when the deer eats the barley, (the farmer) does not hope to nourish the animal....' She has as her attendants a hundred daughters of carvers and charioteers; they insult the carver in return: 'Hey, carver, hey, carver, when the deer eats the barley, (the farmer) does not hope to nourish the animal....' These insulting speeches are for all kinds of attainment, for through the horse sacrifice all desires are achieved. Thinking, 'With all kinds of speech we will achieve all kinds of desires', they make the chief queen get up. Then the women walk back the way they came, and the others utter at the end a sweet-smelling verse, the verse that begins, 'I praise Dadhikravan.' For the life-span and the gods go out of those who speak impure speech in the sacrifice. Thus they purify their speech to keep the gods from going out of the sacrifice."—Satapatha Brahmana

Lord Rama's Mom snf Co-moms Participate in the Queen-horse Sexual Ritual of the Asvamedha in the Valmiki Ramayana To ensure the birth of sons, King Dasaratha conducted both the *asvamedha* and

the *putrakamesti yajnas*. The following quote from the *Valmiki Ramayana* details the first of the two sacrifices that King Dasaratha conducted—the *asvamedha yajna*, in particular the queen-horse sexual portion of the sacrifice. Although all three of King Dasaratha's wives were united with the carcass of the horse, Rama's mom Kausalya was the one who had the honour of spending a whole night with the dead animal's genitals plugged in her vagina:

> *"The prescribed victims—snakes, birds, the horse, and aquatic animals—were bound at the place of immolation; each was dedicated to a specific divinity as is set forth in the ritual texts. The priests then bound them all to the posts in the manner set forth in the ritual texts. Three hundred beasts in addition to Dasaratha's jewel of a horse were bound there to the sacrificial posts. Kausalya walked reverently all around the horse and then with the greatest joy cut it with three knives. Her mind unwavering in her desire for righteousness, Kausalya passed one night with the horse.*
>
> *The priests—the hotr, the adhvaryu, and the udgatr—saw to it that the second and the juniormost of the king's wives, as well as his chief queen, were united with the horse. Then the officiating priest, who was extremely adept and held his senses in check, removed the fat of the horse and cooked it in the manner prescribed in the ritual texts. At the proper time and in accordance with the ritual prescriptions, the lord of men then sniffed the fragrance of the smoking fat, thereby freeing himself from sin. Then, acting in unison, the sixteen brahman officiating priests threw the limbs of the horse into the fire, in accordance with*

the ritual injunctions. In other sacrifices, the oblation is offered upon branches of the plaksa tree, but in the Horse Sacrifice alone the apportionment of the victim is made on a bed of reeds. The Horse Sacrifice is known as the Three-Day Rite; for both the kalpasutra and the brahmanas refer to the Horse Sacrifice as a rite lasting for three days."—Ramayana

ON THE EVE OF RSA ASVAMEDHA YAJNA

Yajna, Mahayajna, Asvamedha Yajna: In ancient times, simple yajnas used to play an important role in inner refinement and self-purification. The mahayajnas used to be performed to purify the social life. But, when the need for complete renovation of the nation (Rashtra) and that of the environment was felt, there was a tradition of Asvamedha yajnas at the universal level. Thus, the yajnas have been classified into three categories; viz, yajna, mahayajna and Asvamedha yajna. The magnitude of their results also increases in the same order.

The importance of yajna has been described in detail in Srimad Bhagwat Purana. Several such events have been described in this scripture, which acquaint us fully with the enormous power of yajna. According to this Purana, the universe was created with the help of yajna. This phenomenon has been described as follows.

In an answer to a query, Brahmaji describes the form of yajna as follows-

"Yadasya nabhyam .... caturhortram ca sattam" —Bhagwat, Skandha 2, Addhyaya 6, slokas 22,23,24.

Meaning: "When I was born from the navel of the all-pervading Brahma, I did not see any articles for oblation except the body of the Purush (the male God). Therefore,

I created the animals, vegetables, Kusa (a sacred grass), the sacred land where gods can perform yajna and the time, which is full of virtues (meaning the time in which the virtues are worshipped). Then I created all the ingredients of yajna, herbs, milk fats, sweetmeats, metals like gold, clay (earth), water, four Vedas (Rig, Yaju, Sama and Atharva), four Brahmans, and such procedures too by which the yajna may be performed."

There is description in the Brahma Purana (Purva Bhag, Addhyaya 1, sloka 5,6,7) that in the beginning of the Kalpa, a very sacred mahayajna was performed for one thousand years. The organizer of this mahayajna was Brahmaji himself accompanied by His wife Ila. The role of Shamitraka was performed by intelligent and radiant Mrityudev himself.

The king Daksha felt very sorry when his yajna was spoiled by her daughter Sati by her self-immolation. After begging pardon from Shiva, he organized Visad yajna as atonement for his sin. Its description is found in slokas 16 to 18 of seventh chapter in the fourth Skandha of Bhagwat; as follows:

Thus Daksha got his sin pardoned, and after consulting Brahmaji, he expanded the work of yajna, beautifully, by taking into account all the aspects, e.g. upadhyaya, ritvija, *agni* for yajna, etc. A Purodasa (an oblation made of ground rice and offered in kapalas or vessels) of three kapalas was offered to Lord Vishnu. In order to complete the yajna, offerings were given to virtuous Brahmans to purify the chief stalwarts. When the Adhwaryu took the Havi in his hand and meditated on God after performing havan with pure intelligence along with the Yajman, he sighted the Virat Purush (Lord Vishnu)".

Rishabhdev is considered the incarnation of God. This country has been named as Bharatvarsha in the memory of his son Bharat. The latter made this country a sacred land through the performance of mahayajnas.

Wherever the mahayajnas were performed, Tirthas (holy places) were established. After removing the suffix 'pra' from 'Prayag', what remains is the word 'yag', (which means yajna). This place has become Tartharaj (the king of Tirthas) because a large number of yajnas have been performed there. The Dasasvamedha Ghat (a bathing place on the bank of the river Ganga) in Kashi (Varanasi) is a proof of the fact that ten major yajnas had been performed there. This is why so much holiness has been attributed to this place. It is mentioned in part 4 of Skand Purana that the king of Kashi, Divodas performed yajan of the Lord Mahayagyeshwar in Kashi city by ten Asvamedha yajnas. From that day, that place became famous as Dasasvamedha Tirtha. Previously, it was known as Rudrasarovar.

The sages asked reverend Sootaji about the place, time, type etc of the first mahayajna. Whatever Sootaji said, in an answer to this question, is described in the second chapter in the first part of "Vayu Purana", as follows:

> *"The creator in the primordial state (i.e. before the actual creation of this universe), performed the sacred yajna for thousands of years with an aim to create this world. In this mahayajna, indeed Tapa (penance) was Yajman and Brahmaji Himself was Brahma of the yajna. In this long and grand yajna of great souls, the 'Nemi' (wheel) of Dharma revolved so much that it shattered and hence that area which was worshipped by the sages and saints, was named as Naimisharanya.*

The fourth sloka in the first chapter in first skandha of Bhagwat says-

Naimishe ninishiksetre rshayah saunkadayah
Satra swargaya lokaya sahastra samamasat

Meaning: Once upon a time, 88000 sages including Shaunak performed a 10,000 years long mahayajna in the sacred area of Naimisharanya, with a desire to achieve Heaven. It is the sacred effect of these yajnas that this area is supposed to be sacred even today.

A description is found about Ayodhya-that this city was the capital of Suryavanshi (descendants of Sun) king Vaivashwat Manu, who established himself as a universal monarch. He used to indulge himself always in Mahayajnas and Dana (donations). That is why in his reign no one suffered from the pangs of death, disease and old age, in the city of Ayodhya.

The rewards of Asvamedha yajna are far more purifying. In the medieval period, Asvamedha was thought to be the war for the expansion of the empire, whereas it used to be a special mahayajna performed for the benefit of the society and the nation, in the earlier ages.

The pages of Vedas, Upanishads, Darsans and Puranas are filled with the description of the importance of these Asvamedha yajnas. In ancient times, they were performed to achieve ecological balance, to seek the grace of God and to unite the nation. The writer of a scripture says that one gets the same sacred reward by participating in Asvamedha yajna as that achieved by visiting the holy place Gaya, taking a holy dip in rivers Ganga and Yamuna and performing one crore oblations (-Matsya Purana).

Ima nu kam bhuvana sishadhamendrasca visve ca devah

Adityairindrah sagano marudbhirasmabhyam bheshaja karat

Yajnam ca nastanvam ca prajam cadityairindrah-Sahasishadhati *-Yajurveda 25-46*

Meaning: Certainly, the whole world gets joy (by performing Asvamedha yajna). Indra and all the Gods alongwith their Ganas (attendants), accompanied by twelve Adityas and forty nine Marutas make the herbs beneficial. Majestic Indrayajna (for ecological balance) surcharges the bodies of the performers and their children with superior virtues. —Mahidhar Bhashya

Sarvan ha vai kaman apnoti

Yo Asvamedhen yajate -Shatpatha13/4/1/1

***Meaning*:** Those who perform Asvamedha yajna, all their desires are fulfilled.

Yajnenasvamedhenayuh kalpatam ....

One's life span is increased by performing Asvamedha yajna. —Mahidhar Bhashya 22-23

Oh dear! The sacred reward of participating in that Asvamedha yajna is matchless, in which the body of Nakul (a mongoose) became golden after it rolled its body in the water left over after eating by ritvijas (priests) who came to conduct the Asvamedha yajna there.

—Mahabharata

Rashtram va AsvamedhahViryam va asvah

—Satapatha Brahmana 13/1/6

The aim of Asvamedha is to increase the power and strength of the habitants of the nation, and the nations at large.

The king Vasu performed the Asvamedha. Vrahaspati Upadhyay was its Hota. The three sons of Prajapati, the superior sages Kapil, Katha, Taittari, Kanva, etc were its rtvikas. This sacred yajna was completed without hurting anyone. "Na tatra pasu ghatoabhuta"-(meaning) no animal was sacrificed therein.

—Mahabharata santiparva (3/336)

The following description is found in chapter 14 of fourth Skandha of Bhagwat Mahapurana. The king Vena had forbidden the performance of yajna etc in his kingdom. He said-"All the gods reside in the king and hence the people should praise and worship me only". In reply to this the sages tried to convince the king Vena thus –

"Oh king! The entire universe and the gods reside in the yajna. The priests perform yajan of the God who is full of Vedas (knowledge), wealth and devotion, through unique yajnas performed by different methods for your benefit and the prosperity of the people. You are in a position to help in such yajnas. Oh brave man if the people in your kingdom perform yajna, all the gods, who are indeed the different forms of Sri Narayana, will get satisfied and will grant the desired result to all. Therefore, you should not disregard these yajnas".

When he did not agree even after much persuasion and still remained adamant in his opposition to yajna, the sages cursed him so that king Vena died. After that, his arms were churned which gave birth to king Prithu.

"Adhadiksat raja tu hayamedha satena sah

Brahmavartta manahksetre yatra praci saraswati"

Meaning: After that Prithu promised to organize one hundred Asvamedha yajnas. These yajnas were performed where the river Saraswati flows towards the west and which is the area of Brahma and Manu, normally called Brahmavarta.

It is a sad story that in the medieval period confusion was created about animal sacrifice in these yajnas; partly due to the foreign invasions and partly due to the gradual decline of the true vedic culture. In this context, Pandit Beniramji in his hook "Yagya mimansa" and reverend

Satavalekarji have given the correct clarification. The learned Satvalekarji, in his book, writes:

> *"The gods of upright thinking and the demon animals of evil tendencies, both exist in the human body. They are shapeless in the human body, but when the evil tendencies, assume the form they become the animals of the visible world.*

That is to say-"It is the evil motives that condemn the human soul to slide back to sub-human (animal) forms. The arrogance results in the shape of hawk. The vulture is the representative of greed. The cunningness leads to birth as a dog. The ignorant souls have to go in the form of owl or donkey. When the animal-like tendencies become universal and assume the powerful shape as that of a horse, the Asvamedha yajnas are organized. The mode of sacrificing these animal-like tendencies is called Asvamedha".

The references, about the purity of preparation of Asvamedha yajna that are available in the ancient scriptures also do not enjoin the killing of any creature in these yajnas.

The Hindu Dharma Kosha States: "Three Ishtis (worships) of *Savita* (the Sun) used to be performed daily in the morning, afternoon and evening from the day the horse of Asvamedha used to be sent for global conquest. *Savita* used to be worshipped by the name of Satya-prasava in the morning, by the name of Prasavita in the afternoon and by the name of Asavita in the evening.

This fact has been described in Ashwalayan shroutsutra (10/6/8), Latyayan shroutsutra (9/9/10) and Katyayan shroutsutra (20/2/6). "This means that Gayatri used to be worshipped for the entire year, following which Asvamedha yajna used to be performed for three days.

Gandharvo asya rasanam gribhanat Suradaswam vasvo niratashta. *-Rigveda 1/163/2*

-Vasus have created the horse of yajna through the Sun. (It is, therefore, necessary to worship Sun (Gayatri) for the success of Asvamedha).

It is in this form that one should participate in the Asvamedha yajnas and attain peace and happiness in one's life.

DASARATHA'S DESIRE FOR A CHILD

Ramacandra appeared in the Iksvaku dynasty. He is known as Iksvaku Kuladhana. Kula means "dynasty" and dhana means "property" or "valuable jewel." So he is the jewel of the Iksvaku dynasty. Dasaratha was known as such because he could fight in ten directions simultaneously.

Dasaratha was such a great fighter that sometimes Indra would summon for him when there was a fight with the demons. So Dasaratha would go to the heavenly planets and fight with the demons. And these demons were so expert with maya, they would create darkness, expand into various forms etc. So Dasaratha would fight in ten directions, and when you looked at his ratha, his chariot, it would look as though there were ten kings and ten chariots fighting simultaneously. Dasa means "ten" and ratha means "chariot". That is how he got the name Dasaratha. So Dasaratha was famous for fighting for demigods and righteous kings. And he married Kausalya. From Kausalya, only one daughter was born. She was named Shanti, or "peace." But Dasaratha had no peace, because he only had one daughter, and that daughter would only get married and go to another dynasty. The Vedic system is that when a woman marries, she belongs to the husband's gotra or family line. So if Shanti married to another dynasty, she would belong to it. What about the Iksvaku dynasty?

Dasaratha was so worried. Then he married Sumitra. At least Kausalya had a daughter, but Sumitra had no child. Then Dasaratha was getting old. He gave up the idea of producing dynasties. As he was getting older he saw that some less powerful kings were doing small yajnas, so he did big yajnas. They were trying to get their name known, because once Dasaratha died Kosala would be broken. The kingdom of Kosala started all the way from what they now call the Dalai lama's line. From up in the north, in Tibet, all the way down to the river Godavari in Andhra Pradesh. So this was Kosala, practically it was the whole of India, not the democratic India but the Vedic India. So he was very worried that this kingdom will be broken to pieces and some small-timers will become emperors. Then Vasistha advised him to go to Kaikeya. This kingdom was right on the border of Afghanistan. They now call it the Sind region. Kaikeyi was the only daughter of the king of Kaikeya. The king's name was also Kaikeya. And when Dasaratha came for marriage negotiation, Kaikeya told him, "You have two queens, and they both have no children. Now you will marry my daughter, but what will happen to her if the other wives have children?"

Dasaratha replied, "I don't think they will have children because they have had none up to now. I am also getting old. They're not going to get any child. Only Kaikeyi will get a child." So Kaikeya said, "That's all right, but you must give this in writing." There is a system in the Ksatriya marriage known as kanya-sulka. Sulka means "will". When you accept a virgin in marriage, you must give in writing what properties she will enjoy as your wife if you are a ksatriya. This is kanya-sulka, the "will of dowry." So Dasaratha wrote kanya-sulka. He said, "Whoever is born to Kaikeyi will enjoy my kingdom, even if my other wives produce children later." This kanya-sulka was known to three people. Of course, now we all know it, but at that time only three people knew it. Vasistha knew it, Dasaratha knew it, and Kaikeya knew it. It was kept a secret, because otherwise they would blame Dasaratha, "What is this? He is giving the kingdom to a younger woman." So this kanya-sulka was kept secret.

But at the time of the marriage, due to great attachment, Kaikeya told his daughter this secret, that whoever is your son will rule this kingdom. Kaikeyi kept this at heart. Once Vasistha advised Dasaratha to perform asvamedha-yajna. He was telling him, "If you perform asvamedha-yajna, then all the demigods will personally come to accept the oblations." There are two kinds of offering oblations to the yajna. One is that Agni will take the oblations and offer it to the different destinations. Another is that the devas will personally come in the sacrificial arena. They will stand in the sky holding their hands open, and when you offer in their name in the fire then the harvest will get up from the fire and go into their hands. And they will eat it right there in front of everyone,. These types of sacrifices are considered first-class, because the devas have come in person. So Dasaratha should perform asvamedha, and all the devas will come. And then Dasaratha will tell them, "You have your kingdom only because of my fighting. So why don't you continue my dynasty and give me blessings that I can get some son?" That was the plan. There was a big arrangement for asvamedha-yajna, and wherever Dasaratha's horse went, no-one objected.

Asvamedha-yajna means that you have to select a horse with certain lakshanas or qualities. The ears have to be a certain way, the nose a certain way. There has to be a black part behind the tail. The hooves have to be a certain shape, 35 degrees bent. There is a whole description in karma-khanda. So you have to find out that horse, and after finding it you have to tie a golden leaf on his head. There it will be written, "This horse belongs to King Dasaratha. He will perform asvamedha-yajna, so everyone should donate liberally. And whoever stops this horse will have to meet the army of King Dasaratha." So this horse will go around the whole world, and if any king dares to stop the horse there will be one army which is following about 100 metres behind the horse.

They will have to meet that army. This army would consist of the best fighters in the army, all the generals, and if one can defeat that then more army would be sent. In this way the challenger would have to fight and prove that he is the emperor. So asvamedha-yajna was already started, and then when the yajna was going on, Sumantra (the minister of Dasaratha) came to Dasaratha and said, "I remember one incident when Sanat-kumara came to our assembly, when you were a prince." At that time Dasaratha was not married, and Sanat-kumara was visiting Dasaratha's father, Aja. Sanat-kumara made some predictions. "Maharaja Dasaratha will become very famous throughout the three worlds, and he will perform a putra-kamesti yajna, a sacrifice for getting a son. So in this sacrifice, the yajna-purusha, the personification of fire, will come there and give him some sweet rice. And out of this sweet rice Dasaratha will get the Supreme Lord as his sons." This was predicted by Sanat-kumara.

At that time Dasaratha was just an unmarried prince, a brahmacari. So Sumantra was a very old man and he suddenly remembered this. He came to Dasaratha and said, "You are doing asvamedha for getting a son, but Sanat-kumara told you that you should do putra-kamesti."

So then there was confusion over which yajna should be performed. In Treta-yuga everything was yajna. For material benefits, for spiritual realization, for anything tretayam yajato makhaih. Makha means "yajna". Now Dasaratha got confused. So he went to Vasistha's house and prostrated himself before him. "Guru maharaja, we have spent 60% of the treasury, and now we come to know that this is not the proper yajna, that there is another yajna. How am I supposed to do this?" So then Vasistha said, "Oh yes, I remember too now. Sanat-kumara said this.

It is not a very expensive yajna, but the purohit, the priest who performs the yajna must be a very special person. That is the difficulty. That person must have not seen a woman until the time of his marriage. He should not have even known what a woman is. Such a great personality must perform the yajna. Then only can the putra-kamesti be performed with the purnahoti and we will get a son." Then Dasaratha said, "You must tell me where this person is." Vasistha was a walking encyclopedia, because he had been there three lifetimes with the same remembrance. There is no-one in this world who knows better than Vasistha. So Vasistha said, "Yes, there is a person like that."

Dasaratha said, "Who is this person? He has never seen a woman or known what a woman is until marriage? At least he must have known about his mother! What kind of a person is he, that he has never heard of a woman yet he has taken birth?"

THE UNIVERSE AS A SACRIFICIAL HORSE

The commencement of the Brihadaranyaka Upanishad is a description of a symbolic placement of the parts of the individual in the cosmic quarters, with the spiritual intention of an undivided meditation, where the subject commingles with the object. The peculiar technique, adopted here in this Upanishad, is ritualistic as it is characteristic of the Brahmanas in the Vedas, and this technique is supposed to be adopted in the case of every individual character in its correlation with the universe. Here the individual concerned is the horse of the Asvamedha Sacrifice, which is the object of consecration and while, exoterically considered, it is one of the items in the Asvamedha Yajna, and it becomes a part of an external act, in the Upanishad it becomes a piece of contemplation, which is the avowed purpose of the Upanishad-to convert every act into a mode of contemplation, to transform every object into the Universal Subject. This is the aim of the Upanishad finally; and for this purpose various methods are prescribed. One method is, here, in this Brihadaranyaka Upanishad, at its beginning, the transformation of the ritual technique into an inward contemplation of the Spirit.

1. aum. usa va asvasya medhyasya sirah, suryas caksuh, vatah pranah, vyattam agnir vaisvanarah; samvatsara atmasvasya medhyasya, dyauh pristham, antariksam udaram, prithivi pajasyam, disah parsve, avantaradisah parsavah, ritavongani, masas cardhamasas ca parvani, ahoratrani pratisthah, naksatrany asthini, nabho mamsani; uvadhyam sikatah, sindhavo gudah, yakric ca klomanas ca parvatah, osadhayas ca vanaspatayas ca lomani, udyan purvardhah nimlocan jaghanardhah, yad vijrimbhate tad vidyotate, yad vidhunute tat stanayati, yan mehati tad varsati; vag evasya vak.

VERSES WITH DIACRITICAL MARKS

This is the first Mantra which is written in prose, the style of the Brahmana portion of the Vedas. Usa va asvasya medhyasya sirah: The dawn is the head of this sacred horse. The idea is that every part of the essential item in the sacrifice is to be identified, correspondingly, part by part, with the sections of the universe outside. In worship, especially that performed in temples, we have also a similar technique adopted, which is known as the Nyasa method-the placement. Nyasa means placement. The parts of the body of the worshipper are correspondingly placed in the parts of the body of the deity, so that the distinction between the worshipper and the deity is abolished. The two become one. Such a Nyasa is done here. The head of the sacrificial horse must be contemplated as the dawn. Here, the dawn does not necessarily mean a particular time of the eve of the rise of the sun at any particular place, but the eastern part, mostly conceivable by the mind, as the world, as it can be visualised by us to the extent possible. Now, if it is not possible to conceive it in this manner, it can be taken literally as the eastern part of the world where we are living. The dawn is the head of the consecrated horse. The dawn, the beginning of the day, is the head, because the head is the beginning of the body. That is the similarity. The day begins with the dawn, and the body begins with the head. This is the similarity conceived here.

The eyes may be compared to the sun. The similarity is very obvious, because the sun is the eye of the day through which perception is made possible; and the eyes, of course, in the body, are the means of every kind of visual perception.

The Cosmic Wind, the Air that pervades, is the Prana within. We should identify the Prana within the horse with the Air that is outside, because the two are essentially the same, one working in the world outside and another working within the body of the individual, here, the horse.

The mouth is the Agni Vaisvanara. In some Upanishads, the Aitareya particularly, we have another cosmological description where we are told that from the Cosmic Virat, Fire broke out through the mouth. And the organ of speech is supposed to be presided over, in every case, by the principle of Fire. So the mouth of the individual horse, here, may be identified with the cosmic fire which is Vaisvanara. Vaisvanara is a word which has two or three meanings. It is a fire principle which is hiddenly present in all things, the principle of fire which manifests itself as the visible fire outside, which, again, is sometimes identified with the Cosmic Being. Vaisva-Nara means the Cosmic-Man, and the derivative of this word is Vaisvanara. The Vaisvanara is the Cosmic Person who represents the energy of all things, manifested outwardly as the fire principle, energy secondarily manifest, again, as the power of speech. And so, the mouth is to be identified with the Vaisvanara, the principle of Divine Fire.

The body is the entire process of the year. The Time process is the body, because the body has many limbs, many parts; and likewise, time can be segmented into parts-past, present, future; and if it is concretised further, it becomes capable of division into years, months, days, nights, etc. The comparison is that, as the time has divisible parts, so the body also has divisible parts. The two are identified.

The Sky is the back, as it were. The comparison is that it is on the top, above the body.

The Atmosphere is the belly, because it is hollow, as it were.

The Earth is the hoofs, on which the animal is placed.

The sides are the quarters of the heavens.

The sides of the body, consisting of the bones, may be compared to the intermediary quarters, which are between the main quarters.

The seasons are the limbs of the body. Even as the Samvatsara, or the year, is constituted of various seasons, the body is constituted of various limbs.

The divisions of the year, namely the month, the half-month, the bright half and the dark half of the month, etc., are the parts of the entire physical body, just as the year may be supposed to be placed on the parts consisting of the months, days, etc.

The day and night are the essence of the calculation of Time, and, therefore, the year may be supposed to be rooted in the calculation or conception of day and night. Thus is also the body rooted, or placed, or supported by the feet. So, the day and night are said to be the feet of the horse.

The constellations in the sky may be compared to the whitish bones which are spread out, as it were, in all parts of the body.

The clouds are the flesh of the whole body.

The sand that you can see anywhere, physically, in the world, may be compared to the half-digested food that is in a seed condition in the stomach.

The rivers are the veins and the arteries.

The spleen and the liver are the mountains, as it were, which are something like an elevation in the body within.

The trees and the plants and the shrubs may be compared to the hairs of the body.

The sun, rising, is the earlier, fore part of the body.

The hind part of the body may be compared to the sun that is about to set.

The horse's yawning is something like the lightening.

The shaking of the members of the body is like the thunder in the rainy season.

Its making water is like the rainfall. The sound that it makes, neighing, is the principle of speech.

This description of the Cosmos as Horse is entirely symbolic, and highly complicated to conceive, because the purpose of the Upanishad is to bring out the psychological element that is present in the comparison that is made between the physical counterparts of the body of the horse, and the body of the universe outside. The difference between the horse conceived here, or to make a wider comparison, the case of any individual, for the matter of that, the distinction between the body of an individual, whether of an animal or a human being, and the world outside, is psychological. If it were not psychological and is really physical, an identification would be impossible. That one person is different from another person, is a psychological division. It is not physical. We have had occasion to discuss this subject earlier in some of our discourses.

I shall give you a small example of how physical division does not exist. It is only imaginary. The bodies of people are constituted of the five elements-earth, water, fire, air and ether. Your body, my body and everybody's body is constituted of only these things, nothing else-earth, water, fire, air, ether. If the body of one individual, 'A', is substantially the same as the body of another individual, 'B', because of its being formed of the same five elements, what is the reason for the distinction or the difference that we make between one body and another body? It is that which exists between the two bodies. The space is the cause. But space is a part of the very constitution of the body itself. So, how does this become an element of distinction? That which we regard as spatial, and, perhaps, the only reason for the distinction that we usually make between one body and another, is an element essentially present in the constitution of the body itself. So to say that space is the distinctive mark of division between one body and another is logically not tenable. It is a peculiar thinking of the minds of people that makes it impossible for them to feel the coextensive nature of bodies, as if they are connected at the bottom, like the waters of the ocean. Inasmuch as physical distinctions are not tenable ultimately, the distinctions are to be regarded as purely mental, or psychological; and therefore, a mental act can abolish the mental distinction that has been thus created.

The entire psychology of meditation is nothing but a setting right of errors in thought; and the details of these methods we shall be considering as we proceed further. So, to come to the point, this distinction between the individual unit and the Universal Substance is to be abolished for the purpose of the removal of the sorrow of the individual. Meditation is the technique of the removal of sorrow in the sense that sorrow is caused by the segregation of the individual from the world outside. For this purpose, one enters into the technique of meditation. Now, here, the context being sacrifice, we are given a method which is ritualistic in its nature, and thus the ritualistic horse of the Asvamedha Sacrifice becomes an object of contemplation, literally, liturgically as an animal in the sacrifice, but psychologically and spiritually, as an element like any other element in creation as a whole. The subject is continued in the next Mantra.

2. ahar va asvam purastan mahima nvajayata. tasya purve samudre yonih, ratrir enam pascan mahima nvajayata, tasyapare samudre yonih, etau va asvam mahimanav abhitah sambabhuvatuh hayo bhutva devan avahat, vaji gandharvan, arvasuran, asvo manusyan; samudra evasya bandhuh, samudro yonih.

Again, this is a ritualistic peculiarity of the Brahmana, concerned with the Asvamedha Sacrifice. Mahima is a term used to designate certain sacrificial vessels, gold and silver, placed in the performance of the sacrifice. The daytime may be compared, says the Upanishad, to the golden cup that is placed in the front of the horse.

The eastern ocean, by which what is intended is the farthest eastern limit of the conceivable world, is the base. The world ends with the ocean. That is how we have to think, because we cannot think more than that. What can a child think? If you ask a baby to think of the world, it will think only up to the ocean. Beyond that, no thought is possible. But this is only a beginning of the method of extending the thought to further and further limits, until we reach the limit of the psychological horizon. The idea is that the eastern ocean is to be regarded as the limit, the farthest possible for the mind in contemplating the horizon of the universe. That is the limit of the horse.

Similarly, the rear part may be compared to the night, and the western ocean, which is the other side of conceivable limit. Thus, the horse is enveloped, encircled by the ritualistic elements, which means to say, in this process of contemplation, the parts of the world are contemplated as associated with the world which is, here, the object of contemplation. Just as the parts in a sacrifice are associated with the element in the sacrifice which is the horse, the parts of the world or the universe are to be conceived as associated with it as parts are associated with the whole. Here is a very difficult passage whose meaning is very obscure. But evidently what its meaning is, is this, that there is a gradual ascent and descent of the degree in the concept of the horse, or rather, the concept of the universe. When you think of the universe as an object of contemplation, you think of it in various degrees-the gross, the subtle and the causal. And the commentators, especially Acharya shankara, and others, tell us that the horse mentioned here is the Prajapati, or the Creator of the cosmos. It is not merely the animal in the sacrifice. That is how we have to think in meditation. So, as there is a descent from the causal condition to the subtle condition, and from the subtle to the gross, and from the gross to the variegated forms of manifestation in this world, so also is the horse to be contemplated in the various aspects of its functions, and the functions are mentioned here in respect of the ritual of the Asvamedha Sacrifice.

When the horse becomes the vehicle of the celestials, it is called 'Hayo'. When it becomes the vehicle of Gandharvas, demi-gods, above the earth, it is called 'Vaji', a peculiar name ascribed to the horse. When it becomes the vehicle of the demons, it becomes 'Arva'. It becomes the ordinary horse, Asva, when it becomes the vehicle of human beings. The substance of all these things is the ocean. Here, the great commentator, Acharya shankara, tells us the ocean means the Cosmic Soul. It does not mean the ocean which is water. The Universal Soul is the basis of the world, as the horse is the basis of the entire sacrifice. It is the substratum; and every activity-name, form, action-is something like a wave in the ocean. But the wave is the ocean. The wave is in the ocean, or on the ocean, as you may think of it. Likewise, all actions, name and form, rise and subside within the bosom of the universal Soul, so that you may say, just as waves are the ocean, actions are the Universal Soul. So the universe is the ocean, or rather, the Universal Soul is the ocean. That is the deepest and the nearest associate. The greatest friend of man is God. That is what is intended here. And He is the support, ultimate resort and refuge-Samudra evasya bandhuh, samudro yonih

YAGNA, DANA AND GOTRA

Every society has passed through a tribal stage at some time or the other. Some societies are still in the tribal stage for instance the Australian aborigines, and the Red Indians living in the preserves or nearer home in India the Nagas and Bhils, etc.,. This stage is normally characterized by a collective way of living where property is under common ownership of the tribes the institution of monogamous family has not yet been accepted and where livelihood depends on tending of cattle, collection of wild fruits and roots and shifting, subsistence agriculture.

THE TRIBAL WAY OF LIFE WAS OF COLLECTIVE ACTIVITY

This Collective way of life is conducive to the birth of many of the folklore and rituals of later stages of development when the tribal way of life is no more. The origins of these folklore and rituals is normally lost and hence they are looked upon as timeless and having divine sanction. The main reason for their origin being lost is the absence of a written language during the tribal stage when most of the folklore is born. Due to the absence of a written language, ideas had to be passed on from generation to generation by means of oral narration. Although the origin of most rituals is lost to us, the nature of the rituals that we perform today is at times eloquent about their origins.

A HARD LOOK AT OUR RITUALS CAN BRING OUT MANY OF THEIR LOST ORIGINS

A hard look at these rituals can bring out many of their lost origins. The practice of oral transmission of knowledge due to the absence of a literary medium itself becomes a tradition in some cases. In India our traditions of smriti (remembrance) and Shurti (listening) and sloka pathan (oral narration) are instances of this. Even during our prayers and sacrificial invocations (Yagna) we rarely see the officiating priests reading out the prayer (slokas and Mantras).

These are generally recited or chanted. In this chapter we take up a set of traditions which we observe in today's society and try to reconstruct the social ethos in which they could have originated. The issues we take up are the ritual of fire sacrifice (Yagna) our traditional practice of charity Dana), the concept of Gotra which is a consideration while arranging marriages, the institution of monogamous marriage (Dwanda-Vivaha) and the worship of the Mother Goddess.

YAGNA AS A SACRIFICE

Yagna is a term we normally hear in today's society. It is popularly understood as a fire sacrifice involving the offering of grains, clarified butter, sandalwood etc, to a fire. This fire is ignited in a special fireplace called the Kund, which literally means a "Pot". Yagna is normally performed with the objective of ushering in prosperity or to avoid disaster. For performing a Yagna a minimum number of five priests are required although many more priests may participate. A Yagna is normally accompanied by mass feeding of people, the food being distributed as Prasad (i.e food which has been sanctified by offering it to the Gods). Rituals similar to yagna are performed during marriage, thread ceremony, vaastu shanti (opening ceremony for a house), etc. when a homa or sacred fire is ignited in a kund.

It is widely known that Yagna is a very old tradition in the Hindu religion and it is looked upon as a Vedic ritual. In Vedic literature there are innumerable descriptions of a Yagnas being performed. The origin of the Yagna though lost in history, the rituals associated with it today throw light as to its nature.

YAGNA CENTRES AROUND A FIREPLACE

Yagna as a ritual centres around a fireplace. Thus, it obviously must have come into being after fire was domesticated. Even the oldest of the Vedas, the Rigveda describes a society where man had no fire, no protection against wild beasts, uncertainty of prey and hence the spectre of being perished. This environment is poetically expressed in Vedic literature. Prajapati, the creator suffered abortion in the act of creation and was threatened with extinction. But the world was saved when he was given milk and roasted meat. Praiapati, symbolizes the Aryan man in his most primitive stage, who to the Aryans became a personification of their existence, the memory of which was kept alive by Prajapati being deified in the hymns and songs that constitute the Rigveda.

THE FABLISED RECOLLECTION OF THE DISCOVERY OF FIRE

This fableised recollection also narrates the discovery of making fire and the art of domesticating animals. Agni-fire has been referred to as an eater of dead flesh (Kravyad). Fire also served as a formidable weapon against wild animals and other tribes. It also helped during the hunt for capturing prey and as a shield against the oppressive cold winters of the higher latitudes. Society obtained a respite from the threat of extinction and was lifted above the margin of sustenance.

SATRA-THE COLLECTIVE LABOUR

However man individually was powerless in the fight; against nature, hence whatever was collected or hunted had to be done collectively in large groups (Gaṇa). Thus the auxiliary practices of distribution and consumption were also performed collectively. The absence of the institution of the monogamous marriage and family life as we know it today was another factor that ensured collectivity in all facets of life. The collective labour that was undertaken by Vedic Aryans was termed Satra which means a session, implying collectivity. Thus there was no question of division of society into Varnas and Jatis, so prominent in later Hindu society.

THE FIREPLACE WAS THE NUCLEUS OF THE TRIBAL SOCIETY

But the domestication of fire provided a gravitating nucleus for the collective life of the tribe (Gana). As to what the tribal Aryans did around this central fireplace can be guessed from the original Yagna rituals which today are kept alive in the Yagnas as performed by Sadhus (i.e. ascetics and hermits).

THE YAGNA RITUAL RE-CREATES ALL ASPECTS OF PRIMITIVE TRIBAL COLLECTIVE LIFE

Contemporary writer describes this Yagna ritual as follows: " The Yagna ritual "... " is a process in which almost all primitive social life has to be recreated. You have to produce fire by friction of two pieces of wood, to build a cottage where no iron is used but only specific wood and grass, to milk cows, make curds, pound corn with stone (not even a stone mill), boil and cook it,..." This description brings out the fine semblance between the original Yagna ritual and the function of cooking for a tribal household. In the public Yagnas, like the Rajasuya and Ashwamedha Yagna that were sponsored in later ages by kings, many alterations and refinements were introduced but the original primitive features stuck fast. These royal Yagnas involved the coming together of innumerable Brahmins, the consigning to the central fire, generous quantities of sandalwood, camphor, ghee (clarified butter), grains, and even sacrificial animals and birds. All this corresponds to the central fireplace theory as the origin of the Yagna.

BEFORE ITS DOMESTICATION FIRE WAS AN OBJECT OF AWE AND FEAR

Fire had, before its domestication been observed by cavemen and savages only as a formidable destructive medium in the gigantic forest fires, volcanic eruptions etc. Hence it had always been looked upon with fear and awe. But after its domestication, fire spelt prosperity for the nomadic people. Hence it could easily become an object of worship. When the nomadic Aryans had progressed towards settled civilized life the fireplace no longer remained the gravitating nucleus of their daily life. But their social memory continued to be ruled by the past reality.

THIS LINGERING SOCIAL MEMORY PERPETUATED THE PRACTICE OF HAVING THE CENTRAL FIRE AS THE YAGNA

This lingering social memory perpetuated the practice of having the central fire, which in the changed circumstances became a ritualised form of worship. The recollection of the extinct past fermented ideas that invocation of the fire would again spell wealth and prosperity as it had after its domestication. In the Yagna ritual of later days up to our own age, the hymns sung in the Vedic days are recited, the collective social life is reconstructed in a ritualised rnanner with the fond hope that all this would spell prosperity for the performers of the Yagna. This is one instance of a past being kept alive in later ages by crystallizing it into a ritual.

5

DANA AND DAKSHINA

At some time or the other during our lives we observe the practices of dana and dakshina. Dana is the traditional Indian form of charity. We are told that giving away of dana secures divine blessings for the giver. As such dana can be given to anybody but the emphasis has always been on giving dana to Brahmins. Hindu tradition has never extolled Dana to Kshatriyas, Vaishyas or Shudras.

Since ancient times kings and noblemen have organised mass feeding ceremonies, distribution of grain and utilities as dana. Such giving away of wealth without expecting anything in return except blessings, was termed Dana.

On any occasions like marriage, thread ceremony, opening ceremony, rites at death etc., we ask a Brahmin priest to officiate over the ceremony and in return for his services we offer him grain, cloth, gold and nowadays even cash. This offering is termed dakshina.

DANA AND DAKSHINA ARE GIVEN IN CASH AND KIND, BUT NEVER AS FREE PHYSICAL LABOUR

Traditionally dakshina was given, and had the nature of a payment in kind for services rendered by a priest. But nowadays with this offering being made also in terms of cash its nature as a payment becomes clear. When it is given in cash, it is in the denomination of eleven, twenty-one, fifty-one, one hundred and one-etc Although has the nature of a voluntary payment it is not looked upon as such and is considered to be an offering to an officiating prbst. In spite of the fine difference between the terms dana and dakshina, these terms are used interchangeably with the same connotation. But the common element in both dana and dakshina is that they are payments in cash or kind articles of use, such as, cloth, grain, utensils etc.

Dana and dakshina are never offered in terms of physical labour in the form of social work. This is where they are different from the Christian concept of charity which involves social work and provision of social services. The custom of dana has always been part of Indian society and like Yagna, its origins seem to be in the collective hunting and common sharing way of life of life of the Vedic period.

THE HAVANA-A METHOD OF DISTRIBUTION OF THE COMMON TRIBAL WEALTH

The Rigveda mentions the incendiary wars that the different nomadic tribes fought in their search for better pastures and hunting grounds. The way of life both during peacetime and war was based on collective activity. In the tribal way of life even during peacetime the share (Havi) of every member of the tribe was distributed in a function called the Havana. Whatever was gathered hunted or cooked was shared among all members of the tribe

The same principle was applied to the distribution of the booty of war. Articles that were plundered after a successful military campaign such as weapons, clothing and other articles of personal consumption were distributed amongst members. This distribution which was carried out in festive atmosphere after a successful campaign is perhaps the progenitor of our custom of offering dana especially on festival days and other auspicious occasions like the crowning of a king, royal birthdays, etc.

DANA ORIGINALLY CONNOTED DISTRIBUTION NOT CHARITY

The term dana is used in Vedic literature to describe the act of distributing such wealth among members of a tribe. The original connotation of the word dana was thus not just to give but to distribute. And in the tribal way of life this distribution did not have the nature of one person giving away his wealth to another but as distribution among members of a tribe (Gana) the captured property that was under common ownership of the tribe as a whole, but for its consumption it had to be allotted to individual members.

That dana connoted only the distribution of proceeds of war is corroborated by the fact that it was not part of daily life and was held on select occasions that called for festivities. The practice of offering of dana especially on festive occasions survived the passing away of the tribal way of life of collective activity and common sharing.

But with the passage of time, the tribal way of life broke up and so did the institution of common property. With the division of labour according to different specialised occupations, war became a profession of a select body of men who constituted the army, the commander of which was the king. In India those of the warrior profession were known as Kshatriyas or Rajanyas and their chieftain was the Rajan.

The proceeds of war and later on the proceeds of tributes and taxes came into the hands of the warriors and the king. These proceeds were no longer looked upon as common property to which every member of society had an equal claim. It now came to be looked upon as Rajasva, literally meaning that which belongs to the king (Raja = king, sva = own or self). But the practice of distributing wealth accumulated in the royal treasury and in the smaller private hoards of noblemen-warriors, among the kingdom's of populace continued. Religious festivals and public events such as coronation were occasions for distributing wealth and this distribution was looked upon as dana. This practice was normally respected but it was not a compulsory or obligatory requirement. If the king followed it he was looked upon as virtuous if not then he was an evil king.

DANA BECAME A TRANSFER OF WEALTH FROM THE NOBILITY TO THE CLERGY

But there was no formal law that made it imperative for the king and noblemen to observe this custom. Dana, thus acquired a voluntary character which was looked upon as an act of piety. With the passage of time Dana came to be bestowed mainly upon the clergy which in India was the Brahmin caste. Dana which under the tribal set up was an instrument for equi-distribution of wealth became one of discriminatory enrichment of a section of the society. This was so as the practice of Dana gradually came to acquire the nature of transfer of wealth from the nobility to the clergy. The clergy by virtue of the psychological hold exercised on all sections of society enforced this transfer though not always successfully. There did exist some justification for this transfer as it was normally the clergy which was a repository of knowledge as under the caste system only it had the right to acquire education. It was mainly the king and the nobility who could sustain the practice of dana although the trading community (Vaishyas) also joined their ranks of donees, when mercantile activity favoured them with disposable surplus wealth. In the later ages the observance of dana was ensured by fostering ideas that giving of dana results in Punya (God's blessings). Hence, it was the holy duty of everybody to offer dana this was especially so for the King and the nobility to give dana. The episode of Karna in the Mahabharata, highlights the overwhelming importance attached to honouring the practice of dana by the nobility in ancient India. Briefly the episode is as follows:

THE STORY OF KARNA IN THE MAHABHARATA

Karna was born to Kunti mother of the Pandavas before marriage. According to the mythological account he was fathered by the Sun from whom he inherited the Kavacha and Kundala which were protective organs as a part of his physical body. It was deereed that as long as he wore the Kavacha (a bony shield on the chest) and Kundala (ear rings), Karna would be immortal. Out of shame, Kunti abandoned the baby Karna by setting his cradle afloat in the Ganges river. He was found by a person from a menial Profession and was brought up as a son. Karna grew up to be a brave and expert archer whose extraordinary talent was spotted by Duryodhana the eldest of the Kaurava brothers. The wily Duryodhana enrolled Karna into the ranks of the Kaurava army in spite of Karna being looked upon as a member of a menial caste for which he was contemptuously referred to as Sutaputra (low born).

Karna's prowess as an archer was superior to that of Arjuna of the Pandavas, who himself was an accomplished archer. During the Mahabharata war between Pandavas and Kauravas, Karna and Ariuna were to confront each other. The outcome of their encounter was a foregone conclusion. When Kunti came to know that Karna was also her son, she rushed to Karna and begged him not to fight his brother Arjuna in what would be a fratricidal war. But Karna was unmoved in his determination to stand by his master, Duryodhana during the war.

Lord Srikrishna who acted as adviser to the Pandavas knew the inevitability of Karna's victory against Arjuna and to preclude this possibility he decided to deprive Karna of his protective Kavacha and Kundala in a way that Karna could not refuse. Srikrishna took upon the guise of a Sadhu and went to Karna before the inception of the battle and demanded that Karna offer him dana. Considering the giving of dana to a Brahmin before setting off for battle to be an auspicious deed, the innocuous Karna told the lord in guise to ask for anything he wanted and consider it to have been granted. Horrified as he might have been when the lord in guise demanded the Kavacha and Kundala.

But Karna refused to go back on his word and gave away his impregnable armour to the malevolent Sadhu. Thus unprotected he proceeded to the battle and the lack of his armour along with the misfortune of a ruptured chariot wheel became the reason for his undoing. Karna preferred death rather than the stigma of dishonour that would have attached to him had he refused to carry out his word and offered whatever the malevolent lord in the guise of a Sadhu had demanded. This anecdote illustrates the moral grip on the psyche that has insured the existence of dana over the ages till today.

GOTRA

Gotra is one of the many considerations that exist during match making in the traditional manner. Janmakundalis (horoscopes) of the prospective bride and groom are compared to see if a match could he made.

Gotras have to be Different while Matchmaking for a Marriage: While in matching Janmakundalis the consideration is for the common and symmetrical features, but surprisingly while comparing Gotras the requirement is that the bride and groom should belong to different Gotras. If their Gotras are identical a match cannot be made. Today most of us may not be aware as to what Gotra is. Its meaning is lost and it is doubtful whether even the astrologers who compare horoscopes can satisfy an inquisitive student as to the origin and meaning of Gotra and the reason why identical Gotras preclude a match in a traditional Hindu marriage.

Gotra Originated as the Common Cowpen or Cow Shed During the Tribal Aryan Past: The origin of this concept of Gotra also seems to lie in a tribal ethos and is linked to the system of common ownership of property. The word Gotra literally means cowpen or cowshed and is derived from "Go" meaning cow.

With the domestication of animals, cattle became an important source of meats and milk. With the rearing of cattle, hunting as the principal source of subsistence lost its importance and the lifestyle became less nomadic as compared to the earlier days when hunting was the main activity of sustenance. With the coming of a pastoral way of life it was possible to have individual ownership of the means of subsistence which was impossible during the days of hunting.

But the older practice of holding property in common could not die out abruptly. Even in a pastoral society the principle means of subsistence-cattle-continued to be held as common property. The members of a tribe had one object for solidarity and this was the cattle they held in common. While in a society of hunters, the prisoners of wars and other fellow travellers could either be sacrificed or absorbed into the tribe so as to increase the strength of the hunt party; the pastoral society ruled out such absorption of new members who would only be additional mouths to feed. The tribe henceforth became an endogamous clan which kept outsiders out and insiders in.

SA-GOTRA (MARRIAGE WITHIN A GOTRA) WAS THE NORM ORIGINALLY

But the endogamous clan still retained some features of the tribal way of life like common ownership of property (and promiscuity). This new solidarity that emerged from the common ownership of cattle, acquired the name Gotra from its very nature. *But then the Gotra which was the foundation of life and livelihood also became its limit.* Sexual pairing was limited to member of a Gotra. This form of pairing was termed Sagotra. Our Present day prohibition on marriage within one Gotra is a later development.

The shift from pairing within a Gotra to prohibition on marriage between two members having the same Gotra must be a result of a variety of factors.

As long as promiscuity survived, society must have been matriarchal as the mother would have been the only identifiable parent. But with the rising productivity and gradual emergence of individual holding of property, this way of life had to make way for another.

The title to the increasing hoard of wealth was held by male members of a clan due to their being the physically dominant sex. It was the efforts of the more powerful males that won for the clan the property of other clans and also enabled defense of their own property from being grabbed by other clans. With the gradual increase in productive power, the acquisition of slaves etc. The title to property also changed from being collective to individual. This change in the title to property from communal to individual must have been the result of evolution over hundreds of years. But why did this change have to prohibit the established practice of marriage within a Gotra?

The answer perhaps lies in Human Social Evolution. Primitive promiscuity as it exists among the lower animals, also existed among humans to begin with. Later on came monogamous marriage. Simultaneously, with the rise in the productive power of human beings there came about accumulation of property initially in the form of cattle. The common ownership of this object of wealth made essential marriage only within members of the clan that held the wealth so as to prevents outsiders from claiming a share of it.

But while this solidarity was based on the common ownership of wealth there still existed a commonality in the title to that wealth. And this commonality was first disturbed with the removal of promiscuous matriarchy which did take place with the passage of time. In matriarchy and its earlier form, promiscuity, there existed no bar on members of a clan (Gotra) whether they be the progeny of the same mother, the father not being an identifiable parent.

But with the eclipse of matriarchy and the coming of individual ownership and monogamy, the father became an identifiable parent and strains of patriarchy appeared. The ethic of matriarchal society that allowed marriage between the progeny of one mother or between paternal cousins now came to be frowned upon as these progeny were now the sons and daughters of one (identifiable) father or of one grandfather. This encouraged marriage outside the clan (Gotra). The prohibition on marriage outside a Gotra was made irrelevant by individual ownership of property and the custom of inheritance whereby property passed from father to son. As the title to property was individual and private and the transfer of this title to property was also fixed, there was no reason why a female member of one Gotra should not be tied in wedlock with a male member of another Gotra. Thus while formerly marriage within a Gotra was the rule, later marriage outside a Gotra became one.

Today it is difficult to imagine that marriage within one Gotra between members who were the progeny of one mother or were immediate maternal cousins by virtue of having the same grandmother could have once been a solemn custom. But the later rigid injunction against marriage within a Gotra itself implies that once the practice of marrying within one Gotra must have existed.

Thus as Sagotra marriage was once the norm, there arose the need for its prohibition. Something that has never existed need not be prohibited. Hence the existence of prohibition on Sagotra marriage itself is one evidence of its existence sometime in the past. With the disappearance of a pastoral society and also the clan ownership of cattle (Gotra as 'cowpen'), the emergence of monogamy and ownership of property and later urban civilization and with it a much wider social unit of human existence, the Gotra as an institution and a consideration for matchmaking vanished and marriage outside one's Gotra became the rule.

But even afterwards the custom of prohibition on marriage within a Gotra continued. Today this prohibition is still observed as a matter of ritual and custom when even the original connotation of the term Gotra is generally not known. —How Indians Lived During Vedic Times

INDIA IS ESSENTIALLY RURAL INDIA

Time and again we have been told in our text books at schools and colleges, and through speeches by our politicians, economists, etc., that "India is essentially Rural India and Rural India is virtually the Cultivator".

URBANIZATION AND INDUSTRIALIZATION

In our century the rate of urbanisation is quite rapid as is witnessed in the thousands of people that pour into our major metropolises in search of livelihood, for better employment prospects, better living conditions, etc. But in spite of this urbanisation and industrialisation, India is still overwhelmingly an agricultural country.

Most rural migrants leave their native villages for various negative reasons like famine, floods, loss of land, indebtedness and exploitation. This migration represents on a smaller scale the migration of European peoples to the New World (America), from the 16th century onwards.

MOST US HAVE RURAL ROOTS

Though a large majority of educated Indians reside in Urban or semi-urban areas most of us still have some roots in our native villages. Some agricultural land, residential property distant relatives, etc. Event like traditional local festivals, marriages in the family, etc., continue to keep alive the links of most urbanites with their rural roots.

But having lived in the cities for most of our lives and in some cases for two or three generations, we have developed an outlook different from that which our rural cousins have. But nevertheless, we come to learn of life of the vast majority of Indians (70% to 75%) who still reside in villages, through text books, mass media, etc.

The Predominance of Rural India is Evident during Elections

The relevance of agriculture and the issues before our rural cousins are brought to the fore, time and again by Indian political which keep public attention focussed on the issues facing agriculturists. The vital role of agriculture is also highlighted by the river water disputes between various states, the agitations for minimum procurement prices, support prices, etc. for agricultural produce, agitations for reduction in tariff for power supply, the election promises of some political parties for waiving off of agricultural loans if they come to power keep reminding us of the relevance of the rural populace as vote banks during elections.

THE LAND REFORM LEGISLATIONS OF THE 1950'S AND 1960'S

The Land Reform legislations of the 1950's and 1960's have now become things of the past of which we come to know only through our text books. These land reforms abolished the Zamindari land revenue system established by the British. Along with this also went other similar land revenue systems like Ryotwari, Malguzari, Mahalwari, etc. These systems, mainly Zamindari were formalised by the British but they had been in existence since long before British rule came to India. They were in fact a result of thousands of years of evolution of land tenure and which along with the caste system shaped the lives of our forefathers. As we have seen how caste and casteism are still alive in our minds-whether consciously or sub-consciously in the same manner, though to a lesser extent our agrarian roots are also still living in the minds of an average Indian. How did the institution of landed property come into being is what we shall try to understand in the following paragraphs.

The Evolution of Landed Property in Ancient India-References in Vedic Literature

Ownership of Land was Common in Vedic Times: To begin with, as long as human beings roamed in tribal clusters from place to place, land must have naturally been looked upon as a gift of nature and thus the common property of everybody. But when settled agriculture became the main occupation a system would have become necessary for the title to land to be allocated to different individuals. Initially, land was considered to belong to the person who first cleared it. In times of peace, this doctrine to establish the title to landed property would have seemed a logical one.

In the transitory stage between nomadic hunting and gathering and the establishment of settled agriculture, there must have existed shifting agriculture. Under the nomadic lifestyle the only items owned by a tribe would have been the weapons used for hunting; and as hunting had to be undertaken collectively even the weapons would have been owned collectively.

In the very next stage of nomadic (shifting) agriculture, the pieces of land that were cleared for cultivation would also have been held under the common ownership of the tribe. Only when settled agriculture became the order of the day would the practice of individual ownership of land could have come into being.

VEDAS PROHIBITED LAND GRANTS

But in an age when in the then recent past all property was under common ownership, the idea of gifting property to any person would have appeared strange.

The tradition embodied in the Shatapatha Brahmana (a Vedic text) and referred to in the Mahabharata that land must not be given away even on the plea of a sacrificial fee, reflects this attitude. The fact that land grants were being scoffed at indicates that up to the Mahabharata period (dated around 1200 B.C.E.) the idea that land could be an object of purchase and sale had not yet been established. This attitude is in direct contrast to the regular practice of making land grants to Brahmins and noblemen, apart from land becoming an object of regular purchase and sale which was the characteristic of later times.

TRIBAL MORALITY INFLUENCED THE PROHIBITION OF LAND GRANTS

The above attitude against Land Grants which was seen up to the time of the Mahabharata seems to typify the attitude towards land ownership in Vedic and the Post Vedic times when land was no longer held as common property of the tribe (i.e. the Gana), but in that scenario, individual (private) ownership of land was gradually being established. The fact that land grant also had started is established by the fact that they were frowned at in the legal literature which goes to prove the ambivalent attitude that existed towards a practice that was not prevalent before those days, but had since then begun to be observed.

The Shatapatha Brahmana and the Mahabharata are chronologically placed in the Post-Vedic period but before the rise of the big monarchical states of Koshala and Magadha. In those days the purchase, sale and grants of land was frowned at as land had been till then held till as common property and when individual ownership had finally come to be established it had been linked to the labour put into making it cultivable, as the statement in the Manusmriti (a later text) reflects.

Secondly, in those days of social stratification and the caste system of the later days of Magadhan imperialism (i.e. after 500 B.C.E.) had not yet come about. In the tribal set-up of the days of the Rig Veda (i.e. before 1500 B.C.E.) every male member of a tribe had to work in the collective activity of hunting.

When the disintegrating tribal society of hunters, took up agriculture to be its prime occupation, land was collectively owned to begin with. Every member of the tribe seems to have had an equal right to whatever the tribe produced collectively.

Even the tribal chief did not wield the absolute powers that characterised the monarchs of later ages. That the Vedic king's authority was limited is clear from the fact that in the Atharva Veda, Indra is invoked to give the king's share (Bhaga) in the village. But in later times the king himself is stated to be the collector of his share according to the Panchavimsa Brahmana.

MANUSMRITI ON RIGHTS TO LAND OWNERSHIP

According to an ancient India text, the Manusmriti "Land belong to him who first cleared the timber and a deer to him who first wounded it." This couplet provides a clue to the understanding of a very important doctrine of ancient Indian economics.

It makes it clear that, at least to begin with the title to property of land was allied to the labour put into making it cultivable. Finally in a society where the title to property in land was linked to the labour put in to make it cultivable; land grants as well as purchase and sale of land would have seemed strange when there existed vast tracts of freely available virgin land which could be cleared and claimed by any person. But as the Aryans society established itself on the Gangetic plains, the population gradually increased and the shortage of arable land began to be felt and frequent transfer in the ownership of land became the order of the day. Transfer of land apart from being a sign of settled agriculture also indicates a shortage of land. When virgin land is abundant the motive to transfer land or to get it transferred is naturally weak.

PATTERN OF OWNERSHIP OF LAND CHANGED FROM COMMON TO INDIVIDUAL

The changes in the pattern of land ownership also brought about corresponding changes in the connotation of words used in day to day language. In this context it is relevant to note the gradual change in the meaning of the words Bhratru and Bhratrivya. These words occur in the Atharva Veda where they stand for brother and brotherhood. But gradually they came to mean rival and rivalry. This change in connotation shows that hostility had started manifests itself with the Vedic Kulas i.e. families, over the division of property, of which, land was the primary constituent in an agrarian society.

The system of landholding also gradually underwent fundamental changes. Whereas to begin with the whole tribe (Gana) held the ownership of land being cultivated, the ownership gradually narrowed down to the Vamshas or blood relations which further disintegrated to the Kulas or families. This narrowing down of ownership must have affected the size of the individual holdings. Tribal holding upon which the entire tribe used to work, must have been much bigger in size. Its fragmentation into separate family holdings must have naturally limited its size. It must have been further limited in the subsequent period with the rise of the individual proprietary rights on land.

THE ASHWA MEDHA SACRIFICE WAS A METHOD FOR LAND GRABBING

But after the individual ownership of land had come to be established parallel to the tendency of fragmentation there was also an opposite tendency of the formation of large landed estates.

As people practiced settled agriculture on individually owned land, it could be grabbed by others. The landed estates must have come into being in this way, as a result of war and the grabbing of land of one kingdom by another. The martial caste of the Kshatriyas would have been in the position of carrying out such plunder. The Ashva-Medha Yagna was another method of extending ownership to the lands under weak kings or over lands which had not come under individual proprietary ownership. Such accumulation of land in the hands of a few landlords created a class of landlords and cultivators.

6

RISE OF THE BIG MONARCHICAL STATES IN THE GANGES VALLEY

With the formation of monarchical states and their capital cities which were the hub of mercantile activities, there emerged a class of absentee landlords who largely lived in the cities but had vast landed properties in rural areas. Such absentee landlords are mentioned in the Pali text of Buddha's time. These absentee landlords had landholdings relatively near the monarchical states of the Ganges valley. These states were mainly Koshala and Magadha. As these landlords came under the sovereignty of the kings of Koshala and Magadha their landholdings came to be integrated with the prospering mercantile economy of these kingdoms. In the Pali texts we find mention of landlord-merchants like Anathapindaka and Kossiyagotta. The state in whose territory these landlord-merchants lived also gained in the form of increasing collection of taxes and the general prosperity.

In these monarchical states, the landlord-merchants played the role of intermediaries between the state and the actual tillers of the soil. Thus a nexus was established between the state and the landed aristocracy. But in the foothills of the Himalayan range which were outside the

Gangetic monarchical states of Magadha and Koshala the landed aristocracy was not under the sovereignty of any outside king. The landlords were their own rulers and had conglomorates of oligarchies. Such oligarchies of the Mallas, Lichavvis, Koliyas, etc. are mentioned in the Pali texts.

THE STRUGGLE BETWEEN THE TRIBAL OLIGARCHIES AND THE MONARCHS

These landholding oligarchs were different from the absentee landlords of the plains, in that they were based on their landholdings, did not have any significant mercantile contacts with the outside world and above all did not owe loyalty to any King as did their counterparts in the Gangetic Valley. These landlords were bound to one another in a tribal oligarchy which refused to yield taxes to the monarchies from the Ganges Valley nor did they acknowledge any sort of sovereignty of any outside monarch. Herein lay the seeds of the struggle between the tribal oligarchies and the monarchical states. Right from Ajatashatru who ruled Magadha in the 6th Century B.C.E. during Buddha's time up to the Nandas of the 4th century B.C.E. we hear of a running struggle between the tribal oligarchies of the Himalayan foothills comprising the Mallas, Lichavis, Koliyas and some other tribes with the monarchical states of Koshala and Magadha.

This struggle brought about the destruction of the independent tribal oligarchies. The victory of the monarchies over the tribal oligarchies was also the victory of a more advanced and organised economy over the closed tribal economy. But as a result of this struggle, land the primary factor of production came under state supervision. While the state did not deny the right to private property, it nevertheless adopted measures which siphoned off a large segment of the produce as revenue to be collected in the royal treasury. This further increased the strength of the monarchical states. Thus in the Ganges valley and in the Himalayan foothills, the administrative suzerainty of the Magadhan King came to be absolute. The nexus between the state and the large landholders came to be firmly established. But the regions to the south of the Ganges valley viz., Madhya-desha and Dakshina-patha i.e. Central and Southern India, were still outside the pale of Magadhan imperialism.

FABLEISED RECOLLECTIONS OF THE ARYAN MIGRATIONS INTO SOUTH INDIA

From the earliest Aryan migrations into the Ganges valley in the Post Vedic period, some Aryan tribes had started trickling down into Central and Southern India. The fableised recollectlon of the Sage Agastya leading the Aryans across the Vindhyas and that of Parshurama retrieving the land of Kerala from the sea so that the Aryans could settle there indicate the migration of the Aryans to Central and Southern India. These immigrants had established pockets of settled agriculture and had mushroomed into small kingdoms. The earlier non-Aryan settlers already had their own kingdoms located in pockets of agriculture, throughout the country. But these kingdoms were relatively small and were separated from each other by dense un-reclaimed forests. Along with this population pressures were being felt in the Ganges Valley by the 4th century B.C.E. This was the general situation when the country's first pan-Indian empire was established by Chadragupta Maurya.

THE RAID OF ALEXANDER THE GREAT

It was in this scenario where the tribal oligarchies were battling the rising Monarchical States in the Ganges Valley, that Alexander and his Macedonian (Greek) phalanxes crossed the Hindu Kush into Punjab after overcoming the Persian Achameanian Empire. The kingdoms that Alexander faced in Punjab were similar in organisation to the tribal oligarchies of the Hills of Mithila north of Magadha, rather than to the proper monarchies of Magadha and Koshala.

The two main tribal-oligarchical kingdoms in the Punjab were that of Taxila which was ruled by Raja Ambastha (or Ambhi-Omphis in Greek) and Arratta which was ruled by Raja Pururava (or Puru-Porus in Greek). While Ambhi decided that discretion was the better part of valour and made an "honourable" compromise with Alexander by joining forces with the invader against his compatriot Raja Pururava who ruled the land between the Vipasha (Beas) and the Vitasta (Jhelum).

Pururava fought a devastating battle with Alexander on the banks of the Jhelum and we are told that the river flew red for a whole day during the battle. Pururava was defeated, but not before he had so demoralised the Macedonian army that it refused to advance forward into India-to the kingdom of the Gangaridans on the Ganges. Alexander retraced his steps after making Pururava his vassal, but the result of Alexander's raid was to destroy the tribal-oligarchical kingdoms in the Punjab which could have posed a hurdle to the growing Mauryan power.

THE RISE OF MAGADHA

Meanwhile for three hundred years before the coming of Alexander, Magadha had been growing in importance in the Ganges valley. Magadha and Koshala were two of the most powerful states that had arisen in the Ganges valley in the 6th century B.C.E. i.e. around the time of Gautama Buddha. Koshala was the stronger of the two, and was ruled by King Prasenjit. (If mythology is to be believed Lord Sri Rama ruled Koshala from Ayodhya in earlier times of the epics). The rival kingdom was Magadha and was ruled by Ajatashatru. The two kings were related to one another and so there was no direct war.

But it so happened that during one military campaign, the army of Koshala was camping on a river bed. Unfortunately a flood came about, and the entire army along with its commander Bimbisara (King Prasenjit's son) was washed away. King Prasenjit died of grief soon after this and as there remained neither king nor army to defend the Kingdom of Koshala, it was taken over by Ajatashatru, the king of Magadha. Magadhan power continued to grow till it became the unchallenged power in the Ganges valley.

THE NANDAS

In around the 4th century B.C.E., the throne of Magadha was usurped by an ambitious general named Mahapadma Nanda. According to the Dharmashastras, Mahapadma Nanda was a Shudra by caste and hence, he is debunked in Dharmashastra literature as an usurper. The Dharmashastras say that, "With the usurping of power by the Shudra Nandas, the Kshatriyas have ceased to exist in Aryavarta." However, the Nandas were powerful, and apparently also just, kings. Mahapadma Nanda's grandson was Dhana Nanda, and he was ruling from Pataliputra when Alexander the Great invaded the Punjab. At that time, Dhana Nanda's kingdom stretched up to the Ganga but did not include today's Western UP and Punjab. Hence, the kingdom of Magadha has been referred to in the Greek chronicles of Alexander as that of the Gangaridans.

The Greeks, however, never reached Magadha. Among the Greeks who came with Alexander, we are told, there was a rumour that the Gangaridans are far more fierce than the soldiers of Porus (Pururava) whom the Greeks had fought with in Punjab. The Greeks had won a very costly victory against Porus and hence as the Ganagaridans were even more fiercer, the homesick Greek soldiers revolted against Alexander and refused to advance beyond Punjab. Thus Alexander had to retrace his steps from Punjab itself.

THE COUNTRY'S FIRST PAN-INDIAN EMPIRE

The Maurya empire was established by Chandragupta Maurya soon after Alexander's departure. Chandragupta, guided by his shrewd mentor, Chanakya, overthrew Dhana Nanda, the last Nanda king and crowned himself king of Magadha. He started off the first known political unification of India. His armies conquered virtually the whole of India. The Maurya Empire, under him stretched from Karnataka to Afghanistan and from the river Indus to Bengal. He even attacked the Greek Governor of Punjab, Seleucus Nikator and defeated him. There was subsequently a treaty between Chandragupta and Seleucus whereby, Seleucus ceded Punjab and Sindh to Chandragupta and also gave his daughter in marriage to Chandragupta.

But now we had an empire that stretched all across India. Revenue collection was now to be a qualitatively different task than what it had been under the small pre-Mauryan kingdoms of the Ganges valley. What made this task more difficult was the fact that dense forests separated the isolated pockets of settled agriculture and as against the dense forests there existed a surplus population in the Ganges valley. This apart the aboriginal tribes that roamed in the forests practiced shifting agriculture. Thus to bring the vast empire under a dependable revenue collection system, the state had to undertake more fundamental tasks beyond simple revenue collection to ensure proper and systematic collection of revenue. Now we move on to examine the change which the first Pan-Indian empire of the Mauryas brought about in the Landholding Patterns and consequently on the Political Set up in ancient India. —The Coming of Feudalism in Post-Maurya Times

THE FALL TOWARDS FEUDALISM

As described above, we find that in the post-Mauryan times, the geographical spreading of farmlands over vast areas, due to which the jurisdiction of tax collection was no longer limited to the tiny isolated Janapadas as in the Mauryan times.

As long as the centralised apparatus of the Mauryan state existed it could carry out the process of revenue collection but with the collapse of the empire and the disintegration of this centralised apparatus, this task became increasingly difficult. This created the necessity for an intermediate class between the tillers of the widespread farmlands and the sovereign monarch. The extension of farmlands on a scale that seemed almost limitless in those days along with the corresponding absence of a centralised tax collecting apparatus was one of the most important reasons for the emergence of intermediaries and the rise of feudalism.

DISAPPEARANCE OF THE SHRENI GUILDS

This expansion of the physical dimensions of the agrarian economy required the large scale supply of various commodities to the countryside. The apparatus of the Arthashastra type with its heavy tolls at every Janapada frontier now became a hindrance for the essential commodity movements due to large scale trade handled by private traders and not by the state as in Mauryan times. The absence of a central authority after the downfall of the Mauryan empire accounted for the absence of good and secure means of transport to all corners of the expanding settled territory. This became an hindrance to extensive commerce.

The only way to satisfy the village demand was for the producer-artisans to move out of the centralized Shreni guilds and spread out into the countryside. With the strengthening of this tendency, the urban based centralised production units of the Mauryan period began to disintegrate. So also did the till now cohesive Shreni guilds.

THE RISE OF THE SELF-SUFFICIENT VILLAGE ECONOMY

The individual producers who resulted from this falling mode of production, settled in the scattered villages throughout the countryside. In the absence of good means of communications. The village now began to get the characteristic of being itself self-sufficient closed economic unit which produced all its required commodities internally. Without any exchange or trade. While trade did exist it was a much smaller and irregular scale than it was in the Mauryan times. Thus while in Europe the coming of feudal relations in the middle ages saw the rise of craftsmen-guilds, in India the rise of feudal relations was marked by the disintegration of the Shreni guilds.

Rise of a Class of Hereditary Revenue Collectors-the Feudal Lords

This shifting of economic activity was accompanied by the shifting of political power to the rising class of village feudatory revenue collectors who stood one above the other in a hierarchy in place of the salaried bureaucrats who collected revenue for the Mauryan State. In the changed circumstances the practice that was gaining ground was of appointing revenue collectors who would not be paid a salary by the king but who would be entitled to a share in the revenue collected by him. Thus the position of a revenue collector changed from being that of a salaried employee of the king to that of a petty chieftain himself. Such hereditary revenue collectors were called "Samant". They also maintained a fighting force which could be called upon by the king when needed to defend or attack other kingdoms. The Samants were the feudal nobility.

ROLE OF TEMPLES IN REVENUE COLLECTION

When such revenue collectors were to be appointed for the first time, the opposition of the tax paying tillers was smothered by making religious institutions like temples, Ashrams, Viharas, Chaityas, etc., perform the function of collecting revenue. Hence the practice of generous land grants to temples, ashrams. individual Brahmins, etc. Along with the right to collect revenue there was an obligation to pass on a part of the proceeds to the king who had given the land grant. Only in rare cases was the obligation to pass on part of the revenue to the donor-king was waived. Thus these temples and monasteries served both as the institutional and ideological arms for establishing this new mode of revenue collection. Thus the administrative costs of overcoming the opposition to this new revenue system was also reduced by making ecclesiastical institutions as intermediaries.

BRAHMADEYA, DEVADANA AND AGRAHARA LAND GRANTS

These land grants were to religious institutions were called Brahmadeya, (i.e. donated to Brahmins) Devadana (donated to Gods) and Agrahara (Settlement-of priests) These lands donated to the temples and monasteries apart from being used as normal tenancy also carried a right vested with the temple authorities to call for unpaid labour (called Vishti) as a religious service to the temple from the tillers on the donated land.

This unpaid labour, became an important method of enrichment of the intermediary revenue collectors, which the temples were, apart from having the rights of revenue collection.

RIGHT TO CARRY ARMS FOR THE NOBILITY 'SAMANTS'

But the physical muscle of this method of revenue collection through intermediaries, was the right to bear arms which was given to the feudal lords and the petty local chieftains. These armed feudal lords could be called upon by the king to render military service to quell a rebellion to defend the kingdom from attack or to launch an attack on neighbouring kingdoms.

The armed retinue of every feudal revenue collector-administrator was maintained out of the revenue collected locally. Thus the local feudal lord was the paymaster of this armed soldierly, and not the king whose kingdom they might be called on to defend. This undermined the power of the king and we hear of rebellious nobles in this period. This was unthinkable during the centralized administration of Mauryan times.

Ultimately the maintenance of armed guards and the obligation to render military service became the qualification for making grants of land with revenue collection rights. These grants were made in recognition of valour displayed by the various feudal lords in the battles in which the particular kingdom was involved. The Jagirdari, Subahdari and Inamdari grants of the Muslim period which came later were also of this type. But the feudal relations were established in the Post-Maurya period, much before the coming of the Muslims.

THE KING WAS AT THE MERCY OF HIS NOBLEMEN

But the political consequences of this type of dependence of the king on the feudal lords in military matters often turned out to be unfortunate for those kings who did not have sufficient control over their vassals and their private armies of retainers. Many a times the vassals did not pass on the revenue collected to their king, this led to a perpetual struggle between the king and the feudal lords under him. Often the feudal lords would switch loyalties from one king to another whenever circumstances favoured this.

The feudal system as a whole was characterised by the diffusion of executive authority in the hands of innumerable petty chieftains vastly reducing the absolute power of the king.

Summing up of the Landholding Scenario in the Ancient Hindu (Pre-Muslim) Period

To sum up we can say in the period of 2200 years from the post-Vedic Period (i.e. 1000C.E.) upto the establishment of Muslim rule in India (around 1200C.E.) Indian socio-economic development passed through the following three stages.

The 1st Stage: In the post-Vedic age with the rise of caste divided society, to begin with, cattle and later largely land became the object of ownership. There existed large landholdings of two types-the first were the tribal oligarchies like the Mallas and Lichhavis as depicted in the Jataka stories. These oligarchies were eliminated by the pre-Mauryan monarchical states of Koshala and Magadha.

Alongwith these oligarchies in the hills, there existed on the plains within the kingdoms of Koshala and Magadha, large landed estates owned by absentee landlords. These were the second type of large landholdings. Such absentee landlords are mentioned in the Pali text of Buddha's time. These absentee landlords had landholdings relatively near the monarchical states of the Ganges valley. As these landlords came under the sovereignty of the kings of Koshala and Magadha their landholdings came to be integrated with the prospering mercantile economy of these kingdoms.

In the Pali texts we find mention of landlord-merchants like Anathapindaka and Kossiyagotta. The state in whose territory these landlord-merchants lived also gained in the form of increasing collection of taxes and the general prosperity. In these monarchical states, the landlord-merchants played the role of intermediaries between the state and the actual tillers of the soil. Thus a nexus was established between the state and the landed aristocracy.

The corollary of these large estates of the absentee landlords were classes like the ardha-sitika share croppers. This indicates the existence of a society sharply polarised into two classes. Extensive landed estates in the Ganges Valley which were under private ownership were tilled by the labour of classes like the ardha-sitikas. Indepedent small peasantry seems to be largely absent in the civilized belt of the Ganges valley in that period.

The 2nd Stage: The imperialism of the Mauryas marked the second stage which led to the extinction of the big landowners and also of the urban merchants. The object of this was to eliminate centres of potential opposition to the state, through the almost complete elimination of this intermediate class between the state and the peasantry. The Mauryan state itself assumed the role of this class which it had successfully eliminated. But after the departure of the Mauryas and alongwith them of the highly centralised multifunctional administrative apparatus, a void was left between the state power and society (of peasant cultivators).

The 3rd Stage: The filling up of this void marks the beginning of the third stage. This void was filled up by the policy of giving land grant; followed by the emperors in the post-Maurya period and continued by the Gupta and Post-Gupta Kings. The titles assumed by the Gupta kings also indicate that they ruled their large empire by proxy. The Gupta kings did not call themselves Samrat as Ashoka, Maurya and Chandragupta Maurya were called. The titles of the Gupta kings like Samudragupta and Vikramaditya included Param-Eshwara (The Greatest-God), Param-Bhattaraka (The Greatest-Protector of the Brahmins), Maharaj-Dhi-Raj (King of Kings). All this indicates that the Gupta kings recognised themselves not as undisputed absolute monarchs, but as Chieftains of many other lower (and defeated) chieftains who paid tribute to the Guptas.

But now the social relationships were of a qualitatively different nature than those prevailing in the pre-Maurya period. During the Maurya period too land was granted to farmer cultivators. But what was granted was not the right of revenue collection, but the right to cultivate and pay a part of the produce to the Mauryan state in the form of tax. The land grantees of the Gupta age were not owners of the lands and the villages granted to them. They were not interested in actual cultivation of the land themselves. They were only invested with the rights of revenue collection and exacting of forced labour, etc. A part of this revenue collected they gave to their overlord-the Gupta Emperor. In this respect they were neither land-owning aristocrats, nor were they absentee landlords, they were feudal intermediaries between the state and the peasantry.

It can thus roughly be summed up that in the pre-Mauryan period the landholding class in the tribal oligarchies comprised mostly the Kshatriyas. This must have been so as the passage from a tribal to a settled agrarian society the social class that could have established, through muscle power, its ownership over property (mainly land in an agrarian society) would have been that which wielded arms. (But in the kingdoms they seem to have been mainly Vaishyas like Kossiyagotta and Anathapindika).

In the later periods i.e. in the Gupta and Post-Gupta Periods, the grantees must have been largely, though not necessarily individual Brahmins and temples as they constituted the class which commanded royal patronage and had a lesser tendency to rebel against the king, unlike the nobility which had a martial attitude. The temples also exercised religious influence and hence were most acceptable as revenue collectors to the God-fearing peasantry.

These land grants along with the rights of revenue collection and the free forced-labour services of nearby villagers and the generous offerings of devotees had made Hindu temples into conglomorates of vast collections of wealth in terms of gold, silver, gems, artifacts apart from acres of land and the rights of revenue collection.

SATI (PRACTICE)

Sati (also suttee) is a Hindu funeral custom, largely defunct in Modern India, in which the dead man's widow used to immolate herself on her husband's funeral pyre.

The term is derived from the original name of a goddess, who immolated herself, unable to bear the humiliation of her (living) husband. The term may also be used to refer to the widow herself. The term *sati* is now sometimes interpreted as 'chaste woman'.

Origin: Few reliable records exist of the practice before the time of the Gupta empire, approximately 400

CE. While a couple of instances of voluntary self immolation by women as well as men are mentioned in the Mahabharata and other works that may be considered at least partly historical accounts, it is known that large parts of these works are relatively late interpolations into an original story. Also, the immolation or desire of self immolation is not regarded as a custom in the Mahabharata and as such the word 'sati' as a custom never occurs in the epic as compared to other customs such as the Rajasuya yagna. Rather, the instances are viewed as an expression of extreme grief on the loss of a beloved one.

Aristobulus of Cassandreia, a Greek historian who traveled to India with the expedition of Alexander of Macedon, recorded the practice of *sati* at the city of Taxila. A later instance of voluntary co-cremation appears in an account of an Indian soldier in the army of Eumenes of Cardia, whose two wives vied to die on his funeral pyre, in 316 BCE. The Greeks believed that the practice had been instituted to discourage wives from poisoning their husbands.

Voluntary death at funerals has been described in northern India before the Gupta empire. The original practices were called *anumarana*, and were not common. They were not necessarily practices that would be understood as *sati* at present, since it was not necessarily a widow who died. Those who died could be anyone, male or female with a personal loyalty to the dead person. They included other relatives of the dead person, servants followers or friends. Sometimes these deaths were bec of vows of loyalty taken in life. Compare wi Japanese seppuku.

Widow burning, the practice as understood today, started to become more extensive after about 500 CE, and the end of the Gupta empire. The neo-Buddhists have ascribed to the decline of Buddhism in India, the rise of caste based societies, and the idea that sati was used to reinforce caste status. There are also suggestions that the practice was introduced into India by the Huna Buddhist invaders who contributed to the fall of the Gupta empire.

At about this time, instances of *sati* began to be marked by inscribed memorial stones. The earliest of these is in Sagar, Madhya Pradesh, though the largest collections are some centuries later, in Rajasthan. These stones, called *devli*, or sati-stones, became shrines where the dead woman became an object of reverence and worship. They are most common in western India.

By about the 10th century *sati*, as understood today, was known across much of the subcontinent. It continued to occur, usually at a low frequency and with regional variations, until the early 19th century.

Practice: The act of *sati* was supposed to take place voluntarily, and from the existing accounts, most of them were indeed voluntary. The act may have been expected of widows in some communities. The extent to which any social pressures or expectations should be considered as compulsion has been the matter of much debate in modern times. It is frequently stated that a widow could expect little of life after her husband's death, especially if she was childless. However, there were also instances where the wish of the widow to commit *sati* was not welcomed by others, and where efforts were made to prevent the death.

Traditionally, the funeral of any dead person would usually have taken place within a day of the death. Thus a decision by a widow to die at her husband's funeral would often have to be made quickly. In some cases, such as when the husband died elsewhere, it was still possible for the widow to die by immolation, but at a later date.

The connection with the original marriage between the widow and the deceased was emphasized. Unlike other mourners, the *sati* at the funeral was often dressed in marriage robes or other finery. Her death may have been seen as a culmination of the marriage. In the preliminaries of the related act of Jauhar, both the husbands and wives have been known to dress in their marriage clothes and re-enact their wedding ritual, before going to their separate deaths.

There are accounts of many different approaches of the widow to her death. The majority have the widow seated or lying down on the funeral pyre beside her dead husband. There are also many descriptions of widows who walked or jumped into the flames after the fire had been lit, and there are descriptions of widows who lit their own funeral pyres after seating themselves on it.

Some written prescriptions to the practice exist; a recent one has been quoted at a mailing list.

Compulsion: *Sati* was supposed to be voluntary, but it is agreed that in many cases it may not have been voluntary in practice. Leaving aside the matter of social pressures, there are many accounts of widows being physically forced to their deaths.

Pictorial and narrative accounts often describe the woman seated on the unlit pyre, and tied or otherwise restrained to keep her from fleeing after the fire was lit. Some accounts say that the woman was drugged. There is one description of men with long poles preventing a widow from fleeing the flames.

Royal Funerals: Royal funerals sometimes have included the deaths of many wives and concubines. A number of examples of these occur in the history of Rajasthan.

Symbolic Sati: There have been accounts of symbolic *sati* in some Hindu communities. A widow lies down next to her dead husband, and certain parts of both the marriage ceremony and the funeral ceremonies are enacted, but without her death.

Jauhar: The practice of jauhar, known from Rajasthan and Madhya Pradesh was the collective suicide of a community. It consisted of the mass immolation of women, and sometimes also of the children, the elderly and the sick, at the same time that their fighting men died in battle. It is detailed in a separate article.

Burials: In some Hindu communities, it is conventional to bury the dead. It has been known for similar widow deaths to occur in these communities, but with the widow being buried alive with the husband, in ceremonies that are otherwise largely as in the immolation.

Prevalence: Records exist of *sati* across most of the subcontinent. However, there seem to have been major differences historically, in different regions, and among different communities.

Numbers: There are no reliable figures for the numbers who died by *sati* across the country. A local indication of the numbers is given in the records kept by the Bengal Presidency of the British East India Company. The total figure of known occurrences for the period 1813 to 1828 is 8,135, thus giving an average of about 600 per year. Bentinck, in his 1829 report, states that 420 occurrences took place in one (unspecified) year in the 'Lower Provinces' of Bengal, Bihar and Orissa, and 44 in the 'Upper Provinces' (the upper Gangetic plain). Given a population of over 50 million at the time for the

Presidency, this suggests a maximum frequency of immolation among widows of well under 1%.

Communities: It is said by some authorities that the practice was more common among the higher castes, and among those who considered themselves to be rising in social status. It was little known or unknown in most of the population of India and the tribal groups. According to at least one source, it was very rare for anyone in the later Mughal empire except royal wives to be burnt.

However, it has been said elsewhere that it was unusual in higher caste women in the south (quoted from Kamat).

Regional Variations: It was known in Rajasthan from the earliest (6th century) to the present. About half the known *sati* stones (about 150 in total) in India are in Rajasthan. However, the extent to which individual instances of deaths resulted in veneration (glorification) implies that was not very common.

It is known to have occurred in the south from the 9th century through the period of the Vijayanagara empire, which fought Islamist kingdoms up to the 17th century. Madhavacharya, who is probably the best known of those historical figures who justified the practice, was originally a minister of the court of this empire. The practice continued to occur after the collapse of the empire, though apparently at a fairly low frequency. A record exists of a minister of the kingdom of Mysore giving permission for a widow to commit *sati* in 1805.

In the Upper Gangetic plain, while it occurred, there is no indication that it was especially widespread. The earliest known attempt by a government to stop the practice took place here, that of Muhammad Tughlaq, in the Sultanate of Delhi in the 14th century. In the Lower Gangetic plain, the practice may have reached a high level fairly late in history, it appears possible, based on available evidence and the existing reports of the occurrences of it, that the greatest incidence of *sati* in any region and period, in terms of total numbers, occurred in Bengal and Bihar in the late 18th and early 19th centuries. This was during the earlier period of British rule, and before the abolition. The Bengal Presidency kept records from 1813 to 1829. The frequency increased in periods of hardship and famine. Ram Mohan Roy suggested that it was more prevalent in Bengal than in the rest of the subcontinent. An unusually large number of the surviving reports for this period are from Bengal, also suggesting that it was most common there.

In modern times, *sati* has been largely confined to Rajasthan, mostly in or near Shekhawati, with a few instances in the Gangetic plain.

Recent Incidence: *Sati* still occurs occasionally, mostly in rural areas. About 40 cases have occurred in India since independence in 1947, the majority in the Shekhawati region of Rajasthan. The last clearly documented case was that of Roop Kanwar. However there are claims that other more recent deaths have also been cases of *Sati.*

Roop Kanwar, a childless 18-year old widow, committed sati on 4 September 1987, some allege forcibly, dressed in her red wedding dress, in Rajasthan's Deorala village. Several thousand people were said to have been at the event. After her death, she was hailed as a 'sati mata', meaning pure mother. The event quickly produced a public outcry in urban centres, pitting a modern Indian ideology against a traditional one. A much-publicised investigation led to the arrest of a large number of people from Deorala, said to have been present in the ceremony, or participants in it. Eventually, 11 people were charged.

On January 31, 2004, a special court in Jaipur acquitted all of the 11 accused in the case, observing that the prosecution had failed to prove charges that they glorified *sati*.

On 18th May 2006, Vidyawati, a 35-year-old woman allegedly committed sati by jumping into the blazing funeral pyre of her husband in Rari-Bujurg Village, Fatehpur district in the State of Uttar Pradesh.

On 21 August 2006, Janakrani, a 40-year-old woman, burnt to death on the funeral pyre of her husband Prem Narayan in Sagar district.

Justifications and Criticisms: Brahmin scholars of the second millennium justified the practice, and gave reasonings as to how the scriptures could be said to justify them. Among them were Vijnanesvara, of the Chalukya court, and later Madhavacharya, theologian and minister of the court of the Vijayanagara empire, according to Shastri, who quotes their reasoning. It was lauded by them as required conduct in righteous women, and it was explained that this was considered not to be suicide (suicide was otherwise variously banned or discouraged in the scriptures). It was deemed an act of peerless piety, and was said to purge the couple of all accumulated sin, guarantee their salvation and ensure their reunion in the afterlife.

Law Books: These are relatively late works. Justifications for the practice are given in the Vishnu Smriti.

> *Now the duties of a woman (are)... After the death of her husband, to preserve her chastity, or to ascend the pile after him. (Vishnu Smriti, 25-14).*

There is justification also in the later work of the Brihaspati Smriti (25-11). Both this and the Vishnu Smriti date from the first millennium.

The Manu Smriti is often regarded as the culmination of classical Hindu law, and hence its position is important. It does not mention or sanction *sati* though it does prescribe life-long asceticism for most widows.

Scriptures: Although the myth of the goddess Sati is that of a wife who dies by her own volition on a fire, this is not a case of the practice of *sati*. The goddess was not widowed, and the myth is quite unconnected with the justifications for the practice.

The Puranas have examples of women who commit *sati* and there are suggestions in them that this was considered desirable or praiseworthy: *A wife who dies in the company of her husband shall remain in heaven as many years as there are hairs on his person.* (Garuda Purana 1.107.29) According to 2.4.93 she stays with her husband in heaven during the rule of 14 Indras, i.e. a kalpa.

It is notable that in the Ramayana, Tara, in her grief at the death of husband Vali, wished to commit *sati*. Hanuman, Rama, and the dying Vali dissuade her and she finally does not immolate herself. Examples of the act in the puranas include the following.

In the Mahabharata, Madri, the second wife of Pandu, immolates herself. She holds herself responsible for the death of her husband, who had been cursed with death if he ever had intercourse. He died while performing the forbidden act with Madri, who blamed herself for not having rejected his advances, although she was well aware of the curse.

Passages in the Atharva Veda, including 13.3.1, offer advice to the widow on mourning and her life after widowhood, including her remarriage.

Argument that the Rig Veda Sanctions Sati: It is often claimed that this most ancient text sanctions or prescribes sati. This is based on verse 10.18.7, part of the verses to be used at funerals. Whether they even describe *sati* or something else entirely, is disputed, The hymn is about funeral by burial, and not by cremation. There are differing translations of the passage. The translation below is one of those said to prescribe it.

> *Let these women, whose husbands are worthy and are living, enter the house with ghee (applied) as collyrium (to their eyes). Let these wives first step into the pyre, tearless without any affliction and well adorned.*

The text does not mention widowhood, and other translations differ in their translation of the word here rendered as 'pyre' (*yoni*, literally "seat, abode"; Griffith has "first let the dames go up to where he lieth"). In addition, the following verse, which is unambiguously about widows, then contradicts any suggestion of the woman's death; it explicitly states that the widow should return to her house.

> *Rise, come unto the world of life, O woman — come, he is lifeless by whose side thou liest. Wifehood with this thy husband was thy portion, who took thy hand and wooed thee as a lover.*

A reason given for the discrepancy in translation and interpretation of verse 10.18.7, is that one consonant in a word that meant house, *yonim agre* "formost to the *yoni*", was deliberately changed by those who wished claim scriptural justification, to a word that meant fire, *yomiagne.*

Argument that Sati was an Act of self Defence: Hindu scholars such as Prabhat Varun have tried to show [26] that Sati was not part of Hindu doctrine at all, but a practice of voluntary immolation by Hindu women as a means to avoid the humiliation and stigma associated with rape. The argument is that the practice came into effect during the Islamic invasion of India, to protect their honour from Muslims who were known to commit mass rape on the women of cities that they could capture successfully. It is argued that the prevalence of sati has been exaggerated by Europeans and Muslims as a canard against Hinduism.

Counter-arguments within Hinduism: No early descriptions or criticisms of the practice within Hinduism, (or in the other native religions of Buddhism or Jainism), are known before the Gupta period, as the practice was little known at that time.

Explicit criticisms later in the first millennium, included that of Medhatithi, a commentator on various theological works. He considered it suicide, which was forbidden by the Vedas:

One shall not die before the span of one's life is run out.

Another critic was Bana, who wrote during the reign of Harsha. Bana condemned it both as suicide, and as a pointless and futile act. There does not seem to be any thought or suggestion among any of these critics that the act would not be voluntary.

Reform and bhakti movements within Hinduism tended to be anti-caste, favoured egalitarian societies, and in line with the tenor of these beliefs, they generally condemned the practice, sometimes explicitly. The Alvars condemned sati, in the 8th century. The Virashaiva movement in the 12th and 13th centuries, also condemned it.

In the early 19th century, Ram Mohan Roy wrote and disseminated arguments that the practice was not part of Hinduism, as part of his campaign to ban the practice.

Non-Hindu Views and Criticisms: The Sikh religion explicitly proscribed the practice, by about 1500.

The principal foreign early visitors to the subcontinent whose have left records of the practice, are from Western Asia, mostly Muslim, and later on, Europeans. Both groups were fascinated by the practice, and sometimes described it as horrific, but often also as an incomparable act of devotion. Ibn Battuta described an instance, but said that he collapsed or fainted and had to be carried away from the scene. European artists in the eighteenth century produced many images for their own native markets, showing the widows as heroic women, and moral exemplars.

As Islam established itself in the subcontinent, their opinion of sati changed to regarding it as a barbaric practice. The earliest known governmental effort to halt the practice were by Muslim rulers, including Muhammad Tughlaq.

Europeans also showed a change in their attitude to local customs as they became dominant local powers. The earliest Europeans to establish themselves were the Portuguese in Goa. They tried early on to override local customs and practices, including *sati*, as they attempted to Christianise territories in their control. The British entered India as a trading body, and in the earlier periods of their rule, they were largely indifferent to local practices. A campaign against *sati* was however set up by the evangelical movement in Britain, particularly by William Wilberforce, as part of a campaign to increase missionary activity in India. The practice of *sati*, and its later legal abolition by the British (along with the suppression of thuggee) went on to become one of the standard justifications for British rule. British attitudes in their later history in India are usually given in the following much repeated quote, usually ascribed to General Napier-

You say that it is your custom to burn widows. Very well. We also have a custom: when men burn a woman alive, we tie a rope around their necks and we hang them. Build your funeral pyre; beside it, my carpenters will build a gallows. You may follow your custom. And then we will follow ours.

SUPPRESSION

Mughal Period: Humayun issued a royal fiat against sati, which he later withdrew.

Akbar required that permission be granted by his officials, and these officials were instructed to delay the woman's decision for as long as possible. The reasoning was that she was less likely to chose to die once the emotions of the moment had passed. In the reign of Shah Jahan, widows with children were not allowed in any circumstances to burn. In other cases governors did not readily give permission, but could be bribed to do so. Later on in the Mughal period, pensions, gifts and rehabilitative help were offered to the potential sati to wean her away from committing the act. Children were strictly forbidden from the practice. The later Mughals continued to put obstacles in the way but the practice carried on in the areas outside their capitals.

The strongest attempts to control it were made by Aurangzeb. In 1663, he "issued an order that in all lands under Mughal control, never again should the officials allow a woman to be burnt". In spite of such attempts however, the practice continued, especially in conditions of war and upheaval.

British and other European Territories: By the end of the 18th century, the practice had been banned in territories held by some European powers. The Portuguese banned the practice in Goa by about 1515, though it is not believed to have been especially prevalent there. The Dutch and the French had also banned it in Chinsurah and Pondicherry. The British who by then ruled much of the subcontinent, and the Danes, who held the small territory of Shrirampur, permitted it into the 19th century.

Attempts to limit or ban the practice had been made by individual British officers in the 18th century, but without the backing of the British East India Company. The first formal British ban was in 1798, in the city of Calcutta only. The practice continued in surrounding regions. Toward the end of the 18th century, the evangelical church in Britain, and its members in India, started campaigns against *sati*. Leaders of these included William Carey and William Wilberforce, and both appeared to be motivated partly by a desire to convert Indians to Christianity. These movements put pressure on the company to ban the act, and the Bengal Presidency started collecting figures on the practice in 1813.

From about 1812, the Bengali reformer Ram Mohan Roy started his own campaign against the practice. He was motivated by the experience of seeing his own sister-in-law commit *sati*. Among his actions, he visited Calcutta cremation grounds to persuade widows not to so die, formed watch groups to do the same, and wrote and disseminated articles to show that it was not required by scripture.

On 4 December 1829, the practice was formally banned in the Bengal Presidency lands, by the then governor, Lord William Bentinck. The ban was challenged in the courts, and the matter went to the Privy Council in London, but was upheld in 1832. Other company territories also banned it shortly after. Although the original ban in Bengal was fairly uncompromising, later in the century

British laws include provisions that provided mitigation for murder when "the person whose death is caused, being above the age of 18 years, suffers death or takes the risk of death with his own consent".

Sati remained legal in some princely states for a time after it had been abolished in lands under British control. The last such state to permit it, Jaipur, banned the practice in 1846.

Modern Times: In modern India, following outcries after each instance, there have been various fresh measures passed against the practice, which now effectively make it illegal to be a bystander at an event of *sati*. The law now makes no distinction between passive observers to the act, and active promoters of the event; all are supposed to be held equally culpable. Other measures include efforts to stop the 'glorification' of the dead women. Glorification includes the erection of shrines to the dead, the encouragement of pilgrimages to the site of the pyre, and the derivation of any income from such sites and pilgrims.

Enforcement of these measures is not always consistent however. The enforcement of some measures, such as the possible stopping of worship at ancient shrines, is a matter of modern controversy.

Influences on Art and Culture: A famous fictional depiction of sati is found in *Around the World in Eighty Days* (1872). The English gentleman Phileas Fogg and his servant Passepartout are travelling India when they find a sati. They risk their lives battling the Indians and rescue the drugged princess Aouda from death.

In Tom Robbins' 1984 novel *Jitterbug Perfume,* the main character Alobar witnesses and attempts to intervene in an act of sati. George MacDonald Fraser's character Flashman witnesses a mass sati by the wives and concubines of an Indian ruler, Jawaheer, in the Punjab in *Flashman and the Mountain of Light*, which is set during the First Sikh War. In *Flashman in the Great Game*, he questions the widowed ruler of Jhansi, Lakshmibai about why she, when her husband died, did not follow the custom; Lakshmibai's response is to ask whether Flashman thinks she is a fool. (While Fraser is normally a most meticulous researcher, whose books are quite accurate on matters of historical fact, the Sikh prohibition on sati mentioned above indicates that, in this case, he may have been in error—or that the Sikhs' prohibition did not apply at this time, or not to royalty.)

Rudyard Kipling wrote a poem entitled "The Last Suttee" in 1889. In this poem, the Boondi Queen escapes her British captors (who are seeking to prevent her carrying out sati, and keep her alive) and throws herself upon her husband's burial fire, to become his foremost queen in the afterlife—"To rule in Heaven his only bride, while the others howl in Hell."

SUMMER ROSES ON THE BLUE MOUNTAINS, 1976 OPENING ADDRESS

Without getting rid of your *Thamo Guna* and your anger, how are you going to understand the spiritual background? Without getting rid of your *Rajo Guna* and of your temper, how are you going to take any interest in spiritual aspects? In fact, the best of the three *gunas* or qualities is the *Sathwa* and that itself promotes *Bhakthi* or devotion and that is the best *sadhana*. What I am telling you is the simple and elemental truth. Divyaatma swarupas, boys and girls, who are the future citizens of this country:

The first thing man does soon after he is born, is to try and understand his mother and father. In the wider context of the community in which we live, after understanding one's parents, one should make an attempt to understand the full significance and meaning of one's mother country and mother civilisation. The history of our country and the history of our traditions and culture are our true parents. Although more than twenty-five years have lapsed since we have attained the independence of our country, it is a great misfortune that in our entire period of independence, we have not been able to produce one single text or scripture which is typical of the culture of our country. Although, we, in this country, have been listening to real history in many ways, yet we are truly not able to recognise the essence of our civilisation. Such permanent truth, which does not alter with time, such permanent truth which is not affected or altered by revolutions, is the only truth which is the essence and true form of our culture. The inner meaning and significance of such truth represents the history of our country. Forgetting this sacred history of ours, we are taking two alternatives which are temporary, transient, and artificial. Because of this change, no student has been able to assert and say what the true picture of our country is. Unfortunately, today every student makes all attempts to pass an examination. They do not make any attempt to understand the wisdom that lies behind true

Education: The students of today are spending their lives in trying to acquire some cheap texts or notes and somehow or other, by hook or by crook, and by copying from such cheap texts or even by terrorising the teachers, they just want to pass the examination. From the time he wakes up from sleep till the time he goes back to bed, man spends all his time in such a trivial manner. Today, man's way of living is such that he becomes dependent on others. Man is always in a hurry, he is simply spending his time in running from one thing to another. He runs for a seat in a bus, he runs for a seat in a cinema hall, he runs for a seat in a college, he runs all his life for acquiring one thing or another. Even while undertaking to do things in such a hurry and running for everything, they have the misfortune of having to wait for everything. Our life appears like the life of a bird or of an insect dependent on others for everything. We spend all the time today in reading useless stories. One does not find time to read useful history and useful aspects of one's culture. Not only this, man also wants to take a short cut for everything that he wants to achieve. Man does not want to make an effort in growing crops. He wants to go and steal the harvest prepared by someone else. He does not want to take the trouble for anything. He wants to earn his money by picking the pocket of someone else and such are the shortcuts that he wants to adopt for everything.

How is the breadth of vision of a man going to enlarge if he wants to lead a life like that? A man whose *Atma* has not blossomed and a man whose spiritual background has not blossomed will never understand the whole purpose of his life. Today people think that acquaintance with a large number of books is education. Acquaintance with books can never be called education. For this enormous creation that we see in this universe, that there is an invaluable strength behind it all, is a truth that we should recognise. Although man's birth and death look to us as common things, yet to understand the secret of birth and of death is a very difficult matter. No one is making an attempt to understand the reason for human life and for human birth and death. No one is trying to understand the basis for this. Man is not making an attempt to understand the duties and responsibilities of himself as a human being. Why is there so much anarchy and confusion in the world today? Why is there no peace?

Is it because there are no educated people, and is it because there are no educational institutions? No, there are plenty of them, but the educated people do not have the necessary culture and breadth of vision along with their education. Our country has been known as the spiritual treasure house. Yet today we are forgetting the spiritual treasure and the real strength of our country.

Children are not understanding even the meaning of education. For the root word "*Vid*" if you add "*Ya*" then you get *Vidya*. Here "*Vid*" stands for illumination and "*Ya*" stands for that. Therefore, that which gives illumination and light is *Vidya*. That which gives you light and sheds your ignorance and that which gives you wisdom and superior knowledge can alone be called *Vidya*. What promotes ignorance and darkness cannot be called *Vidya*. From time immemorial, our country had been the leader of all the countries in the world. It had enjoyed the position of leadership in this world, and that is the kind of sacredness that we have enjoyed in the past. Because there are no leaders today who can set an example of such ideal life and who can hand on such ideals to other countries, we have fallen on bad times. The main reason for this is that in the people, there is no coordination between the words that they utter and the acts that they do. You are all the future citizens of Bharath. You are the citizens who will bring up the welfare of Bharath. The entire prosperity and welfare of the country rests on your shoulders. Your lives and your hearts are pure and sacred. They are unwavering. I am hoping that you will not allow the confusion and anarchy prevailing in the country to confuse your pure, unwavering, and sacred minds; and I am hoping that you will develop into ideal citizens of this country.

We keep on talking about discipline. Simply to keep on talking about discipline and not have the strength and faith to accept discipline is not going to do any good. To discipline and duty we should also add devotion. It is only when these three D's—Discipline, Devotion, and Duty—are together and firmly implanted in your heart, that your heart will be able to develop into a sacred one. Today, unfortunately, even persons who claim to be, and boast of being highly educated, appear as weaklings in practical life. Such people do not understand the value of true education. As one student has just mentioned, the entire education has turned into one begging bowl.

Students, after having a degree in their hands, should undertake to be of some service to the community. If, on the other hand, you search for a job or beg for a job, it is not correct. For the chariot of this body, the axle, namely the *Atma*, has become very distant. It is for rectifying this defect—namely to remove the distance between the body and the axle, we will have to undertake *Yoga*. *Yoga* does not mean that one should give up his family and his house. It does not mean going to a forest and sitting in meditation. Today man faces many problems in the community that he lives in. To be able to face those problems courageously, and to meet and solve them, is the true meaning of *Yoga*. Every man aspires for happiness and a peaceful life. Every man wants a respectable position in the society in which he lives, and every man wants good health; but to be able to deserve this happiness, this health, and this peaceful life is a part of *Yoga*. To be able to enjoy this peace and happiness, we will have to adopt a path, and the path that we have to adopt for this will constitute the *Yoga* of which we are talking.

In the *Bhagavad Gita* the *Yoga* that was taught to Arjuna was to give him the strength by which he does not turn his back on the problems that he was facing. The lesson that was given to Arjuna was that he should face the problem and find a solution for the problem. This kind of *Yoga*, which the students should undertake in their lives, should enable them to face the country and community and the problems thereof. You find the solutions to the problems, and by God's grace, these problems will be solved. One should regard the country's problems as one's own problems. Put away the selfishness and ego in you and regard the problems of the society as your own problems, and you must solve them.

It is necessary that students take the lead in solving such problems. I hope that those of you who are students will be able to imbibe the messages given by the older people in sacred congregations like this, and that you will shape your lives in such a manner that you will become useful citizens of the country. I hope that this will be possible for you. Of all the animals that are born in this world, to be born as a human being is the most difficult and fortunate thing. Having been born as human and having acquired that special gift of intellect, you must sanctify your human birth and human existence. You must be prepared to put into practice one out of the ten things that you preach in preference to just saying ten good things.

You must be prepared to serve as servants for all your lives. Never think of being a leader. Without becoming a servant you cannot become a leader. You must first learn to follow before becoming a leader. We find the world in an unfortunate state because, today, people become leaders without knowing how to become good followers. In that context you must be prepared to spend all your lives in the service of humanity. In the first instance, you must serve your own home, then you must serve your village, then your state, and then the country. Without acquiring the ability to serve in your own home and produce results in your home, how can you serve your country and hope to produce results?

Students: In the first instance you must give satisfaction to your father and mother. According to our traditions, mother and father who have gifted us this human body are to be treated like gods; and if we cannot show them gratitude, our lives are meaningless. Many great saints have sacrificed everything else in order to satisfy their mother and father. Saints like Chaitanya and Pundarika have sacrificed everything to be of service to their parents. In the first instance, you should show gratefulness and provide satisfaction to your mother and father. Then you can make an effort to serve the country. You should be sure that the kind of work that you undertake does not cause waste of time. Everything is time for us, in fact, time is the very basis of all that we see in this creation. If we waste time, we will be wasting our entire life and body. The significance of our commencing the summer classes today is that we recognise the spiritual strength in us. We should take such steps as would promote this spiritual strength and let it blossom out and become useful to others. In the world there are many organisations which are devoted to the service of the community; but our organisation, the Sathya Sai Organisation—should have something specific and distinctive—showing an ideal to other organisations. We are commencing our summer classes today and many experienced and elderly people will come, and they will give you their messages. I am hoping that you will imprint their messages in your heart. Not only imprint them in your heart, but also try and put them into practice. I bless you all and bring this discourse to a close.

BROTHERHOOD OF MAN AND FATHERHOOD OF GOD

Children who do not have good qualities, education which does not have character as its objective, and life which has no morality are purposeless and without any use. An individual who has no peace of mind and the world which has no moon shining in it are similar and are without use and purpose in this world.

Pavitratma Swarupas!: Every item of creation in this world has some distinctive feature and a character of its own. If any item in this world gives up this distinctive aspect, it will destroy itself. Here are some examples for this.

Fire has the ability and quality to burn. Water has the ability to flow. Man has got the quality of human nature, and an animal has the quality of being a brute. When the ability to burn disappears, you cannot call it fire. When the ability to flow disappears, you cannot call it water. When the inner vision or the basic human nature disappears, you cannot call him a man. When the external vision or the brute nature disappears, you cannot call it an animal. Here we see that for everything there is an inherent quality, and this constitutes the life for that particular item. To have an inner vision is the natural quality of a human being. By its very definition, an animal can look only externally. One may, in form, be a human being; but if he has only external vision and is unable to see within himself, he cannot be called a human being. He will be called an animal. Because a prescribed quality is being exhibited or worn as a cloak by each one of these items, this quality is also being called its *dharma*. This *dharma* takes many different forms. When any one item exceeds the natural *dharma* or quality characteristic of itself and promotes something in excess, then that will be referred to as an attempt to promote *dharma*. Just as by effort, a student in a particular class can be promoted to a higher class, an individual by promoting his own natural *dharma* and giving attention to something higher and nobler can earn promotion to a higher level. A lifeless piece of iron can be converted to a set of several useful implements by successive heat treatments.

Out of a piece of iron which has not been properly treated, and therefore worth only a few annas, by making suitable changes, we can produce a watch which is worth 300 rupees. You should notice here that it is the *samskara*, or the change that we give to the substance, that brings the value to it and not the inherent value of the untreated material. As in this analogy, an ordinary and unsophisticated human being can, by seeking the company of elevated beings, get an opportunity of elevating himself to the position of a *Paramahamsa* (Realised sage). Man's mind aspires to get such sacred wisdom through the use of the sensory organs. In such a situation, because the mind is not able to distinguish between the good and bad, the intelligence comes forward and puts itself ahead of the mind for the purpose of distinguishing good from bad. Even the intelligence cannot, by its own accord, decide between the good and the bad; but it is able to make a judgement of everything that is put before it. In the case of a judge, we know that he will decide between right and wrong only on the basis of facts that are put before him. As in this analogy, the nature of intelligence is such that it can decide between good and bad only on the basis of facts that are put before it; and it cannot go outside the facts. Conduct and practice of *dharma* is the quality of the mind; and the decision between good and bad, on the basis of facts put before it, is the quality of intelligence. But in the world today, this kind of intelligence can be classified into four different categories. These are—the first is a selfish type, the second is a selfish-selfless type, the third is a purely selfless type, and the fourth is based upon *Atma*. The first category is always thinking of what is good for one's own self and makes a decision of being good for one's own self. It is like the intelligence of a crow.

This is very common today, and we find this category in large numbers in the world.

The second category partly selfish and partly selfless—will think of the good of one's own self along with the good of others. This appears as the ordinary way of life. The third category, which may be described as selfless intelligence, always thinks of others and will think of the kind of happiness that he wants for himself as also the kind of happiness that others must get. The kind of sorrow that he wants to get rid of is also the sorrow that he wants others to get rid of. So long as you feed and look after a dog, it will follow the master.

So long as you give a salary to a servant, he will be with you and serve you. If you do not show affection, do not give food, and beat a dog with a stick, even a dog will bite you. Similarly if you do not look after the servant well, and if you push the servant to a distance, the servant will stop serving you. In the same manner, when you wish good for others, you will get good for yourself, and when you wish ill for others, you will get ill for yourself. In that context, realising that the human body is given to you for the sake of causing benefit to others, this third category of persons will always be trying to do good to others. This has been described as the kind of *buddhi* (intelligence) which is all the time doing and thinking of doing good to others.

The fourth category—the *Atma Buddhi* is always concerned with the aspect of *dharma* and the necessity for safeguarding *dharma*. He always thinks of himself as a messenger of God; and forgetting his own selfish interests, he always thinks of sacrifice and does good to the rest of the world. In this category only truth has the right to make a decision as to what is good and what is bad. Others have no right to make such a decision. It is in this context that our Sruthis have stated *Sathyam nasthi paro Dharmaha* (There is no *dharma* other than truth). It is because of truth that the sun and moon are shining. It is because of truth that the earth is revolving round itself. It is because of truth that the world is going on in the way in which it is going on. Truth is the basis of everything. But today man has no faith in truth and does not want truth. The one thing that man does not like today is truth. He is always taking a backward step even in regard to finding out and getting the truth regarding himself. He is afraid of coming to know such truth.

How then can such a man, who is afraid of truth within himself, take to the path of truth? On the platform we speak, like a parrot, words like truth, *prema* (love), *ahimsa* (non-violence); and in our daily life we do not have faith in truth, we do not practise *ahimsa*, and we do not follow the path of buddhi. In that context, the young people of today must learn to put into practice these words and not simply utter them in a meaningless way.

Man's life depends upon three things—his words, his thoughts, and his deeds. Whatever desires one gets, one will exhibit them and take them to his mind. For getting a thought, mind is the basis. The thought that comes to your mind will be exposed to the world as the word of the mouth. Once you utter this word of your mouth and expose the thought that has come to your mind, in order that you put it into practice, action comes on. It is only when there is a harmony between this thought, word, and action that man will be in a position to recognise his own true nature. When one is able to put these three—thought, word, and action along the right path, then do we earn *punya* (merit from good deeds); but if we put them along the wrong path, then we will earn sin. We come to the clear conclusion that for good and bad, the three basic things are thought, word, and deed. In order, therefore, to purify our thoughts, words, and action, we should undertake some kind of *sadhana* (spiritual practice). We should make the right attempt to bring about the harmony between thought, word, and deed. This is what was meant when they said that the proper study of mankind is man..

There is a necessity for us to enquire whether this kind of human nature is present today or not. The cost of all items in this world is going on increasing, but the value of man is going on decreasing. Because man has not got the fortune to understand the real value of human nature, he himself is acting in a manner causing the value of a human being to come down day after day. In the very first instance, we must make an attempt to purify and ennoble the thoughts that come to our mind. When thoughts come surging to your mind, you should spend at least a few minutes enquiring whether such thoughts are good thoughts or bad ones, and whether they are for the good of your country, and whether they are going to be helpful or not to the community around you.

Students!

As soon as thoughts come to your mind, you must make an attempt to spend time and decide whether those thoughts are good or bad. If they are bad thoughts, you must immediately put them aside; and if they are good thoughts, you must make an attempt to promote them. When a thorny plant is seen, it is removed the moment it is recognised as a thorny plant; but when a good fruit tree comes up, we try to take care of it and promote its growth. In the same manner, in the field of your heart, as soon as bad ideas sprout, you must pull them out and throw them away. As the seeds grow into a big tree, man also must try to grow and become *Madhava* (God) ultimately. For both these paths, our own qualities have the basic responsibility. Whether in lifeless matter or in living matter, the promotion of good qualities will depend on the way in which you promote and nurture those qualities. Everything that is born in this world must change. Change is a natural quality of all things that are born in this world. How can things that change from moment to moment give permanent happiness to people? Permanent happiness and bliss can be got only from permanent things and not from changing things. Today, in the very first instance, we should make the necessary attempt to make sacred the thoughts that come to our mind.. The young people of today get all kinds of meaningless thoughts into their minds. For those who get these meaningless ideas and thoughts, sacred ideas will be of great help. Man has no rest and peace. Man who is suffering from such an anguish can be helped very much by his entertaining such sacred ideas. Our sacred thoughts have prescribed a *Karma Kanda*, the path of work, by practising which, we will be able to generate good ideas and sacred thoughts. Our body has not been given to us for only eating in the morning, afternoon and evening. The body of ours must be sanctified by doing good work at prescribed times. Time, action and duty should be regarded as man's primary responsibility.

From time immemorial, there have been sacred sayings in our ancient texts; and it is not appropriate for us to forget these and not pay any heed to such sacred things. If we make our thoughts, words, and deeds sacred, there can be no better way for man's emancipation. If each student asks himself the question as to why he is going through the process of education, he will get the answer that it is for securing such and such a degree or for securing such and such a job or authority; and he will, all the time, think of what he will get in return as a result of the education and degrees that he is seeking. This cannot be the right attitude of a student. For him, the right attitude should be to ask himself how his degree will be of use to the community and the country in which he lives, or how he can be of use to others. Life should be a process of give and take, and it should not be a one-way traffic with you being at the receiving end always. All the different branches in education, unfortunately, look as if they have no essence in them. They appear as things which are simply enabling us to just carry on in this world. Good education must be such that it covers both worldly and spiritual matters. Out of education comes humility, and out of such humility comes the right to acquire good qualities and from such a right, you will be able to acquire wealth. Once you acquire wealth, you will be able to follow the path of *dharma;* and once you follow the path of *dharma,* you will be happy in this world as well as in the spiritual world.

Students!

Do not be under the impression and illusion that your education is for the sole purpose of begging for a livelihood. Remember that the education that you get should enable you to do some good to the community that you live in, and the world that you are born into. Just as there is a flash of lightning in the sky whenever clouds gather in the sky, so also, where there is education, there should be wisdom like a streak of lightning. When such sacred wisdom shines in the clouds of your heart, then only will your education enable you to do some good and be of some service to other people.

Today we regard education as just that which we learn in a school or a college or a university. No, this is not right. The entire universe is a place of education for us. Whether it is a workman, or an agriculturist, or a businessman, there are so many things that he has to learn in this world. In fact, every moment in this world we are learning so many things irrespective of what our profession is. In fact, in our lives that kind of education which goes under the name of general knowledge is very essential. Here is a small example. Let us take the case of a student who has taken an M.A. degree and marries a girl who has taken a B.A. degree. In due course, they have a son. If this son gets a cold or a fever, they will be in a terrible confusion not knowing what to do. They will take the son and run to a hospital.

If you have not got the courage and the capacity to handle a situation in which your child gets sick, what is the use of an M.A. degree or the B.A. degree that you acquire. The meaning of this is that in your daily life, if you want to meet a situation and face it, you do not have to take an M.B.B.S. degree; but you have to acquire general knowledge in addition to the knowledge in your own subject. The very first thing that the student has to understand is what is essential for him in his daily life. Let us ask ourselves a question. If we want to acquire a B.A. degree, we can purchase text books, read in our house and pass the examination. For this, why should we go to a college? By going to a college, you have the company of students of different types, we have different attitudes; and by being with them, you get the necessary discipline by which you can face and find solutions to situations which you might face.

While you will get a pass by getting marks in subjects like Physics, Chemistry, Zoology or Botany, there is something else which constitutes the basis of all these subjects and that basis is discipline. If you do not get the necessary qualifications in this broad subject, there is no use of getting marks in a specialised subject. Our students should take care of this aspect. It does not matter even if you do not get marks, but you should have the proper discipline and see that you do not earn remarks. You should make an attempt to respect your teachers. You should make an attempt to satisfy your teachers by your behaviour and conduct.

Prahlāda had said that one who teaches you the very basis of education is the real teacher, and one who tells you that all that you have to do is to reach the divinity of God, is the true father. Such is the teacher and such is the father that you have to seek. But unfortunately, today neither such teachers nor such fathers are available to you. Teachers of today are themselves not following the correct path, and accordingly, the students who learn from such teachers are also not following the correct path. Both are really deceiving the community in which they live. In this young age of yours, while you are still in your youth, the kind of sacred thoughts that generate in your mind and the sacred experiences that you go through will determine the future for you. A young lad by name Mohandas Karamchand attended the drama of Harishchandra, whereby he learnt the importance of truth. He went back to his mother and told her that he would stick to truth in his later life, and by sticking to truth, Mohandas Karamchand evolved into being known as Mahatma Gandhi. Even in those days, there were teachers who wanted to put Gandhi on the wrong path.

When the teacher tried to put him on the wrong path, Gandhiji did not yield. He stuck to the truth, and because of this, he ultimately succeeded even though it meant disobeying his teachers.

Maybe today some teachers will try to give you the wrong path; but if your conscience tells you that it is the wrong path, then it is better for you to disobey the orders of the teacher and follow the right path. The kind of pictures that we witness today, and the kind of dramas that we see today, or the kind of wall posters that we see are such that they cause distortions in your mind and destroy the very human nature and the sweetness of your heart. Because of the destructive nature of what you see, you are getting such bad ideas.

The pure, unwavering, and clean minds of people are being changed and spoiled by the atmosphere around us. The kind of attraction is very transient and can never be true. Such artificial attractions can cause great harm to us. This is responsible for several accidents that occur. Because there are several such things that happen in your daily life, there is a necessity for me to tell you about these common incidents. Some persons, either to go to a library, or to a college, or to fulfil some other duty, go on the motorcycle in the bazaar. In such a situation, the person who is driving the motorcycle must keep his attention on driving and must ensure that he reaches his destination without harming others. He should concentrate on reaching his destination safely. But the person concerned is not accepting and following this duty. He goes on his motorcycle at a great speed and he does not have his attention on driving. His attention is directed towards the wall posters and he gets involved in an accident by hitting against a car or another automobile. The only result of this attracting wall poster is harm.

There is a necessity, at this point, for me to narrate an incident which actually took place. In Kerala, the bus accidents used to be very large in number. This issue was taken to the assembly and several people pointed out the reasons for this large incidence of accidents. Following the advice given by the people, the government followed many approaches but still the accidents were not reduced.

When I visited Trivandrum and went to the house of a responsible person, he asked me the question, why, in spite of all that they had done, were accidents not reduced? I gave a seemingly trivial advice. Immediately this advice was followed, all the accidents stopped. In the Kerala state, women made a special appeal to the authorities that they should be given reserved seats in the front area of the bus, just behind the driver, so that they may travel comfortably and avoid the jolting that one gets in the rear seats of the bus. Because of this, all the time the driver was looking in the mirror to see these ladies and hence accidents occurred in large numbers. You can see how such a foolish attraction by the driver was causing so much harm.

In man's mind today, he is giving room for and promoting foolish thoughts. In the minds of young men, who are the future citizens of this country, such thoughts are coming and they are becoming traitors to their own country. Today you call yourselves students, but in fact you are not seeking Vidya, you are seeking material pleasure.

Students!

You should set aside imitation and you should develop your own inner strength. Whether it is in our conduct and behaviour or in the way in which we dress and talk, all seems to depend on imitation. You have a life of your own, you have desires of your own, and you have a mind of your own; but by imitating and following the mind and actions of someone else, you simply turn yourself into a slave. You are an independent person. Where does this come from and what is the meaning of *swatantra* (freedom)? You have freedom of thought or *swechha*. This word *swechha* comes from a combination of "*Swa*" and "*Ichha*." You follow the dictates of your own desires but never undertake to follow the desires of others. Introspect well on your desires and think carefully; and if you feel that it is good, follow it; but if you think that it is bad, give it up. But man today does not take such a step. He is ever ready and is always attempting to imitate others.

What you see with your own vision cannot represent the ultimate truth. Your vision is looking at the entire creation. When the whole creation constitutes what you see, then you change yourself into the one who sees. When the eye itself becomes what is seen, then your intelligence becomes that which sees. There is an example for this. You are all sitting in this congregation. Your ears are here. Your eyes are here. If at this instant of time, your mind is thinking about something in your village, then even while you are here and while your ears are here, you will not be able to listen to what Swami is speaking. Even though you have your eyes here, you will not be able to see what is in front of you. Thus, while the mind is elsewhere, even if the sensory organs are here, they cannot function as one who sees or one who hears. But sometimes even the mind is seen and the intelligence becomes the seer. In some cases and instances, even the intelligence becomes the seer and the *Atma* becomes the seer. Thus what witnesses everything is the *Atma* and nothing is superior to this. Intelligence is useful to you as seer only with regard to worldly matters, and intelligence is indeed very superior to the sensory organs.

There is a small story to illustrate this. In a village, a blind man and a lame man become friends. The blind man had legs and the lame man had eyes. The lame person sat on the shoulders of the blind person. The lame person was serving the purpose of seeing the passage and steering the blind person. The blind person had his legs, and he was using his legs to move about. In this way they were moving and begging. They were moving from village to village in this manner. In the middle of their journey, the lame man saw a heap of large cucumbers. He said, "Dear brother, if we can stray a little and go to the left, there are many cucumbers there; and we can collect some cucumbers and then go our way." The blind man said that if there are so many cucumbers, it is not likely that they are unprotected.

Just think a little before we go near the plant. The lame man then said that there does not appear to be any fence or protection. The blind man then suggested the possibility of a watchman keeping watch over the plants.

The lame man then said that there was neither a fence nor a watchman keeping watch over the cucumbers. He wanted to go and eat the cucumbers. The blind man then said that if they were truly good cucumbers, would they be left in such large numbers in an unguarded manner? They are surely likely to be bitter cucumbers unfit for eating. Indeed here, the intelligence has worked and the sensory organs have not worked. When they tasted the cucumbers, they were found to be indeed bitter. It is obvious from this story that intelligence is superior to sensory organs. *Atma* is superior even to intelligence. Following the dictates of the ultimate *Atma* it is called *Svechha*. We have changed this word into freedom a kind of freedom that is enjoyed by an animal.

Students!

We all have the form of a *manava* (man). We have the form of a human being. We have the superior intelligence and even after using this intelligence, we still conduct our lives in an inferior way. That cannot be the true nature of human beings. Your desires and thoughts should reach the level of being sacred and good. You should look upon the whole world as a conglomeration of brothers and sisters. In the human family, you should understand and experience this brotherhood of man and fatherhood of God. This should be the spirit of all human beings. Only on that day when you are able to practise and proclaim these ideals to the world can we say that you have re-established the glory of this country. Our *Vedas* and *Sastras* have given us the answers to questions like how a man should live, how a man should conduct himself, and how he should die.

Birth is not the important thing for man. He should promote a good mind and good thoughts throughout his life and should have it at the time of death. To man, death is more important than birth. Your rebirth is determined by the type of death that you get. If you want a good rebirth and a good life in the next birth, you must also desire a good death. We should not die an uncared for death like a death of a dog. We should not devote our life to fulfilling meaningless and sensory desires. Our sensory organs should become our slaves, but we should not become slaves to our sensory organs. The day we become slaves to our sensory organs, we will become slaves to the whole world. If we become slaves to our own sensory organs, what kind of strength can we claim?

We should be masters to our servants, but should not become servants to our servants. Today, we should make an enquiry as to whether we are living in our house as a master or as a servant. The servant of the house can know and will be able to tell you where certain external things are present in the house. But the master of the house will know where the valuable things are kept in addition to knowing the articles of daily use. He knows where each of the valuable things is locked up. Today, we talk of many things which are external to ourselves but we are unable to take or recognise the valuable spirit that is present inside of our hearts. In that context, we are living like a servant of the house of the body rather than as a master of the body. If we are really the master of the house in which we are living, why is it that we are not aware of the good ideas and good thoughts that are present in us?

God is not something present outside you. He is present inside you. Similarly sin is not something which is external to you. It is decided by your own action. The moment you realise these two truths, you will not be a servant to your sensory organs. They will be your servants.

Students!

The things that you listen to here must be proclaimed to the community and you must be prepared to put them into practice. If you want the lamp to shed light on all places, then you should keep the lamp at a height. If you put this light in a pit, how is it going to shed light around? So the sacred ideas in you should be put at a height, in an elevated place, so that the whole world can see them. You should not put them inside the pit of your heart and make them stagnant.

Our body is like a machine. We have the machine of a radio and through the radio we listen to several programmes. Where are these coming from? Is the radio generating them or are they generated elsewhere? These programmes are being generated in some other broadcasting station, and those programmes are being transmitted to us through the radio.

The radio is not generating the programmes. Like this, when we listen to a person's thoughts or ideas, we must realise that they are not coming from his mouth. They are being transmitted through him after they are generated from his heart. He only transmits them like a radio. There is an origin, there is a source from where these sounds are generated. Radio is only an instrument through which these sound waves are transmitted to us. The human body is like this radio. The source is the *atma* and all ideas and thoughts are being generated at this source, the *atma*. You may ask the question as to what are good thoughts and bad thoughts if they are all coming from the sacred *atma*. But why should you classify them as good and bad thoughts? In the process of tuning the radio, you are making a mistake. In this process, the thought that we want to listen to is something, and the station to which we tune is something different. Not only this, in order to enable us to listen to the right thing, the manner in which you make the tuning and the adjustment should also be proper. Our desire is one thing, and if our action is not in tune with that desire, we are having this difficulty. We want to listen to one station, and we tune to a different station. It means such sacred ideas which you want to promote and such sacred ideas which you want in your mind should guide your actions. That is, whatever you do must be to promote such sacred ideas. The ideas and thoughts will not be called good if they are good only to you. They will be called good only if they do good to the whole world.

In man, there are four kinds of desires that emanate. One aspect is to regard the faults of others and one's own faults as being on the same footing and speak on that basis. Another aspect is to speak about the good that is in him and speak about the faults that are in others. The third aspect is to speak about the good in him as well as the good in the others. The fourth aspect is to claim the good that is not in him and speak about the faults that are not in others. This is the worst aspect of the whole lot. Today, we must make a determined effort to root out this fourth aspect. We must be prepared to put into practice the ideas that we want to proclaim to the world.

DIVYA ATMA SWARUPAS

When Sankaracharya wanted to propagate his philosophy in the entire country, he did it with only four disciples. In each college, even if we get ten students who are willing to practise and proclaim these ideals to the rest of the world, that is enough. Every student should make an attempt to make this determination. It is not as if there is no obvious reason for organising this summer course in Ooty. As soon as the summer vacation comes, it is customary for students to plan for different things, and they have many ideas.

They want to have the pleasures of life in this vacation. Submitting oneself to these desires and wasting one's time is one aspect. There are ample opportunities for the students, in the summer vacation, to misuse the facilities that they have. Wasting time is like wasting life. In order to make sure that you do not waste your time, we are making efforts to convert these holidays into holy days in this sacred place. In this sacred time, you should acquire sacred and good ideas and you should be prepared to communicate these ideas to others with whom you come into contact. From tomorrow we will take some specific topic like the *Mahabharatha* or the *Bhagavatha* or the *Ramayana* and will make it possible for you to have sacred ideas and thoughts. Today is your first day, and I have given whatever is necessary for you to lay a strong foundation for what you are going to get in the rest of the days. Without spending more time, I will bring the discourse to a close.

DHARMA NEVER DECLINES

Do you know why this life has been given to you? It is not for searching for food all through nor for eking out a livelihood, but it is to enable you to search and search for God.

7

GREAT INDIANS

PAVITRATMA SWARUPAS

The moment we hear the word Bharath, the name of our country, the Himalayas come to our mind. For centuries in the past, the essential and the great principles of Hinduism were symbolised in truth and *ahimsa*.

These two great principles of truth and *ahimsa* are also symbolised in the silvery mountains of the Himalayas. These lofty mountains are the places where great men and great saints have performed their *thapas* (austerities and sense control). Those mountains appear to us as the symbols of purity attained through truth and through *dharma*. When we look at those mountains, we get the feeling that those silvery mountains are lost in the meditation of Madhava. In those mountains, where the *rishis* (sages) had performed their thapas, lies the origin of Ganges, the sacred river. Ganges is the flowing symbol of Hinduism. Ganges also symbolises what flows through the blood vessels of our country from its spiritual heart. We have to compare the blood vessels and the arteries of Bharath and of its citizens to the flow of the sacred Ganges. The moment we hear the name of Ganges, we are reminded of the two banks thereof on which are the centres of pilgrimage, and on which lie the great places of learning. We visualise, when we think of Ganges, the great spiritual centres like Benares, Prayag, Rishikesh, and Hardwar.

In the same manner, as in this analogy of Ganges, we should also recognise the great pilgrim centres of our mind which lie on either side of the blood vessels.

Our own intelligence and *Anthahkarana* (inner consciousness) are the great pilgrim centres of our body. It is customary that in these sacred places of pilgrimage, sacred tasks are performed; and as a consequence thereof, sacred ideas are generated. In the inner body, alongside the life flow of blood, our mind, our *Chitta* (mind), our *Anthahkarana,* etc., can all be recognised as places where good ideas can be generated.

The fact that Ganges flows in our country has itself got a spiritual significance. The moment we hear about the name of our country, Bharath, we are reminded of the great epic the *Mahabharatha.* The hero of this epic is Lord Krishna. However, the great deeds of Lord Krishna are being pictured in a distorted fashion, and one gets the feeling that we are forgetting the true nature and true character of Lord Krishna. Krishna is one who had mixed with the *gopis* (cowherd maids) and *gopikas* (cowherds) as water mixes with milk. He moved intimately with *gopis* and *gopikas.*

In order to recognise the sacred truth behind the actions of Krishna, we should realise that in the great battle between the Kauravas and the Pandavas, he took Arjuna to the centre of the battlefield and has taught the philosophy of *Karma* or the path of work to Arjuna and to us in the world at large, through the ears of Arjuna. It is said in this context that Dhritharashtra asked a question and described the battlefield as *Dharmakshetra* (Field of virtue)—*Kurukshetra* (Field of action.)

Dhritharashtra asked a question according to which he wondered about the name Kurukshetra. We should understand the hidden meaning and significance of this question. The question says "*Mamaka*"—that is, those people to whom I am bound down by attachment and Pandavas who are known for their *sathwic* (pure) qualities—what is it that these two groups are doing in the battlefield of Dharmakshetra? We have to understand here that Dhritharashtra, in his ignorance, asked a question which really means, from an inner significance point of view, what are the *thamo* (slothful) and *rajo* (passionate) *gunas* (qualities), represented by the Kauravas, doing in the battlefield with the Pandavas who represent *sathwic gunas.* His ignorance was about what these *thamo* and *rajo gunas* were doing in the battlefield of his heart along with the *sathwic gunas.*

In this context, to limit this battle between these qualities to a period of eighteen days is not correct. This battle between the *thamo* and *rajo gunas* on the one hand and the *sathwic gunas* on the other hand, is continually being waged, for all time, in the body which is the Dharmakshetra, in Kurukshetra which symbolises the sensory organs. This continuous battle is always going on and when the battle is on, Lord Krishna in the form of *atma* or the witnessing consciousness is a witness of this battle all the time. Krishna here should be understood as the very essence of *Mahabharatha* come in the human form. This Krishna symbolises the inner consciousness, the unseen *atma* of Hinduism.

With a view to propound this aspect of the cult of Krishna in an ordinarily understood language to the people of the world, to the people in the political, in the cultural, and social spheres, Krishna, the Lord, has come in the ordinary human form.

When we think of the situation in the world today, we see that it is a very diverse and a complicated situation. We are trying to create a new society in the name of socialism wanting to make all human beings come to the same level and wanting all human beings to be exactly the same in regard to their food, requirements, wealth, etc. We are regarding this as socialism, but truly this aspect cannot be called socialism. There is no support in our history or in our traditions to call this socialism. Today, we may be ready and in a position to distribute the wealth and property and to distribute the houses equally among all human beings, but we are not in a position to distribute the totality of desires of all humanity equally between all human beings.

Only when all the human beings have the same desires, can we say this. In fact, all the material wealth, earthly possessions, etc., will be distributed automatically if the desires of all human beings are the same. The process of equitable distribution between all people from the worker to the agriculturist, really started with the French revolution. With this original concept as the starting point, the feeling has arisen that, with every individual, there must be a position of authority.

It has given rise to desires, and the feeling grew that authority and power should not be concentrated in the hands of a few people, but that it should be distributed equally among all men. Gradually this concept underwent several changes; and when it took a distorted form, it acquired the name of Communism.

During both these revolutions, the ideas that gave birth to them are indeed good and sacred and are worth accepting; but in practice, the original concept and the ideals got distorted. As a result of this, the revolutions were unsatisfactory.

These basic ideas of giving equal opportunity and of distributing wealth equally amongst all human beings are being regarded as something new and novel, but this is not correct. Fifty centuries ago, Krishna, in fact, did these very same things and started these ideals.

This historic figure, whom we call Krishna, really established the root of what we, today, call the new society of Bharath. This great figure in our history brought the worker, the agriculturist, and the educated person to the same level and exposed the political hypocrisy which the rulers of the country showed even at that time; and brought them to understand these concepts well. He ruled like an uncrowned king. From ancient times, we have had the sacred idea of referring to Krishna as Gopala. In the word *Gopala,* we have traditionally come to regard *Go* as representing a cow or an animal. This is not correct. In the historic times, everything that gave us prosperity and happiness we regarded as *Go*. We now regard *Go* as meaning an animal; but in reality whoever looks after the happiness of humanity and provides for the prosperity of humanity should be regarded as Gopala.

In those days, Krishna propagated the view that what gives prosperity to the world is the Cow. Man, today, is ignorant and is unable to recognise what is true wealth and what gives true prosperity to humanity. We are now in an unfortunate position of looking at currency notes and thinking that they constitute prosperity or wealth. Krishna pushed aside the foolish concept that these artificial printed notes constituted wealth. This is not wealth; and he regarded the cow which gives us milk as wealth, and this wealth was distributed equally among the people. Not only do we get milk, ghee, butter, curds, and other food material from the cow, but from the cow emanate the cattle; and we use these for purposes of agriculture. We generate all the food that we need from the cow and the cattle. When we talk about the harvest and the milk and the curds, these are in two different categories. The requirements of humanity are essentially of two kinds. One is the milk and related products and the other is the agricultural harvest. These were distributed between the two brothers. Gopala looked after the milk and other related products and the cows; and Balarama, symbolised by the plough, looked after the agriculture and the various products that come through agriculture.

Truly the prosperity of the human race depends on the harvest and the milk and milk products. These requirements of the people do not drop from the sky nor do they generate out of the earth of their own accord. They must come through the cattle and the land.

Balarama and Krishna were examples who showed that they do not care about their own physical strength and that they would sacrifice everything. They were willing to do hard work and showed through hard work that prosperity can be achieved by sincere hard work.

The Lord Krishna was all-knowing, all-powerful, and divinity incarnate, and yet he worked as a charioteer for Arjuna. Krishna was one who recognised the importance of service to the community; and by his own practice and by setting an example to others, he showed that service to others was important. After the battle of *Mahabharatha*, these were the people who took the horses to the river, washed them and tended their wounds and applied medicines. They thereby demonstrated that hard work and compassion to all living beings constitute the duty of all human beings. These two people set such an example in those days.

If we hear of Krishna or Balarama, we immediately think that they were just ordinary sons of either Yasoda or Devaki. This kind of feeling is on an ordinary human level. But if we look at the root meaning of the name Krishna, we understand that "One who is an object of attraction to everyone is Krishna." There is another meaning for this and we can say *Karshayateethi Krishna*. According to this, Krishna is one who ploughs the field. Of course, we must realise that the field that Krishna ploughs is the field of your heart. By this ploughing of your heart, he produces the fruits of peace and distributes them amongst the human beings. Krishna symbolises the great person who planted the seeds of peace in the hearts of the people, and he distributed the fruits of peace among human beings. Such is the ideal picture of Krishna which we should form in our mind.

He used to talk to great people and tell them that this represents the thinking of the great sages of this country, Bharath. There is another aspect to this. He made a sacred determination that he would bring peace and happiness to all human beings by setting an example. He was unmindful of the obstacles that came his way and was always showing a happy and blissful life.

Such was the Life of Krishna

He had the nature by which he radiated happiness, irrespective of whether he was in a battlefield, or a cremation ground, or in a peaceful place. This was a great quality of his. This is the reason why even in the midst of a battlefield, he taught the *Gita* to Arjuna. *Gita* means and stands for a song. We sing only in our happy moments, but Krishna was singing even in a battlefield and was radiating happiness. He was permanently in bliss and he was permanently happy. This is the reason why he was also called *Sath-chithananda* (Being awareness bliss).

As a human being, the divine power that was present in him can be seen more in the *Mahabharatha* than in the *Bhagavatha*. In a story of *Bhagavatha,* he was simply showing some childlike *leelas* (Divine sport), but in the *Mahabharatha* he exhibited a unique combination of human nature and divine nature. In order to proclaim and establish *dharma* from time to time, he himself stated in the *Gita* that he will come again and again. It has been said that he will appear and reappear every time that *dharma* declines. He appears in order to save the good people and punish the bad people and re-establish declining *dharma*.

Here we should understand what *dharma* is. If *dharma* is destructible, then why should the embodiment of *dharma*, God, reappear to establish *dharma*. If *dharma* can disappear like all other destructible things, then it will not be *dharma* at all. *Dharma* is not something which can be destroyed or weakened. If *dharma* is not destructible, then where is the question of *dharma sthapana* (establishment of *dharma*)? We should interpret this as the establishment of the practice of *dharma* and not the establishment of *dharma* itself.

What is declining is the practice of *dharma*, but not *dharma*. When we look in the traditional way, we see that *dharma* in the earliest times, in the *Kritha Yuga*, was on all four legs, and we believe that later in the *Thretha Yuga*, *dharma* was standing only on the three legs. Still later in the *Dwapara Yuga*, it was only on two legs; and it is believed that in the *Kali Yuga* it is standing only on one leg.

We are also learning from our *Puranas* and sacred texts that *dharma* was declining in the *Kritha Yuga* and that Rama came to save *dharma* and re-establish *dharma* in the *Thretha Yuga*. But if Rama re-established *dharma* in the *Thretha Yuga*, what is the meaning of saying that *dharma* had only three legs in *Thretha Yuga*? Once again, as *dharma* was declining, we believe that Krishna came in the *Dwapara Yuga* to re-establish *dharma*, and yet we believe that in *Dwapara Yuga, dharma* stood on two legs only. What is the meaning in saying that one leg has disappeared in the *Dwapara Yuga* in spite of Krishna coming to save it. Krishna came in the *Dwapara Yuga* and came for the purpose of re-establishing *dharma* and yet we say that in the *Kali Yuga, dharma* has only one leg. If this is so, what is the great thing that Krishna has done in *Dwapara Yuga* for the protection of *dharma*? These legs have to be interpreted as relating to the practice of *dharma*.

These *Avatars* never come to re-establish *dharma*—*dharma* was never destroyed—but the practice of *dharma* went on decline. In the *Kali Yuga*, only one way of practising *dharma* remained and that is *Namasmarana* (Remembering God through the Name), and hence we say that there is only one leg in the *Kali Yuga*. When man is born, he is born on two legs. After a few months he walks on four legs. After a few more months he gets back to the use of two legs. When he gets old, he walks on three legs as he uses a stick. All these legs cannot be called legs. They are simply supports to enable him to move his body in the daily life and do his duty. They are instruments which enable him to fulfil his life. So also, as *Yugas* went on, in order that *dharma* might be practised by people, various methods have been introduced, and these methods have, from time to time, been described as legs which enable him to carry on in his life.

The basis for *dharma* is truth and truth is something which is permanent and so *dharma* is also something which is unchangeable. Today some people give a meaning to *dharma* which is different from the original meaning. But at the time when Krishna lived, he was explaining the meaning of *dharma* in a different way.

Today we want to interpret *dharma* by saying that such and such a person is entitled to be happy, and such and such a person is entitled to all comforts. Today's question is why should a wealthy person alone enjoy life? Why should a rich man alone enjoy the pleasures of life?

Why should not a poor man also be given wealth? The wealth should be distributed equally between the poor and the rich people. These questions constitute what we call socialism of today.

In today's socialism, we find a hidden and concealed intent of wanting to provide prosperity to only a certain kind of people, and not wanting the same prosperity for another category of people. But the embodiment of *dharma* in the human form of Krishna was one who desired the well-being of the entire humanity. The true interpretation of *dharma* is to ask for the well-being of the entire human community in the universe. In this context, you may begin to argue that Krishna himself behaved as if he wanted to like some people and favour some people and dislike other people. But the situations were such that Krishna, who was all-knowing, had to make the determination of taking a certain line of action. We should look back and see what Krishna said when Arjuna, in a state of great despondency, refused to go to battle against his own kinsmen, kill them, see their blood and yet become a ruler. Krishna told Arjuna, "I am giving the future of Dhritharashtra and his family. Listen to it. He has one hundred sons but they are all selfish. There is no place for selfishness in this world, and all these must be killed. Even though Dhritharashtra had one hundred sons, there will not be even a single son left to perform the obsequies for him when he dies. Good or bad, *punya* or *papa* are not something which others will give you. These are simply direct results of whatever actions we perform." What Krishna said and agreed to was that under such circumstances, to fight a battle was the right kind of *dharma*. The reason for this is that these people were born to destroy such a nice family.

For this process of destruction, the one, who is born of a slave, has become the help. And in order to add fuel to this fire, there was Sakuni. The battle that was going to come up, the fire that was about to rage was something that cannot be stopped. If you want to save the world and the destruction thereof by this fire, battle cannot be avoided. You have to accept the power of the battle and of the arrows. The fire of *adharma* has spread and taken possession so much that if you want to remove this fire, the only way that can be done is to have a heavy rain and not just ordinary drops of shower. Also this rain must be the rain of arrows. Krishna believed that the battle and this shower of arrows was necessary to stop the fire of *adharma* engulfing the whole world.

The youth of today may get a doubt. Krishna wanted the peace of this world and yet he encouraged this big battle in which forty lakhs of people were killed. Is this called *himsa (violence)* or *ahimsa* (nonviolence)? Even then, Krishna gave an appropriate answer to this. He said, "Arjuna! Let us take the case of a cancerous growth on the body. This cancerous growth gives pain to the whole human body, although the growth itself is confined to a localised area. In that cancer, you have so many small germs present in the wound. When the doctor performs an operation on this cancerous growth, he will no doubt kill millions of germs. He will not think that he is going to kill a million germs and therefore stop the operation. If he does not perform the operation, the germs will be saved but the patient will suffer. He will surely kill the diseasecausing germs and save the patient." Krishna further said, "In this body of the world this is the situation now. The cancer has come in the form of the Kauravas who are ruling. The whole world has got upset, and a state of anarchy is prevailing in the world now. There is also a decline of *dharma*. All families who are living peacefully are being broken up. Therefore, I will be the doctor, with Arjuna as the compounder. I will perform the operation of cancer in the form of the battle of *Mahabharatha*. In this battle or the operation, 40,00,000 (four million) of disease-causing germs will be killed for the benefit of the world. Is this bad or is this good for the world?"

We can also look at this from another angle and we will see that all kinds of attachments and relationships are only bodily relationships. God is present in everyone and some people suffer because of their past actions while the others will not suffer because of the good actions done by them. In this context, we cannot decide what is right and what is wrong. Right and wrong depend on the actions. One body gets relationships with another body because of the bodily relationship, but there is no such relationship between one *atma* and another *atma*. There is only one *atma* in every human body.

In our body there are several organs. Although the body is composed of so many organs, if one of the organs gets sick and has to be separated, we will be prepared to cut it away and remove it. In the same way, if we recognise that the very ancient *jiva* (individual soul) who has entered this body, taking it as a temporary residence; and if a portion gets diseased, there is nothing wrong in cutting away and removing the diseased part of the body. Here Krishna is only demonstrating his authority.

It is a very difficult matter to recognise and accept authority. There is a small example for this. In a hospital you may find a very proficient and capable doctor. He may be a very reputed person in his field. He comes to a decision that for a particular person an operation has to be performed at a particular time the next morning. This will be notified in the notice board and all concerned relatives will be informed. There is no secret about this. Everybody will know about this and the patient will be carried into the operation room. The doctor takes him into the operation room and performs the operation; but due to some misfortune, the patient dies. As a result of this, the police will not come and arrest the doctor. In the same context, if two people enter into a quarrel and one of them inflicts a small wound on the other man with a razor blade, the police will immediately come and register a case and arrest the man who has caused the injury. In the second example, the person does not have the authority to inflict a wound with a razor blade while in the first case, the doctor has the right to perform the operation, even in public.

Sometimes we interpret and call one of these as a help or a good deed while the other one is called a harm. We take the case of a diabetic patient with a wound on his hand. The wound may not heal and may spread to the whole body in the form of gangrene. The doctor will have to come and say that to prevent further spreading of this, the hand will have to be removed. He will then amputate the whole hand, and this is a good deed done to the body.

In another case, if there is a lady who is wearing bangles on her hand, a thief may come and decide to take away the bangles by cutting the hand and taking away the hand with the bangles. While the thief and the doctor have both done the same thing, what the thief has done is harm and what the doctor has done is good.

When there is a young child who unknowingly sets fire to a house, we think that he has done great harm and we begin to punish him. However, when Hanuman burnt down the whole of Lanka, which was as prosperous as heaven itself, we not only did not punish him but we regard him as a sacred person. The reason for this is that in the first case something good was burnt down while in the second case what Hanuman burnt down was the sin itself. He caused injury to the demons and the Rakshasas while the small boy caused injury to good people.

Thus, in order to remove or promote the demoniac qualities in us, we have the complete right and power. It is in the context of recognising these various conflicting situations, in order to preach the inner meaning of these conflicting situations, Krishna gives various instances which will proclaim to us what good things are. Krishna was a selfless person, and he always desired the well-being of the human community. In that context, whatever he may haye done, was always good, and there was never anything bad in what he did. He himself conquered many kingdoms, but he never became a king of any of these kingdoms. He gave those kingdoms to several people. Whatever he may have done, there was always an inner meaning.

All his actions were directed towards preaching an inner meaning. To take another instance, the battle went on for eighteen days, the Kauravas were defeated and the Pandavas were victorious. In the victory, Krishna was the charioteer and Arjuna was in the chariot. After the victory, they came back to their mansion. Arjuna was in the nature of a human being and there was a little remnant of ego in him. As is the common practice even today, the driver of a car is expected to come and open the door of the car when the owner will get down from the car. In the same way, on that day also, when the chariot came and stood in front of his house, he insisted on Krishna getting down first and opening the door.

Krishna did not agree to this; and, in fact, in somewhat strong language, he admonished Arjuna, asked him to get down first and go inside. Not recognising the inner significance of what has been given to him as a command, Arjuna still indulged in an argument with Krishna. Arjuna thought that in the battle, victory was on their side because of Krishna; and he was afraid that some danger might come to him if he enters into an argument with Krishna; and so somewhat reluctantly, he finally accepted what Krishna has said. As soon as Arjuna got out and no sooner did Arjuna go inside, Krishna, in one leap, jumped out of the chariot. As soon as Krishna jumped out, the entire chariot was in flames. All the Pandavas who were witnessing this were surprised and asked Krishna why the chariot had burnt away like that. Then Krishna explained that during the battle, very powerful weapons were sent by heroes like Karna, Bhishma, and others and all these weapons were subdued and kept under his feet. If he had not got down first, the weapons would have exploded, killing Arjuna and the others. Krishna explained that this was the reason for asking Arjuna to jump out first and his jumping out later.

In order to save his devotees, God plans so many different actions in several different ways. Devotees, not being able to recognise and understand the inner meaning of such actions, misunderstand and think that God is giving them unnecessary difficulties. Man has only external vision. God has inner vision. *Paramatma* is always caring for the well-being and good of his people. Whatever he does, he does it for the well-being of his devotees. Even if a son, who has been brought up very carefully by the mother, makes a mistake, the mother will punish the son by giving a slap. When we see this, we feel that a mother who has brought up the son with such care, love, and tenderness is harsh in beating the child; but the mother who beats the child does so with affection. In the same manner—God, the universal father, will punish his devotees, when need be with *prema* and with love. Just as a consequence of that, we should not get the idea that God is wanting to punish people. God is always full of grace. He never gets angry. However, at times He uses words which are harsh, but He is not harsh. It is only the words that are harsh, His heart is soft like *Amritha* (Divine nectar). We must first acquire competence to understand the kind of love and tenderness which God entertains towards His devotees. Pleasure comes out of pain. We should recognise that all pain will ultimately end in pleasure. Because the Pandavas were in the jungles for twelve years and were hiding themselves unrecognised for another year, the people had an opportunity to see their divine qualities.

Because of the many obstacles and troubles that came to Prahlada, and because of the punishments that were given to him, it was possible for the rest of the world to know how great Prahlada's devotion was. Prahlada never had tears in his eyes and he never exhibited any pain when the Rakshasas were harming him. He was only uttering the name of the Lord and was asking the Lord to come to him. Because of such a situation, he was able to promote devotion and show others what real faith and devotion can do. On the other hand, had Prahlada been looked after by his father with care and tenderness and if he took him in his lap, how would Prahlada's devotion and faith be known to the rest of the world?

So all the pains and difficulties that we get will ultimately turn out as means of getting happiness and pleasure. Even a quality diamond does not get its value unless we cut the facets on it. Even pure gold will not be turned into a beautiful ornament unless it is repeatedly beaten hard and put into fire. In all pains and troubles, we should recognise only paths for getting ultimate happiness. So we should be prepared to accept pain. To seek pleasure alone and not to welcome pain is not right. This sacred content of the *Mahabharatha* and the sacred teachings of Krishna regarding the conduct of devotees and other aspects will be given to you from tomorrow. I hope that the students will listen, understand, and benefit by this story of the *Mahabharatha*. I will bring this discourse to a close now to guide us is a very rare thing. When we take an overview of our ancient history, we find that there is one such individual who was able to give a lead and set an ideal example in all spheres of activity.

Krishna was a rare individual. He could be regarded as an ideal for the entire world. But to be able to understand these aspects of Krishna, we have to make some attempts and effort. Truly, if we want to comprehend these ideal aspects of Krishna, we have to push aside, to some extent, the divinity present in him and concentrate on the human aspects of his life and work. So long as we concentrate on his divine aspects, the good human qualities in him will not come to our attention in the proper perspective. Also, if we remain in the position in which we now are, and if we want to experience the great human qualities which he exhibited, this is not possible.

We will have to make a journey backwards in time and move to the times in which he lived. It will be a difficult matter to make a comparison between the time and environment in which he lived and the time and environment in which we now live. Today, the citizens of this country are prepared to worship man; but they are not prepared to understand man. Understanding the kind of divine strength that is present in human beings is possible only if we attempt to do so through human nature.

TWO GREAT HUMAN QUALITIES OF HUMILITY AND OBEDIENCE CHARACTERISED

The Krishna Avatar

Do you know why you have been given your vision and your eyes? Is it for seeing everything that is around you? No, certainly not. It has been given to you to help you to see the supreme one, the omnipotent Divinity.

Pavitratma Swarupas,

Today what our country requires is idealism. In the social and political sphere, we have to have a goal which will be our ideal which we have to aspire for. In any country and in each sphere, one particular individual may be an ideal. But an individual who in all spheres—in the social, political, spiritual, and economic—is able Therefore, if today we want to understand and comprehend the human aspects of Krishna, we will have to make a journey into the times in which he lived. Many may not have understood this; but if we look at the legends around Sri Krishna, then it will become perfectly obvious to us that humility and obedience were two characteristic features of him. People of these times are likely to get some doubt whether humility and obedience are qualities which were, at all, really present in him.

The reason for this doubt is that the kind of Krishna which we see depicted in the cinemas today, and the description of Krishna that we read in the texts of today, differ very much from facts, and hence we get this doubt. In that context, we are also likely to get a doubt as to whether there were such sacred ideas in those times, in Bharath. Just for the sake of earning some money and for the sake of temporary pleasure, we have been distorting our own sacred history. In fact it has become common practice for us to misrepresent our sacred history. When we see these things, we get the picture that Krishna was always fighting with kings and removing them from their thrones. We also think that he was blindly worshipped by his devotees. These are the only two features that we notice. But if we carefully look at the contents of the *Mahabharatha,* written by Vyasa, we get the unmistakable feeling that humility and obedience were present in Krishna in a large measure. In fact, we will see that they were present in excess of what a common man would accept.

There is one simple illustrative example for this. One day, the battle was raging in a terrible manner, and on that day, Karna was using his deadly weapons. Unable to withstand the fury of Karna, the Pandava army was running hither and thither and the Pandavas were very hurt. Dharmaraja hurried to his camp. When he returned to his camp, he found that Arjuna was engaged in another part of the battlefield and Dharmaraja had no help. Dharmaraja was suffering from his wounds, suppressed his excitement, and was waiting for Arjuna's return to camp.

Arjuna returned to the camp after some time. Dharmaraja was, after all, a human being and was suffering a great deal from the physical injury that was caused by the weapons and could not bear it. In his excitement, he started blaming Arjuna and his Gandiva. Dharmaraja looked at Arjuna and said, "What is the use of your Gandiva and all your penance by which you acquired these sacred weapons? Karna has been causing havoc in our camp and you have not been able to retaliate." In this manner, when Dharmaraja showed excitement, Arjuna also showed excitement, and both of them were in an excited mood. Each one tried to console the other. Arjuna went into such a fury that he could not contain himself and was about to hit Dharmaraja with the Gandiva.

At that critical moment, Krishna entered the camp and the humility which was shown by Krishna was such that the Pandavas could never forget it thereafter. Krishna held the hands of Arjuna and pleaded with him and said that in the excitement of war, he should not disobey his brother; and then he went to Dharmaraja and touched his feet and said that he will not let go of his feet till he has excused Arjuna with the fullness of his heart. He told Dharmaraja that the Five Pandavas are like the five *pranas* (vital airs). If among the five brothers, who are like the five *pranas*, such differences come up and if these differences be known to the world, what was going to happen to this world? He would not leave the camp until he was assured that Dharmaraja had excused Arjuna.

In that situation, when Dharmaraja found that Krishna was showing an unprecedented amount of humility and obedience, tears came out of the eyes of Dharmaraja. He said that the humility and obedience shown by Krishna were because of the great love which Krishna had for the Pandavas. Immediately he went up to Arjuna and asked him to forget about the quarrel and apologise to him. We should ask ourselves why Krishna put himself in this situation where he had to go and touch the feet of Dharmaraja. We will then get the answer that this is because of the affection and love which Krishna had for the Pandavas.

As a result of his *prema* to his devotees, God will be willing to put himself in any objectionable position. Krishna is one who demonstrated that as a result of his *prema* to his devotees, he is willing to subject himself to any situation. Here, we should ask ourselves whether we should take the human qualities in Krishna and appreciate them or take the divine qualities in Krishna and take that as an example. In the later case, we will immediately get a doubt as to why he is submitting himself to these things if he is a divine personality. In the context of the society in which we are living, a society which is decrepit in many ways—we should take the human qualities of Krishna and study them.

Such a study will benefit us.

He never modified what he wanted to say either to please others or displease others. He always uttered the truth, irrespective of whether it pleases or hurts others. On one occasion Dharmaraja wanted to perform a *Rajasuya yagna.*

He called all his brothers and told them that they should support him. The brothers immediately accepted the orders of the eldest brother and said that he was the right person to perform such *yagna,* and they were ready to help him. The next day he called for various pundits and priests, and he mentioned to them his intention of performing the *yagna.* The pundits also praised the idea and said that Dharmaraja was the right person to do such a thing. They said many things to please him. Next day he also sent for Dhaumya and Vyasa and told them of his intention of performing the *Rajasuya Yagna* and sought their blessings.

However, Dharmaraja was not satisfied with the approval which he got from these quarters. He thought that Krishna was the very basis of all things and he asked Arjuna to go and bring him. When Krishna came, Dharmaraja touched his feet and told him of his intention of performing the *Rajasuya Yagna.* Krishna listened to all that Dharmaraja had to say, very quietly, and with a smile. Krishna was not prepared to approve the idea just to please Dharmaraja. For a moment he lifted his eyebrows and told Dharmaraja that he should give up the idea of performing the *Rajasuya Yagna* because he did not yet have the right to do so. So long as Dharmaraja was not the undisputed king of this country and so long as there were other kings like Sisupala, Dantavakra, and so on, who were equally strong or stronger than him, he would not have the right to perform the *Rajasuya Yagna*. When he is able to conquer and subdue these other kings such as Sisupala, Dantavakra, and Jarasandha, he will acquire the right to perform the *Yagna*. The reason for this is that to perform any *Yagna*, a certain amount of right was required. To perform a certain *Yagna*, there has to be a lot of wealth and a lot of help coming from the other kings. At that time, Dharmaraja could not count on the support of many powerful kings. So long as there were kings who did not regard themselves as his subjects and were ready to help, there would, in fact, be a lot of trouble for the people. Here, we should really enquire as to what the reason was for Krishna to tell Dharmaraja to go and conquer powerful kings like Sisupala, Dantavakra, and others. These kings were intensely selfish and would do anything in order to maintain themselves in the ruling position. In that process, they were doing a lot of harm to the people with the ultimate objective of selfishly retaining their possessions.

Krishna had the idea that if there are kings who do not have the welfare of the people in their minds, who are only selfish in their approach, there will not be any peace in the world. He thought that such rulers were undesirable and felt that they should be removed. When the ruling power is in the hands of selfish people, knowing that the king will do things which will simply help him in his selfish ambitions, even at the cost of the interests of the people, Krishna told Dharmaraja that such rulers should be removed. Krishna felt that the people in a country are like the organs of a body of the ruler, and the ruler of the country is like the heart of the country so far as the people are concerned. The intimate relationships that exist between the heart and the body should be the kind of intimate relationship that should exist between the ruler and the ruled in a country.

The country and the body are like the object and the image. Just as an individual makes all attempts to escape from an injury that may be coming to his body, so also when there is some harm that is foreseen for the country, the people of the country should make all attempts to remove such danger. Without any personal motive, Krishna very clearly stated that so long as there are such selfish rulers in the country, the country is not going to have any peace and security. So, if Dharmaraja wanted to have the right to perform such a *Yagna*, he must first remove such kings.

Dharmaraja accepted the orders of Krishna. With the blessing of Krishna, he started to first conquer and remove King Jarasandha. With the help from Arjuna and Bheema, it was possible for Dharmaraja to remove king Jarasandha from the kingdom. Having done this, Dharmaraja prepared for the *Rajasuya Yagna*. Krishna himself was ready to give all help to Dharmaraja in the conduct of the *Rajasuya Yagna,* and Krishna was helping him in every way.

Dharmaraja was entrusting each individual with a specific task. Vyasa was nominated as the chief priest. Arjuna was asked to attend to all the preparations for the *Yagna*. Sahadeva was entrusted with the task of receiving the guests. Kripacharya was given the task of giving gifts to various people. As each individual was being given tasks, Krishna was also standing with folded hands, and he said, "Dharmaraja, you are now the undisputed king of this country and I am one of your subjects, I stand before you and ask that I be given an appropriate task."

Dharmaraja was somewhat hurt and said that all the territory and Kingdom of which he was the ruler and all the wealth which he was enjoying were all the result of the divine blessing of Krishna, and it was not right for him to ask to be entrusted with work. Then Krishna said that at that point of time, Dharmaraja should see only the human aspect of Krishna and forget the divine aspect. He further said, "You should not look at me and regard me as one individual citizen amongst your people and you should not think of me in the aspect of the divine *atma*." Dharmaraja then addressed Krishna and said that he should choose any work that he would like. Krishna said that he would like to serve everyone, and that he would like to wash the feet of all the guests and sprinkle the water on his head. He requested that this duty be given to him. He stated further to Dharmaraja that he was the leader while Krishna was the follower and that as a follower he would like to serve people.

Krishna was all-knowing and all-powerful and one should try to understand the meaning of Krishna offering to do such service and the humility that underlies such an offer. Truly, in the books that we read, or the cinemas that we see, or in the dramas that we see, when we look at Krishna, we come to the conclusion that all the aspects in which he is portrayed are indeed divine aspects and that there is nothing human in him. Krishna lived in the *Dwapara Yuga*; and for us who live in the *Kali Yuga*, it will be very difficult to understand the human qualities of Krishna. If we want to understand Krishna's conduct, then the right thing for us to do is to go back to Krishna's time and not bring Krishna to our time.

The young people who really want to understand and comprehend Krishna as an ideal human example must be prepared to travel back and look into the times when Krishna lived. He was the great individual who set up an example for ideal conduct in the social, political, and spiritual fields.

On one occasion, Arjuna was very despondent and he was preparing to commit suicide. Realising and feeling that if this was to be allowed, it would be a very shameful act and a blot on the entire family of the great Pandavas, Krishna went and entreated Arjuna to refrain from such an act, and convinced him that it should not be done. Under many circumstances and in many difficult situations, he was protecting the Pandavas as eyelids protect the eyes.

On one occasion when Krishna went as an Ambassador, Dhritharashtra insulted him and told him that the Pandavas and Kauravas were all brothers, and one set of brothers should not be looked at in any special and privileged manner. Even in that situation, Krishna was prepared to tell the truth to Dhritharashtra without fear or favour. He told Dhritharashtra that there can never be friendship between fire and water. He said that he was always on the side of Pandavas because the Pandavas were the embodiments of *dharma* and they always protected *dharma*. On the other hand, the Kauravas were evil and bad people. While the evil and bad people were giving trouble to those who follow the *dharmic* way of life, Krishna could not remain a passive witness to such a situation. In the body, Dharmaraja was like the head, Arjuna was like the shoulders, Bheema was like the tummy, Nakula and Sahadeva were like the legs, and in that body composed of the Pandavas, Krishna was the heart. So the kind of close relationship that existed between the Pandavas and Krishna was like the relationship that exists between the various parts of the body and the heart. If the Pandavas that constitutes the body are not true, there is no heart called Krishna; and if there is no heart called Krishna, there is no body called the Pandavas. This kind of a relationship that exists between the Pandavas on the one hand and Krishna on the other was told without fear or favour in an assembly where evil people were sitting, with the intention of hurting Krishna and insulting Him. For this, we should take Krishna as an ideal example of a person who is willing to speak the truth, irrespective of the consequences.

This was not a one-way love. The Pandavas were also regarding Krishna as their very life. It is only as a consequence of the *prema* which the Pandavas had for Krishna that such a two-way relationship existed. The kind of tree that sprouts will be determined by the nature of the seed. The smell which one gets when one has a belch will be determined by the kind of food which one eats. The kind of cake you will get will be determined by the kind of flour you will use in making the cake. When Krishna was sent to undertake peace negotiations, the amount of trouble and the hesitation which the Pandava brothers had is not easily understood by others. It is very well-known to Krishna. The Pandava brothers, particularly Nakula and Sahadeva, were worried that their elder brother was sending Krishna, the Paramatma, into a court filled with evil people. They were greatly worried about a possible harm these people might do to Krishna. Until Krishna returned safely after completing the negotiations, Nakula and Sahadeva did not even take a sip of water. They were living in fear and dread of getting bad news about Krishna and were constantly thinking of Krishna and his welfare.

When Krishna returned, the youngest of the Pandavas, namely Sahadeva, embraced Krishna and expressed himself in the following terms, "I was in great hesitation and doubt when Krishna, my brother-in-law, was being sent to negotiate peace. I was worried that harm would come to him. Indeed, I was wanting to ask them to drop the idea of sending him for the negotiations; but I thought that if I gave rise to such an expression, it would have been considered a bad omen. So I kept quiet. However, I am glad that Krishna has now returned safely." So saying, he embraced him and expressed great pleasure.

Because the Pandavas had such great faith and affection towards Krishna, Krishna in turn was also protecting them at all times. The kind of connection that exists between God and his devotees is always strengthened by the bonds of *prema*. Even Lakshmi could not bind Narayana to herself, but Narayana was bound down by the *prema* of Prahlada. When we look at the *Avatar* of Narasimha, we get a feeling of terror. When we look back at the story of Prahlada and Narasimha, we will realise that when Narasimha was giving *darshan* (Seeing the Lord) to Prahlada, he showed great kindness. But it looked as if Prahlada was standing in a corner full of fear. At that time, Narasimha looked at Prahlada and asked him if he was afraid of the fearsome figure which had come to punish his father; but Prahlada explained that he was not afraid of the Lord as it was the sweetest form one can comprehend. He said that he was indeed happy to be able to see the Lord. Narasimha then asked why Prahlada was afraid. To this Prahlada replied that he was afraid because the divine vision which he was then having was likely to disappear in a few moments and he would soon be left alone. The fear which was troubling Prahlada was that God will leave him in this world and disappear. Prahlada wanted to ask God not to leave him. God's divine vision and divine beauty are such that only his devotees can appreciate.

Hiranyakasyapu went on saying that God does not exist anywhere. On the other hand, when Prahlada said that God will be found wherever we want, to him indeed, God was present wherever he sought him, and this is simply the result of *Yad Bhaavam tad Bhavathi* (The thoughts will determine the action). Whatever you have in mind will be reflected back to you as a reality. Today, we are performing *Puja* (ritual worship) to God, and we are worshipping and wanting to follow him. For whose benefit are we doing all these? We are doing all this for our own benefit and not for the benefit of God. The reason why we do all this is that by thinking of the good qualities that are present in God, we will also get such good qualities. There is a small example for this. When we have a thought in our mind about something which is exciting, then we find that our words show excitement and our actions also show excitement. On the other hand, if in our mind there are thoughts which are sorrowful, then our external body will show the sorrow that our mind is experiencing. We need not go so far. If we think of a lime and think that we are cutting it, you will find that there is saliva on the tongue in your mouth. Actually, the lime juice has not come and touched your tongue.

The thought of the lime juice makes your tongue water. If we think of some dirty matter while eating our food, there will be some disturbance in our mind. That is why it is our traditional practice that while people are eating their food, no one should go and talk to them of dirty matter. The reason for this is that the moment we think of something and a thought passes through our mind, our heart attunes itself to that kind of thought. When we are sitting here, if somebody shouts out that there is a scorpion which is seen, irrespective of whether there is a scorpion or not, the very word will make us all shudder and go away from here. Therefore, a particular thing which enters our mind will make us get attuned to that thought in all our actions. So it follows that if we keep on thinking of the divine qualities of God, there is a chance of ourselves developing those divine qualities in us.

It is in this context that it has been said *Brahma vid Brahmaiva Bhavati*. The knowledge of *Brahman* will turn you into *Brahman* himself. Therefore, we should promote good ideas, good ideals, and good thoughts. The result of that is that good will be promoted in us. The real meaning of this is not that God is somewhere and listening to our prayer and that he will come all the way from somewhere to solve our difficulties. In a worldly plane, if someone goes near a person in a position of authority and praises him then he may do some good for the person who praises him, but God is not like this person who is in a position of authority. Even if you pray to God in your mind, His grace will help you. Therefore, prayers to God, singing the glory of God, and thinking of the divine qualities of God are being done by us for our own good and for the purpose of acquiring some of them for ourselves.

Students!

In many ways you are attempting to understand various sacred aspects like the *Mahabharatha*, *Gita*, etc.; but so long as you just listen to them and do not put them into practice, there will be no good at all. Will the Brinjals described in the *puranas* help you in any way? However hungry a tiger may be, will it eat a poori? There may be any kind of attraction, but a real devotee will never think of things which are worthless. Whatever obstacles may come in your way, provided you do not bend in the context of those obstacles and have your faith firmly implanted in your mind, then we can build up a Krishna army.

You must all make up your minds to have an unwavering faith and a steadfast vision. This is an attempt which you should make. Whatever you have grasped in your hand, you have already got. Until your objective is achieved, do not let go the hold. Whatever you have desired for, you have expressed it; and until your desired objective is fulfilled, do not turn back. What you have asked, you have asked. Until what you have asked is granted to you, do not give up. Whatever you have in your mind, you have already thought of it. Never move away from that thought till it is fulfilled. Seeing your determination and devotion, God will yield and grant your desire and what you want, or it may be that you will be tired and you may collapse. Until then, do not change your mind. That is the right path, but to give up your determination is not the right path.

Students!

I am hoping that you will turn back a little into the history of Bharath and look at the ideal life and ideal example which Krishna has set before us. You should have that as your objective and develop yourselves as future citizens of this country. I bless you and bring this discourse to a close he took to prevent war between the Pandavas and Kauravas and to establish security and peace in the country, at that time, will be evident if only we look at Vyasa's Sanskrit text.

Krishna started for Hastinapur in order to negotiate for peace. When Duryodhana, Dussasana, and other Kauravas learnt that Krishna was coming to negotiate peace, they made all preparations and arranged a reception and welcome for Krishna in the very outskirts of the city of Hastinapur. When the great chariot came, it was brought to the front of the city so that a fitting welcome could be given. As soon as Krishna got out of the chariot, Duryodhana and Dussasana met him and appraised him of the fact that a special welcome had been arranged for him and a spacious mansion had been prepared for his stay. They invited him for a special dinner on that day in the palace.

Krishna, who was the very embodiment of peace, appraised Duryodhana and Dussasana that he came there as an Ambassador to negotiate for peace and that it was not right for one who had come in the role of an Ambassador to accept their hospitality even before one's mission was completed. He said that he would gladly accept their hospitality after the mission was completed as it would be proper to do so. With these pleasing.

Krishna was Always a Lover of Peace and Never a Warmonger

Do you know why you have been given legs? Are these legs given to you to go round all the streets and the narrow lanes in a purposeless manner? No, they have been given so that you may visit the temple of God.

Prema Swarupas!

By superficial observers, Krishna is not regarded as a peace-loving person. People generally think of him as one who encouraged battles and fights. They also think that the bloodshed that was caused in the battle of *Mahabharatha* was due to Krishna's love for war. This is not a true picture of Krishna. In fact, he was very peace-loving; and the efforts he made and the trouble words, he went to the house of Vidura. It was a great surprise to Vidura to see Krishna come to his house for he never even dreamt that Krishna would come to his house. He was overjoyed, and he thought that it was his great fortune, and he made all arrangements accordingly.

Vidura gave a hearty welcome to Krishna and they both sat down for a meal. After the meal, both Vidura and Krishna sat together for conversation. Then Vidura said that to him it did not appear proper that Krishna should come, for negotiating peace, to the house of bad people who may do him harm. He felt that knowing everything, Krishna should not have come there to negotiate for peace.

Then Krishna said that it was not as if he did not know that Kauravas were people with bad qualities and evil intentions. Despite this, he felt that when innocent people were being troubled and bloodshed was forthcoming, then everyone who had a responsibility should try his best to prevent injustice and bloodshed, and it was in this context that he was trying to negotiate.

If we really look at the inner significance of what Krishna had said at that time, we will find that Krishna was really concerned with the peace and security of the people; and we will understand that Krishna was truly peace-loving and that he was not a warmonger. All these aspects and acts of Krishna, which were being done on a human plane, should be understood by us as having been done by a human being on a human plane and not by divinity.

Vidura then expressed his doubt and said that these peace negotiations were not going to reach a successful completion because he kne · that the Kauravas had everything ready. All those who were connected with them were also invited to be ready. The weapons were made ready. Under these circumstances, he did not expect any peace.

Krishna then told Vidura that according to *Dharma*, which was only too well known to Vidura, all efforts should be made to establish peace. He said that irrespective of the success or failure, we must do our duty.

The day dawned and Krishna got into his chariot and moved into the city of Hastinapur. That day the city looked gay, the streets were decorated with arches, and all the streets were a pleasant sight to see. In Hastinapur, the people came forward to welcome him like the waves of an ocean would welcome the moon. In that environment, he moved on, smiling and looking at the people of Hastinapur. As soon as he came near the Palace, Duryodhana and Karna were standing there to welcome him.

Women were bringing flowers so that they may be showered on Krishna. Fragrant flowers were showered on Krishna from the terraces. It appeared to Krishna that all this was prearranged by the Kauravas to please him. However, all these external symptoms did neither elate him nor bother him; and he entered the mansion. As Karna and Duryodhana were showing him the way to go into the assembly, Kritavarma was following Krishna. As soon as Krishna entered the assembly, all the kings and subordinate kings stood up and made obeisance to him.

As soon as Krishna entered the assembly, Dhritharashtra, with the help of others, came to greet him. He embraced Krishna and was moving ahead of Krishna with the help of Bhishma, and Drona requested Krishna to occupy the seat of honour. Krishna did not occupy the seat of honour and told Drona that, as he very well knew, there were very learned and eminent Maharishis and yogis who were gathered in that assembly to observe what was going to happen to the peace and prosperity of the country; and it was not proper to offer the seat of honour to him. In accordance with Krishna's instruction, Bhishma called various persons and arranged to seat them in accordance with their importance.

As soon as all these persons were seated, Krishna made obeisance to the members and then occupied his seat. After that Duryodhana, Karna, Bhishma, and Drona occupied their respective seats. After all these elders were seated, the other subordinate kings also took their seats, making obeisance to the assembly. In that assembly, everyone was anxious to hear what Krishna was going to say and know what message Krishna had brought. In their anxiety to listen to him and not miss anything, they all maintained pin-drop silence. Every individual in that assembly had probably looked at Krishna many times earlier, but they were all still looking at Krishna anxiously with wide-open eyes, expecting something very special from him. While his black curly hair and pearl-white teeth were attracting people, he turned towards Dhritharashtra.

The first words uttered by Krishna were that there should be peace between the Kauravas and the Pandavas. He then said, "Let the two families of Kauravas and Pandavas remain friendly forever and establish peace and prosperity in the world. The entire world wanted peace and this was the only word that they were looking for." He further said that he had come there as a messenger and ambassador in the context of wanting peace. He did not stop at this. He went to Dhritharashtra and said that whatever was going to be decided in that assembly was a matter of great concern to him and that Dhritharashtra should think carefully before arriving at a decision. The Pandavas lost their father when they were children. Such innocent children were brought up by Dhritharashtra, and he was responsible for their well-being. The Pandavas were happy that, although their natural father was not alive, there was someone who was affectionate to them.

Krishna went on to say, "Like your natural sons, you have looked after these adopted sons as well as brought them up. It is not right for you to show hatred towards such children whom you have yourself brought up. In obedience to you, they were in a forest for twelve years; and they lived incognito for one year; and because you told them that you would give them their kingdom if they came back after those years, they have now come back.

I am now going to tell you what Dharmaraja told me before I came here. Dharmaraja asked me to convey to you, if they had committed any mistake knowingly or unknowingly, they should be forgiven and all that they were seeking was the affection of Dhritharashtra. He said that your love and affection were more important to them than any kingdom which may or may not be given to them. Dharmaraja said that there were no reasons whatsoever for any hatred on the part of Dhritharashtra towards the Pandavas. If there were any, they were prepared to come and ask for pardon from Dhritharashtra. When we hear such words from the Pandavas, we see how good and how sacred they were.

We will also realise that Krishna, the negotiator of peace, was in no way interested in promoting war. People, particularly students like you, should understand how much trouble Krishna took, and to what extent he went in the promotion of peace. All the kings and monarchs assembled in the hall heard all this; and while reflecting on the circumstances of negotiations, their eyes were filled with tears of sorrow.

All those who were sitting in the assembly were deeply moved at the noble qualities of Krishna who was showing great respect to the elders and great love to everyone. But what could they do in the presence and in the context of the evil-doers, the Kauravas? No one could object to what the Kauravas were doing. Every individual in that assembly developed good feeling towards the Pandavas.

In this manner, Krishna was telling Dhritharashtra in addition to negotiating for peace, various things which will help the cause of the Pandavas. It is not as if Dhritharashtra did not know the truth and strength of what Krishna was saying, and it was not as if he did not understand the sacredness thereof. He also knew that his sons were undertaking something which was wrong. But he had no alternative. He had become a weakling and had to submit himself to the wickedness of his sons. Although Krishna told him in so many words to accept peace, he could not do so, because he was surrounded by his evil children.

When things became unbearable, Krishna told Dhritharashtra, "When a person had no right over a kingdom and still wanted to have the kingdom, he was to be regarded as a thief." The meaning of the word Dhritharashtra is, "one who thinks that a kingdom which does not belong to him is his, and enjoys it." He further told him, "As a consequence of what your sons are doing, the entire country was going to be thrown into confusion and bloodshed. A situation is coming when innocent women and children are going to be involved in this bloodshed. You are taking the world to a situation where the sages and the rishis, who are generally confined to the forest in their *thapas,* will also be drawn into this bloodshed.

"The battle is not going to be confined to the Kauravas and the Pandavas only. Every individual in the kingdom will be drawn into the battle. The forest fire, when it starts raging, will not think that the mango trees should be saved from the fire because they give fruits. This fire of war is going to spread to the entire population and all the people will be burnt." In this context, Krishna advised Dhritharashtra that he should not undertake this war. Dhritharashtra did not know how to meet this situation and what reply to give, and he asked for some time to take rest. Krishna who understood the inner meaning of Dhritharashtra wanting rest took him aside and explained to him the background of the situation.

Then Krishna consoled him and talked with him. In this context, Dhritharashtra said that he realised that his sons were bad people and that they had evil intentions; but being their father, he could not go against their wishes.

Krishna then thought that it was an opportune moment, and he was prepared to use some harsh words. He asked, "If bad things are emanating from our body, are we protecting them and keeping them simply because they have come from your own body? The excreta and urine are coming from our body and are we not throwing them away and cleaning ourselves? Simply because they have come from your own body, are you protecting them and keeping them with you?"

To that, Dhritharashtra said that excreta and urine were lifeless but his sons were living beings. Then Krishna asked, "If bad living bodies are born from us, are we going to keep them and protect them? Similarly, your living sons who were born out of your body are like evil bugs." Because of these words of Krishna, the mind of Dhritharashtra changed a little.

The Kauravas guessed that Krishna was trying to change the mind of their father, and they were planning to catch hold of Krishna and bind him down so that he did not further attempt to influence their father. Vidhura was afraid that some physical harm may be done to Krishna, and he was making attempts to pull Krishna back from the assembly. But Krishna's main purpose was to secure peace and prosperity for the people, and for this he was prepared to sacrifice even his life.

By just reading what people write in sundry books, without recognising the essential basis of all these negotiations, we think that Krishna was promoting war rather than peace. This is quite wrong. Unfortunately, because in our country there are no people who are willing to present even historical events in the proper perspective, we are prepared to regard Krishna, this embodiment of peace, as a warmonger. The generality of people unfortunately do not know Sanskrit and are, therefore, not in a position to read the original text of the *Mahabharatha* as written by Vyasa.

There is one other instance which can be cited to illustrate the peace-loving nature of Krishna. The Pandavas prepared an assembly, and they were preparing to give the first respectful salutation to one who was most respected. The Pandavas did all preparations and wanted to choose one who was universally regarded as the top person in that assembly. Many of the elders in the assembly like Bhishma, Drona and others were all indicating that this honour was to go to Krishna. So Dharmaraja went to Krishna with a view to honouring him.

At that instant, Sisupala, who was sitting therein, got up to decry Krishna in many ways. He was preparing to talk in a very irresponsible and irrelevant manner. People sitting in the assembly could not even bear the harsh words which were being uttered by Sisupala. In a few moments, such irresponsible words spread throughout the assembly. However, Krishna was not at all affected by this tirade and he stood smiling. Sisupala did not stop at this. He got up and shouted, "For what great act of yours are you going to be honoured? Is it for stealing the clothes of the gopis when they were bathing? Is it for stealing the butter from the cowherds that you are going to be honoured today?" Immediately he walked up to Bhishma and asked him to stop his praise of Krishna. At that point, Bhishma started to say something and Sisupala retorted, "Do not be arrogant. Shut your mouth."

At this fearful and most disrespectful situation, all those sitting in the assembly were afraid that something serious was going to happen and they were all showing great concern. But Krishna was completely unperturbed and he was seen smiling. There was no anxiety in his face nor was there any hatred or fear seen in his face. He was regarding all that was going on as something that was being done by Sisupala out of ignorance.

Arjuna and Bheema, from among the Pandavas, were very angry. Krishna, noticing that they were getting very excited, signalled to them not to get excited and that they should remain peaceful.

At this instance, the grand old man, Santanu, Bhishma's father, got up and said that the only person in the assembly deserving the honour was Krishna. He said that Sisupala was so excited because of personal jealousy caused at the time of Rukmini's marriage, and he challenged Sisupala to show even one person in the assembly who deserved the honour better than Krishna. Every king sitting in that assembly had already been subdued by Krishna. If you talk of good qualities, no one else had better qualities than Krishna. If you take the question of learning of the *Vedas* or *Sastras* or even the sixty-four different types of art, no one can equal Krishna. If we talk of the practice of *Dharma*, Krishna is the embodiment of *Dharma*. If we talk of selfless service, Krishna stands right on the top. If we talk of *prema* and love, then the entire blood flowing in the body of Krishna exhibits peace and love at all times.

Krishna who possesses all these good qualities is the only one in the entire assembly deserving this honour. Santanu again challenged Sisupala to show another individual who deserved this honour more than Krishna. To these words, all the kings sitting in the assembly nodded their agreement; and Drona and Bhishma also said that there was no one who deserved this honour more than Krishna. Sisupala was very disturbed and behaved madly, because his end was drawing near. He was still wanting to talk like a madman. Because his end was drawing near, he challenged Krishna to a duel and pulled at Krishna's hand. Even then, Krishna was completely unperturbed and was smiling. But time was passing and Sisupala's conduct was becoming more and more unacceptable.

Noticing this, Arjuna started moving closer to Krishna. At that time, Krishna told Arjuna that he should not get excited and should not worry about what Sisupala said, particularly because that was an assembly and not a battlefield. Their reputation was not going to be lowered just because of what Sisupala says. But if we read the modern text and the description of this event therein, we learn that Krishna was very angry and that he simply threw the disc in his hand at Sisupala and killed him. This is very untrue. In fact the peace-loving nature and the composure which Krishna showed were indeed a surprise to many of the people in the assembly. Here again, the unperturbed attitude exhibited by Krishna, under those trying conditions as a human being, is an ideal example to the world.

In another situation, one other king wanted to imitate Krishna in many ways and his name was Poundarika Vasudeva. He thought that, after all, Krishna was not the only Vasudeva and that he was also a Vasudeva; and in that belief, he used to behave and dress himself exactly like Krishna. He was going everywhere where Krishna went and was saying that he was Krishna. He was behaving as an exact prototype of Krishna. He did not stop there and he was creating a lot of confusion. He was saying that he was the real Krishna and that the real

Krishna was, in fact, putting on a show as an imitation. This was the confusion that he was creating.

This was going beyond all limits and many people came to ask Krishna about the meaning and purpose of all this. Krishna gave them a reply in perfect composure and was not in the least perturbed. "Who has the right to say that the kind of dress that I wear should not be worn by me and who has the right to say that I should not do such and such a thing? So, if someone is wearing exactly the same dress as I am wearing and has the same appearance as I have, I have no right to tell him not to do that. Each one has the liberty to wear such dress on his body as he chooses." He told those people that in a matter like that, it was not good to take any action. It was for the people who were undertaking such imitation to see that they should not do so, and it was for them to take proper steps.

But this situation was trespassing all limits, and it came to a stage when the imitator went to the extent of saying that Sathyabhama and Rukmini belonged to him. Even then, Krishna was very calm and unperturbed. He only said that it was not correct for one to interfere in the affairs of another's family. Krishna said that one may do what one likes with regard to one's own self and his family, but it was not right for him to interfere in another's family, particularly with regard to the women members. Krishna thus warned him that he should exercise great care in such matters. It was only in an extreme situation that Krishna interfered.

In this manner, Krishna always demonstrated perfect composure and a peace-loving attitude. It is only when we understand the ideal nature and qualities of Krishna in the proper perspective, that we will be in a position to get a correct assessment of the ideals of our country in such matters. Young people as you are, on whom rests the future of our country, it is very important for you to understand these aspects of Krishna.

Living a selfless life, desiring only the welfare of the country, and taking care of the people amidst kings who were terrorising the people, he wanted to hand over the kingdom to good and honest people. Thus he never wore a crown and was the uncrowned king doing all this good.

Young students, if you really want to understand the true nature of Krishna, you can do so only by travelling backwards in time to the situation when Krishna was living and doing his work, in the conditions which existed at that time. But for us to try and understand the aspects of Krishna from our present position is not possible. What I am now telling you is contained in what I have often been stating in the words, "You may worship a picture as a God but never worship God as a picture." What you should do is to elevate whatever you see to the position of God. Thus you may worship this tumbler, this table, or this cloth as God; but do not attempt to lower God to the stage of this table or tumbler. You must elevate all things to the high position of God.

If you understand the ideals for which Krishna stood, what you should do is to make a journey and put yourselves in the context of where Krishna lived. If you want to remain where you are and understand various aspects of Krishna, who lived five thousand years ago, it is not the correct way. If you want to understand an ideal, it will be possible only when you make a journey, mentally, to a period when the person who demonstrated those ideals lived.

There is a small example for this. A boy of eleven years of age was married to a girl of nine years of age, but unfortunately the boy died in an accident. The girl had a photograph of the eleven-year-old boy. As time went on, the girl grew up and attained the age of seventy. This seventy-year-old woman takes the photograph of the eleven-year-old boy and says that he is her husband. This statement looks ridiculous if you look at the form of the seventy-year-old woman. When she says that the eleven-year-old boy is her husband, the statement has meaning only when she regards herself as the nine-year-old girl. It is not as if the seventy-yearold woman was married to an eleven-year-old boy. The nine-year-old girl was married to a boy who was eleven years old. In the same context, the statement has a meaning only if she puts herself back in time in the position of a nine-year-old girl. In the same manner, those of us who are born now, if we want to understand the ideals of Krishna, we will be able to do so only if we take ourselves back to the times of Krishna.

Whatever ideals which he demonstrated to the world, be they in the political sphere, or the economic sphere, or the social sphere, will be appreciated only if we take ourselves back to the environment and time— politically, socially, and economically when Krishna lived. Therefore, young people like you should make an attempt to read and understand the sacred text of the *Mahabharatha* in the proper perspective. As a result of our foolishness and lack of understanding, we regard *Mahabharatha* as a very insignificant text and compare it with the ordinary food like a Vadai that we eat. There is a proverb which says, "If you listen to a text, you must listen to the text of *Mahabharatha*; and if we eat anything, we must eat a Vadai." This comparison is ridiculous. If you really want to understand the level at which the *Mahabharatha* was written, you should recognise the sacred contents. One who cannot understand the value of the *Mahabharatha* and of its sacred contents is ignorant and foolish. There is one small example for this. A shepherd took his sheep and goats and went into the forest. One day, when he was looking after the sheep and goats, there was a heavy rain. As a result of this, some stones on the hill became loose and started rolling down. He found that a particular stone was shining very brilliantly. That particular place was known to be a place where diamonds were found. But the shepherd did not know anything about diamonds. He took this bright stone and tied a string round it and put this bright shiny diamond round the neck of a black goat. This bright stone round the neck of the black goat was shining and the goat was attracting him very much. He frequently went to this goat and was looking at it affectionately.

While showing such affection to this goat, he was sitting under a tree and relaxing when a group of people were passing that way. Among those passers-by was one individual who knew the value of diamonds. This person was a diamond merchant, and he quickly realised the value of the diamond tied round the neck of the goat. He recognised the fact that this stone was worth several lakhs of rupees. He thought that poor shepherd boy would not know the value of the stone and he offered him ten rupees in return for the diamond. The shepherd boy said that this bright stone was very beautiful round the neck of the goat, and that he was not going to part with it. The diamond merchant tempted him and offered him a hundred rupees. The shepherd boy thought that with a hundred rupees he could buy a hundred such stones and tie each stone around the neck of each goat and he agreed to part with the stone for a hundred rupees.

We see that in the hands of the shepherd who did not know the value of the diamond, it was happy, safe, and sound. The moment this stone came into the hands of the diamond merchant, he thought that he had secured a valuable thing; and as soon as this thought came into his mind, the stone suddenly broke into several pieces. When the stone broke into so many pieces and fell to the ground, the merchant was surprised. This diamond, in a formless divine voice, said that as long as it was in the hands of person who did not know its value, it was satisfied; but when a person who knew its worth paid only one hundred rupees, its heart broke into pieces at the unjust act.

As in this analogy, in the vicinity of a person who does not understand divinity, it does not matter how things are; but if, knowing the nature of divinity, we begin to communicate and trade with it in a cheap manner, how can we obtain God's grace? How can God's grace come to individuals if we do not conduct ourselves well? Thus, after knowing the greatness and value of Krishna's ideals if we do not put them into practice, we will really be making a mistake. When one is moving with you, you regard him as an ordinary man and only when you see something extraordinary, you ascribe divinity to him. When you recognise divinity, you should make all efforts to follow the divine injunctions. When we read the lives of *Avatars* and when we are told such stories, we should learn their ideals and put them into practice. Only then will we be responding to divinity. But merely to read any text which comes our way and not put it into practice is not the right thing for educated people to do. In *Mahabharatha*, we must understand the human aspects of Krishna. I am hoping that by understanding this true form of Krishna, you will also follow the ideals of Krishna. I am blessing you in this manner and bringing this discourse to a close.

8

RELIGIOUS CULTURAL HERITAGE

MAHABHARATHA CONTAINS MANY VALUABLE LESSONS FOR US

Do you know why you have been given your hands? They have not been given to you so that you may continually feed your mouth with those hands. They have been given to you so that you may perform *puja* with flowers to the Lord.

Students!

It is not easy or possible for us to understand the level at which *Paramatma* functions because we are at a human level. If we recognise that the level at which divinity operates is different from, and higher than, the ordinary human level at which we all operate, there is a possibility of raising ourselves to a level in which we can try and understand divinity.

For doing any kind of work in this world, there should be some order and discipline. Any work that you may do without discipline will not yield good results. In order to get this limitation in the worldly plane, some discipline is necessary. That which rules the world is the rule of law. What is required to control oneself and put oneself under the rule of law, is discipline. This control of oneself is like *thapas*. A life, in which there is no discipline and control, will fail and fall one day or the other. If you put yourself on the wrong side of *thapas* which is "*pata*," it means that you are going to fall. One must recognise the truth that there should be controls on, and limits to, human nature. The five elements that constitute the earth are also controlled by certain laws. Even the infinite ocean moves under certain laws and regulations. In the context of the whole world, man's life is only a part. Therefore, man's life has to be regulated. Whether it is for *prema*, for hatred, or for anger, some regulation is necessary. Such regulation has been shown to us, as an example, by Sri Krishna in his lifetime. It has become the tradition of our country to accept the stories of the *Mahabharatha* as ideal examples. Since this kind of respect and tradition has come to us from the time of the *Vedas*, our citizens are always anxious to listen to such stories and welcome an opportunity to do so. It is also very necessary for us to accept and study the human side of such *Avatars,* and the stories about them, and implement them. That day was the *Karthika Bahula Triodasi*. The sacred land of Kurukshetra was close to Panipat. In this sacred land of Kurukshetra, the armies of the Kauravas were lined up for battle. In the front of the army and leading it was a white-turbaned, lion-like man sitting in a white chariot drawn by white horses. This aged, lionlike man was Bhishma.

On the opposite side, the army of the Pandavas was also lined up for battle, and Bheema was leading that army. This aged Bhishma had performed three hundred *Aswamedha Yagas*. The Pandavas were filled with fear when they saw such a powerful person leading the armies. They expected some tragedy to befall them. On the one hand, the roaring battle sounds from the conches were being heard. The horses were neighing and the elephants were trumpeting loudly. The flags symbolising the chariots of each army were being flown. The weapons of each army were shining brightly. In this situation, as if coming from nowhere, a chariot came and stood in the centre of the battle. It appeared that in that chariot there was one individual who was very despondent and discouraged. There was another person who was giving him courage and patting him on the back. Those two were Arjuna and Krishna, the best of men and the best of gods, respectively. These two represented the deserving human of Arjuna and the supreme *Avatar* of Krishna. We should notice here that the *Avatar* has descended from his high pedestal to the level of the best of human beings who deserved to be taught, and the *Avatar* was teaching and giving the necessary encouragement to the human being. After a few moments, Krishna descended from his chariot and began moving towards the chariot of Dharmaraja. It is not known what Krishna told Dharmaraja at that time, but it could be seen that Dharmaraja removed his armour and weapons and started walking with folded hands towards the Kauravas.

When the Kauravas saw this scene, they began to shout loudly. They thought that Dharmaraja was coming to surrender and seek peace on behalf of the Pandavas. Arjuna and Bheema, who saw this situation, were also very perturbed. The thought which Dharmaraja had and the noble feelings which made him undertake this task were not understood by Arjuna and Bheema. In the next few minutes, Krishna came and signalled to Arjuna and Bheema that they should also follow their brother.

In spite of the confusion and excitement in their own minds, Arjuna and Bheema obeyed the injunctions of the Lord and followed their brother. Dharmaraja, followed by his brothers, went along to Bhishma. When Bhishma looked at the brothers, he understood what was in their minds, and he knew the noble ideas that were passing in the mind of the eldest brother, Dharmaraja, and was praising Dharmaraja within himself.

They went close to Bhishma, touched his feet, addressed him as grandfather, and said, "Ever since we lost our father, you have looked after us and brought us up; but today, unfortunately, we have to fight with you. Please give us permission for this battle." Bhishma's heart was very much moved when he saw that even under those terrifying battle conditions, Dharmaraja was willing to do his duty by *dharma* and came all the way to seek his permission.

Bhishma embraced Dharmaraja and said, "Even in the battlefield, you are observing *dharma* and this gives me great pleasure. You will be victorious in this battle because you are acting according to *Dharma*. *Dharmo rakshati rakshitah*. Those who protect *dharma* will in turn be protected by *dharma*. You are protecting *dharma* and so *dharma* will protect you and victory will be yours."

Immediately after that, Bheema, Arjuna, Nakula, and Sahadeva also sought the blessings of Bhishma. They approached Dronacharya and touched his feet and said, "You are the guru and we are the students. Unfortunately, today such bad times have come that disciples have to fight with the teacher. In such a situation we are begging you to bless us." Dronacharya recognised the right conduct in this, and he also embraced them and blessed them towards victory. Such regulatory conduct was shown by Krishna; and this example makes us wonder if we, as human beings, are observing any rules and code of conduct. Why should the all-powerful and all-knowing Krishna undergo all these troubles and tribulations? Did he do all this for himself with a selfish motive? All this was done for someone else and in the interest of promotion of peace. He underwent all these troubles and tribulations in order to help and support those who sought his grace and support. As a result of the love which God has for his devotees, God has been going through several kinds of troubles for their sake.

Moreover, while he taught the *Gita* to Arjuna, there were several occasions when Arjuna had doubts; and there were situations when Arjuna became despondent. Krishna was undertaking this *yoga* in order to enable Arjuna, the human, to overcome the obstacles that were coming in his way, and to take courage and move forward.

We generally think that the *Gita* consists of certain teachings which will help us and teach us renunciation and take us along the spiritual path. This is not the correct aspect. We should recognise that the *Gita* gives us teachings which will help us to run our daily lives and meet the situations which we come across. Krishna established the truth that our spiritual life and our daily worldly life are not two distinct compartments. He demonstrated that our daily life is something intimately connected with spiritual life. He showed the need for harmony and connection between man's thoughts, words, and deeds. He proclaimed that in order that man may have good thoughts, his mind is very important. In order that he may communicate these thoughts to the world, his word is very important. In order to put this into action, his deeds are equally important.

Many people argue and say that God could do anything, and they say that God should have avoided the war by his own *Sankalpa* (Will). Here, we must notice that Krishna was not willing to use his divine strength for the benefit of mankind directly. He was living as human beings do, and he wanted to use the normal human methods by which to control various actions. There are thousands of people in the world who are willing to demonstrate these spiritual aspects in a manner which is quite easy to understand. There are great people who will help you to follow the essence of the *Vedas* in an easy manner. Were there not kings who acquired wealth and ruled over kingdoms? Where have all those kings and kingdoms gone now? What is it that they have taught to the world? Today also, we have a large number of people who preach and say that there are short cuts to teach the essence of the *Vedas*, but there are very few people who put them into practice in their lives.

All these individuals and the lessons that they teach are merely like guideposts. The best that a guidepost can do is to tell you that if you travel in that way, you will reach such and such a destination; and if you travel along another path, you will reach another destination; but the actual ups and downs along a particular path will be understood only by the people who undertake the journey. The guidepost cannot tell you anything about the ups and downs. One can speak about a crore of things, but one cannot put even one of them into practice by merely speaking. You should put into practice what you say and set an example. You should be prepared fully to put into practice what you say and hear.

The situation in the country is not something which you do not know. Today, hatred, injustice, and fear have filled all aspects of our lives, and the young students are the only people who can remove those evils. You have the capacity to do this. You should make an attempt to understand the sacred ideals that are contained in our sacred texts. The spirit of sacrifice which pervaded the lives of the citizens of this country at all times is contained in the blood flowing in you. In such a sacred country, the Pandavas have led lives in a manner which are ideal examples. They were persons who were the leaders in all aspects—the political, ethical, moral, and all other aspects.

On one occasion when Dharmaraja, Arjuna, Bheema, and others were in some other place in the battlefield, Abhimanyu was lured into the *padmavyuha* (Labyrinth of the lotus shape). His mother cautioned him by saying that the situation at this time was very precarious. The times were not very good for them: his wife was in the family way, his uncle Krishna was not present. He was only being lured into the battle, and he should think twice before going into the battle. When the mother was thus entreating him not to go into the battle, Abhimanyu, because of his brave family traditions and because of the sacrificing spirit in his blood, was begging his mother to let him go. He told his mother, "Instead of telling me to be a lion and jump into the battlefield, you are trying to prevent me from going there."

The mother, herself, was a great heroine, and she realised the greatness in Abhimanyu's heroism. She thought that if she let him go forward, it was bad; and if she stopped him, it was also bad. She was unable to decide between the two evils. This was the situation in which she found herself. In this unfortunate situation, you can imagine what the people of today would have done. They would have cursed God and cried out, "Oh, cruel God, why did you put my son in such a situation!" But this heroic mother was blessing her son by saying that he should go and secure victory on the battlefield.

The kind of blessing which she gave her son was an unparalleled one. We should ask ourselves if any mother would give a blessing like that these days.

Every part of the *Mahabharatha* is such that it has an ideal lesson for us. The ideals demonstrated by the Pandavas and taught by Krishna are very essential for the people of our country even today. As I explained yesterday, when Krishna went to negotiate peace and was asked by Duryodhana to accept his hospitality, he said that as he had come on a mission; he had no right to accept the hospitality till the mission was completed.

Until the peace negotiations were completed, he did not want to accept the hospitality offered by Duryodhana; and he went and stayed in Vidura's house. Because such rules of conduct were being observed in those days in the matter of political negotiations, they were always of a very high order. Today, if ambassadors come from other countries, they are driven to the Raj Bhavan straight from the airport; and even before the negotiations begin, a dinner is arranged and other types of hospitality is given to the visitor. In the conditions that are existing today, if we accept and put into practice the ideals that were demonstrated in the *Mahabharatha*, our country will certainly prosper. We are thinking and taking the view that the *Mahabharatha* simply consists of people who were warmongers. This is not correct.

The *Mahabharatha* is an ideal text for people who are peace lovers. The *leelas* and the stories that we learn from the *Bhagavatha* are not as important as the lessons and morals that we learn from the *Mahabharatha*. So long as we are human beings, and have to live as human beings, we cannot understand and follow the actions of divinity. We have to accept and follow the actions done by God as a human being. When the chariot was kept between the two armies, Arjuna begged of the Lord, in many ways, for enlightenment. He accepted that all that was said by Krishna was truth and was backed by what had been said in the *Sastras*. Because Arjuna was an ordinary human being, he could not understand Krishna's divinity; and he prayed that he be given the strength to understand the potency of what was told to him. He requested that the great divine vision of Krishna be shown to him. He also requested that the weaknesses that were in his mind and body be removed. He requested that mercy may be shown to an ordinary human being like him and that he might be elevated. In all humility and in a devoted way, he was begging Krishna.

Arjuna's anxiety and sincerity were noticed by Krishna; and convinced of his devotion, he told Arjuna that his divine form could not be perceived by the ordinary eyes; and he touched his forehead and said that the eye of Wisdom, which he could give, would enable him to perceive the Lord. By this touch of Krishna, the Wisdom eye had entered Arjuna. This gift had come only through grace and did not come by right. Thus, Krishna had given this gift to Arjuna as a Grace.

Through this eye of Wisdom, Arjuna realised that the entire creation was contained in the divine vision. He realised that all living beings—human as well as animal and insect—were part of this vision. He realised that Krishna was responsible for all creation. He perceived that Krishna was present in every minute particle. Arjuna closed his eyes and the divine vision was there in all directions. He then addressed Krishna and said that he did not have the strength to bear that divine vision any longer and said that he had seen his greatness and his divine strength.

Arjuna prostrated before Krishna and was overwhelmed and began singing in ecstasy and said, "How can I know you Krishna? You are smaller than the smallest thing in this world, and you are greater than the greatest thing in this world. You are the very basis of the eighty-four lakhs of kinds of *jivas* in this world. You are infinitely great, and you cannot be compared even with the greatest thing in this world, and you are the source of everything that can be seen. I now surrender to you and will do whatever you ask me to do without any question."

An *Avatar* is capable of all things at all times, yet the *Avatar* will not undertake to demonstrate his powers at all times. An *Avatar* will undertake to demonstrate such powers when exceptional circumstances demand it, and will shed the grace on a deserving person only. Although such *Avatars* were present in our country for thousands of years, and although our people were exposed to such *Avatars*, they have not fully understood all the aspects of such an *Avatar*.

We should examine the reason why the formless Lord takes the form of a human being and comes into the midst of humans. This formless being comes in the form of a human being so that he may mix with the human beings and set up examples and ideals for human beings and convey to them all aspects which they should learn. Many people ask very innocently and ignorantly why an *Avatar,* who possesses all powers, should subject itself to all troubles; and why should it tolerate hunger and suffering all around. An *Avatar* who has all the powers should be able to remove all such suffering in one moment. If there is any meaning in such a question, why should an *Avatar* come in human form at all? The *Avatar* can remain as a formless divinity and do all these things from that position itself. In time, and under certain conditions and environment, whatever has to be done must be done and such acts, at a human level, have to be performed.

Certain things are essential for remedial action and without doing those things, to expect an *Avatar* to simply remove all suffering is a very foolish thing. First of all, you should make an attempt to make good use of the mental and physical strengths that have been given to you. When you are so lazy as not to use the mental and physical strengths that have been given to you, what are you going to do with divine strengths?

Suppose that you have been given food and drink by the divine grace and strength of the Lord. Because God has given you enough food on your plate, for you to think that God has also to help you in transferring this food to your stomach is a very lazy idea. For taking the food to your stomach, God has given you hands, a palate, and a mouth. You should make good use of them. If you are not able to use the organs that have been given to you, and if you are not able to use the mind and mental strength that have been given to you, it is better to die than to live in that condition. That we may learn to make good use of our mental and physical strengths and other organs, God comes in human form to demonstrate how these may be used.

The essential quality of an *Avatar* is to teach you how to make good and proper use of your thought, word, and deed. Depending on the conditions in the country and the environment in the country, the *Avatar* comes to teach you and show you the right use of all your organs. In Bharath, a country which is like heaven on earth, so that you may be able to make good use of the facilities and faculties that have been given to you, I am hoping that the sacred texts of the *Bhagavatha* and *Mahabharatha* will provide good examples.

Divya Atma Swarupas, Boys and Girls

To some extent you should make an attempt to master your sensory organs and not become a slave to them. I am hoping that by mastering your sensory organs, you will become ideal citizens and representatives of our ancient culture. The ideals that have been demonstrated to us in the *Mahabharatha*, and the close relationships between the Pandavas and Krishna that have become evident from this sacred text, and the lessons from such a relationship must be understood by us and put into practice in our daily lives. The *Mahabharatha* is not an ordinary text. In fact, it has come to be known as the fifth *Veda*.

Every individual character in the *Mahabharatha* has some powers which are attributed to God. They are not people who are born like other ordinary people. As they are not just ordinary people, every act that they perform is an exemplary act. They are individuals with superhuman powers, and so whatever they had done should be taken as an ideal act. That text has, in the context, been compared with the *Vedas*. As days go on, you will hear more stories from the *Mahabharatha*, and you will learn how Krishna had set aside his divinity, and as a human being, taught how human beings should behave and conduct themselves. I am hoping and blessing you that you will take these lessons and put them into practice and develop yourselves into useful and worthy citizens of our country.

A GOOD AND PEACEFUL DEATH IS COVETED BY ALL SAINTLY PEOPLE

Do you know why you have been given your intelligence? It is not to be used for the purpose of accumulating wealth. Intelligence has been given to you so that you may realise that all that you see around is a very temporary and transient phenomenon.

Pavitratma Swarupas, Students! Boys and Girls, Man is like a seed. As the seed sprouts and then becomes a plant, finally becoming a tree giving you fruit, so also man should grow and blossom and should put out flowers of peace and distribute those flowers to the rest of the world. Man has two aspects of his life. One relates to his livelihood and the other to the ultimate objective of his own life. The former is the ability to get one's livelihood and relates very much to the material world whereas the latter relates to the spiritual world.

But today man develops capacities in the former aspect to be able to eke out his livelihood but does not have the capacity to seek out the objective of his life. The spiritual world and the material day-to-day world cannot be two separate worlds. When we talk of the capacities to suit this world, we mean the capacity to acquire all the conveniences to give comfort to this body. What we do in this world, what we see around us, and what we do to keep our body healthy are all called the ability related to this world. If we want to describe this briefly, we can say that this is the capacity related to the external world.

There is another aspect which can be briefly described as the inner world. But unfortunately today, from the time that we get up to the time that we go to bed again, all our efforts are directed to accumulating the capacities relating to this external world. Whatever we do relates to our daily lives and what we see around us. However, it is not possible to think of the day-today world without thinking of the internal or spiritual world, just as we cannot develop external vision without the help of the inner vision. Religious texts of all categories have been teaching people how to promote and how to develop this inner vision. Most religious texts have always been teaching methods and paths related to the spiritual world.

The *Bhagavad Gita* has not been making a distinction between the external and the inner vision and has been saying that both of them have to be studied together. This spiritual text has been teaching us that whether you stress on the external vision or the inner vision, the ultimate objective is the same. There is also a small story which has been given as an example for this. Let us take the case of a woman who carries a pot filled with water on her head. She will be talking and joking along with other women and is quite free as she walks along. Yet she takes great care of the pot of water on her head.

As in the above analogy, while we live in the normal world taking things lightly as they come, we will have to take great care of the spiritual aspects as well. We cannot forget them. Whatever work and task you may undertake, if you have your attention on divinity, then God will take care of you.

There is one more example for this. A mother will put the baby to sleep. After the baby is asleep, she will go to the first floor and will be attending to her work. All the while, her attention will be on the baby, and her thought is always about when the baby will get up. Even if she is engaged in urgent and pressing work, her attention will be on the baby and as soon as she hears the cry of the baby, she will come running. She will not stop to consider in what *raga* (tune) and *tala* (tempo) the baby is crying. Just as the mother comes running from her work as soon as she hears the baby crying, so also, if man cries to the Lord from the depths of his heart, even if the Lord is busy, he will come out of his place and help the devotee. God does not ask what path this devotee is adopting or what bhajans are being sung by him, etc. But he will only look at the sincerity with which the devotee has cried out.

God is all-powerful and can melt even stony hearts, yet he will not undertake to do so. But man has the strength to correct his path by the *Purusharthas* (Goals of life—*dharma, artha, kama, moksha*), and so God will expect that man should first set right his thoughts by his own efforts. In this context, man should not go on arguing about God's capacity but should examine his own capacity and use it to set things right. God behaves like a human being when he comes amidst them, understands the psychology of the behaviour, and investigates the manner in which he can change the minds and hearts of men.

In the battle of *Mahabharatha,* Bhishma was in a ferocious condition. During the first nine days of the war, Dussasana and Duryodhana went to Bhishma on one particular day and asked why they have been suffering defeat after defeat practically every day and had not seen victory even on one day. Bhishma realised that he was then in the service of the King and said, "Yes I understand your difficulty, I will bring you victory in the war tomorrow." Dussasana then suggested to Bhishma that the objective should be to capture and kill the Pandavas rather than just to secure victory over them in the war.

In that context, Bhishma promised that before the sun rose the next day, he would kill the Pandavas. The Pandavas came to know of this and realised that the promise made by the grand old man would indeed be fulfilled by him. Anyway, the Pandavas had no alternative, and they were preparing themselves to be killed by the grand old man who brought them up. This news came to be known to *Droupadi* as well. She could not sleep or eat her food and she was terror-stricken. The dark night had set in. In the whole drama, Krishna also had a part to play, and he was thinking of how to bring the *Purusharthas* to operate and change the minds of people. Bhishma realised that he had made the promise in the excitement of the moment. He was fully aware of the greatness of the Pandavas and their qualities and was much agitated. He could not eat his food and was moving from one place to another. However, Krishna was divine and he knew what was happening on both sides, and he knew the difficulties on both sides.

Droupadi, anticipating the terrible future, came to Krishna, touched his feet and sat down. Then Krishna said, "Sister, do not get excited. Do what you can and I will do the rest." Although this assurance was given, being a woman, she was very agitated. At midnight, when all were asleep, Krishna came to *Droupadi* and said, "Simply follow me and do not ask any questions." It was dark and it was the battlefield. *Droupadi* did not want to be recognised and so she covered herself with a cloth.

In the battlefield, there were no mansions, and they were living in small improvised tents. However, the place where Bhishma was living was quite a big place. In the dead of night, Bhishma was wondering how he was going to fulfil the promise that he made and perform the act of killing the righteous and goodnatured Pandavas, who were indeed very brave. He was anxiously moving about hither and thither. Krishna noticed this opportunity when Bhishma was very excited and agitated, and he signalled to Droupadi that she should leave her shoes behind, as the shoes of wealthy women in those days made a great deal of noise and could be heard even from a long distance, and go and fall at Bhishma's feet. She was only following Krishna's orders. She left the shoes at one place, covered herself, and quickly ran inside and fell at Bhishma's feet and begged him to save her husbands' life. Because of his inherent good qualities, Bhishma immediately reacted without a thought and blessed her by saying, "May you remain a *Sumangali* (married woman with her husband alive) for a long time!" To *Droupadi*, the assurance coming from Bhishma that for a long time she would be a *Sumangali* with living husbands was quite enough. Bhishma had made the promise that he would kill the Pandavas before the sun rose the next day and also assured that *Droupadi* would remain a *Sumangali* for a long time to come, and now it was for Bhishma to fulfil one or both of these promises. At that moment, when Bhishma saw that the person whom he thus blessed was *Droupadi*, he was in utter confusion as a conflicting situation had risen. The conflict which troubled Bhishma was which of these promises was he going to fulfil. At that moment, Bhishma asked her who gave her this plan of action, for she certainly could not have come alone, at the dead of night, with this grand plan.

At that time, Krishna, the master architect of the whole plan, came inside with a cloth bundle in his hands. Bhishma expressed his pleasure at seeing Krishna and said that this plan was drawn up by Krishna in order to save his devotees and that Krishna was the only person who could save even Bhishma from the conflicting situation. At this moment, he noticed the cloth bundle in Krishna's hands and asked what the bundle contained. When the bundle was opened, it was seen that it contained the shoes of *Droupadi*. In demonstrating his grace and love, God will be prepared, not only to help his devotees, but even to carry the shoes of his devotees if it became necessary.

At this unparalleled grace shown by Krishna, *Droupadi's* eyes were filled with tears and she asked, "Is it not sufficient that you have been taking care of our lives? Is it not sufficient that you made a plan for my husbands to be spared instead of being killed the next day? Did you have to carry my shoes which have no value at all?" Is Krishna doing all these things as God on earth? These are being done by him to show what one human being must do to another human being at a time of need. Man alone can demonstrate the kind of relationship that should exist between man and man. So he was conducting himself like a human being. That *prema* is the very basis for one's own life has been demonstrated by Krishna.

Bhishma fully understood this *leela* of Krishna and came to the conclusion that whatever he might do, the Pandavas will not be subjected to any harm. But he did not make any attempt to get out of his promise, as he was a great adherent of truth. On the next day he went to the battlefield with all his determination to fulfil the promise that he had made. On that day, the battle was very fierce and the Pandava army ran helterskelter, but because of the divine grace of Krishna, the Pandavas were able to save themselves. The evening came and Bhishma fell down. Krishna had to play all this drama to demonstrate that one's physical and mental strength are not very important, and it is the divine strength that was real strength.

The day when Bhishma fell down was the tenth day of the battle. From that day till the eighteenth day of the battle, Krishna was conducting various events of the battle, but Bhishma was lying on the bed of arrows which he made for himself. After the last day of the battle, the victorious Pandavas came to Bhishma. The kind of battle that took place, at that time, was subject to its own rules and code of conduct in accordance with the times. The battle took place 3138 years before the advent of Christ. The war in which Bhishma took part was for nine days, and the period for which he was on the bed of arrows was fifty-eight days. These two together constitute a total of sixty-seven days. After this, the Pandavas along with *Droupadi* went to see Bhishma and had his *darshan.*

Lying on the bed of arrows, Bhishma showed great affection to the Pandavas and preached to them what has since come to be known as the *Shanthiparva.* In that context, while Bhishma was preaching the code of conduct relating to peace in the *Shanthiparva, Droupadi* had some thought in her mind; and she laughed loudly and attracted everyone's attention. The Pandavas thought this to be very inappropriate, and they did not like *Droupadi* laughing in this manner in the presence of the elders. Bhishma was all-knowing and he knew the thoughts that were passing in the minds of the Pandavas. In order that an appropriate explanation might be given to the Pandavas, Bhishma asked *Droupadi* to come closer to him. He blessed her and said that she would remain a *Sumangali* for long and went on to say that she would not do anything without good reason. He asked her to explain why she laughed so that her husbands might know the answer.

Droupadi addressed Bhishma in great reverence and humility and asked Bhishma, "At the time when I was humiliated in the court of Duryodhana, you never spoke of any code of conduct; and at the time when my husbands were banished into the forest for twelve years and were to live incognito for one year, you never preached any code of conduct. You are now teaching the *Shanthiparva* to the Pandavas who are the very embodiments of *dharma*. Why are you now teaching this to the people who do not need to be taught? This should have been taught to Duryodhana and his accomplices. Such a thought came to my mind and I laughed. Not only this, in the court that day Dharmaraja lost in the game of Dice and also lost when he placed himself as the stake.

Then he offered me as the stake. It was then decided that the Pandavas were to go to the forest and I was humiliated. Was this *dharma*? You are an embodiment of *dharma* and right conduct. Do you think that on that day, after losing himself in the game, Dharmaraja had the right to bid me? I was married to five husbands, and in that context, belonged to all of them. If only one husband wanted to bid me, was that right? At that time, what had happened to all your professed adherence to right conduct.

Secondly, Dharmaraja offered me as a stake, after he lost himself in the wager. He had no right to do this. On that day itself, I questioned whether Dharmaraja lost himself first and then offered me as a stake or whether he offered me as a stake first and then lost himself. You did not give me an answer then. What had happened to all your right conduct at that time? Today, when there is no need at all, you are preaching all this to the Pandavas. This, indeed, is a laughing matter and has induced laughter in me."

While Bhishma was lingering between life and death, the fact that *Droupadi* was arguing so vehemently and asking inconvenient questions upset even Dharmaraja. Bhishma, however, laughed loudly and praised *Droupadi* for asking such questions and said that the answers to such questions would be of great importance to the coming *Kali* age and asked the Pandavas to calm down. Bhishma said, "For many years, I had been serving evil kings and sinners and had been living on the food that they had given me. Therefore, all the rights and *dharma* in me were submerged. As a result of the arrow that struck me from your husband's hand, all the evil blood has flown out and now the *dharma* that had been submerged has come up; and I am preaching the need for good conduct."

From this *Shanthiparva*, preached by Bhishma, we have to learn the lesson that if anyone promotes himself with the help of money accumulated by bad and evil ways, then the good in him will be submerged by the bad blood in him. It is in this context that Krishna had taught that the pot in which you cook, the material which you use to cook, and the food itself should all be clean.

In this dialogue, Bhishma had taught to the world that there can be evil in the food that you take. From the food that we take, come the thoughts. From the thoughts that are generated in us comes the action. From our actions, will come our good and our bad. After giving the appropriate lessons to the Pandavas, Bhishma gave up his life.

The day before that was an auspicious day because on that day the sun commences his northward journey. That day is also called *Ratha Saptami.* The previous day to Bhishma's death, *Ratha Saptami,* was a sacred day; and on that day, all the Pandavas came near him and he performed the rituals to his forefathers. On the next day, he gave up his life. But at this time, according to our *panchangas* (almanacs) we think that Bhishma died on an *ekadasi* (eleventh day of the lunar fortnight) and we call it the *Bhishma Ekadasi.* Actually this is not correct. The day on which Bhishma died was an *Ashtami* (eighth day), and the prevailing star was Rohini. Krishna was also born in the star on Rohini. Thus, Bhishma died on a day similar to the day on which Krishna was born.

Also, that was the beginning of a very auspicious period in the year. They regarded that day to be very auspicious for a death. Bhishma had waited for fiftyeight days in order that the sun might start its northward journey. He was thinking of the Lord on all those days and was waiting for an appropriate time to die. In this aspect, Bhishma taught to the world that the time of death was more important than the time of birth. More than being born on an auspicious day, it is to be coveted that one dies on an auspicious day and time as well. If one dies like that, rebirth will be a good one.

Today, we all want a good birth, but we are not seeking a good death. The inner meaning of a good birth is to enable one to have a good death. We must recognise the truth that all the *sadhana* that we do is not for the sake of a pleasurable life but for a good and peaceful death. All the great saints and *yogis* direct all their prayers towards aspiring for an easy and good death, and they pray that they be enabled to merge into the Lord easily. Our attempts should be directed to the objective of ultimately merging with divinity. This is the sacred lesson that is contained in the *Shanthiparva*, and it is my hope that you understand this and put it into practice.

MAN SHOULD PROMOTE INNER VISION FOR HIMSELF

Do you know why you have been given your mouth? Is it to utter all kinds of words? No, it has been given to you so that you might sing the glory of the Lord.

Pavitratma Swarupas,

Today man is very eager to listen to the news that comes to him from all corners of the world. He thinks that it is his mission to know everything that is happening, but he does not make an attempt to hear what is coming from within himself. An individual who cannot understand and recognise his own nature has not achieved anything. All that he is learning by way of education is apparently only for eking out a living. This has become common with us and has become an illusion of our mind. This is something which has no basis worth mentioning. This kind of attitude was criticised in a downright manner by Krishna.

The basis for such a desire is your attachment and hatred. This attachment and hatred are commonly found in one who thinks that he is different from the environment around him. So long as one thinks that a particular car or house or land belongs to him, then there will be attachment to whatever he thinks belongs to him, and he will have a dislike of things which he thinks do not belong to him. Man does not have the capacity to distinguish between things which belong to him and things which do not belong to him. In a human body, there are several organs and the body itself is composed of those several organs. From amongst these several organs, even if one is hurt or damaged, the pain is experienced by the entire body; and this is the reason why man regards all the organs in the body on the same footing; and he desires the well-being of all the organs of his body.

In the same manner, the grace and kindness of the creator will fall equally well on all living and nonliving things with *gunas—sathwic*, *rajasic,* and *thamasic*. Although light emanating from the same lamp, when it falls on a group of white pieces of glass, will be scattered in several different directions, we think that it consists of light from several sources. If the same light falls on a large number of coloured glasses, it appears as if it is composed of different colours. If the same light falls on the ground, we will not be able to see the light, because the ground obstructs and absorbs the light.

In the same manner, if the brilliant shining grace from *Easwara* falls on a *sathwic* person, he will shine brilliantly. If the same grace from *Easwara*, falls on a person with *rajasic* qualities, it will make him develop several desires of the world. If the same grace falls on a person with *thamasic* qualities, it will not only go through without having any effect, but it may even lose some of its lustre.

Just as the various facets of diamonds all scatter light and throw brilliance in all directions, so also the greatness of Krishna was scattered in all directions. As we cut the diamond and polish the facets, the value of the diamond goes on increasing. In the same manner, the culture of Bharath has become more and more through greater and greater exposure and experience. The more we experience it, the more we learn about our culture, newer ideas come to us. We will know, more and more, about the sacredness of Krishna's teachings if we look at them from the aspect of their being object lessons to other human beings.

If you want to remove a thorn from your foot, you will have to do this with the help of another thorn. You cannot use an axe to remove the thorn from your foot. To cut a diamond, you need a diamond. In the same manner, to understand and comprehend a human being, you will have to use the essential qualities of a human being. Krishna, who was born as a *Yogeswara,* came down to the level of men when preaching to Arjuna who was the best among men and holding his weapon, the Gandiva. Krishna wanted to deal with Arjuna in a manner in which a human being will deal with another human being. On the very first day, Dhritharashtra asked Sanjaya who the victor will be in the battle and Sanjaya replied, "Wherever there is the Lord *Yogeswara* and wherever there, in his presence, is Arjuna holding the weapon in his hand and ready for action, there will be victory, good, prosperity, and all that is best." This close and intimate relationship can only be understood by Arjuna, the best among men, and by Krishna, the best among the *Avatars.* Here, Arjuna represents the most deserving of human beings.

So if you want to understand and comprehend the teachings of Krishna, you must either become the best of men or at least a person who acquires the right to understand them. Arjuna had the right, and he was also the best of men; and so he was given the *darshan* of the Universal God. We should also recognise the truth behind the fact that this divinity, while it is associated with the universe, is also something which is inherently present in every human being.

You will have seen many trees. Certain big banyan trees look as if they are very big, and they also have many sub-branches and look as if they are a big mansion. Such a banyan tree gives us the impression that it is very big, having many branches; but if we take the seed, we see that it has a very small dimension like a mustard seed. Is it the truth that such a big tree is contained in such a tiny little seed or is it just an illusion on our part? No, this is not an illusion, it is a truth. But in what form is this seed seen? It is in the infinitesimal form. If we put this tiny seed in the earth, feed and nourish it, it will sprout, become big, and grow. The fruit, the flowers, and the leaves all come out of this tiny seed. Therefore, it is not as if the branches, the fruits, and the leaves are all different.

They are all parts of the same seed. Thus, everything that you see in this big tree of the universe has all come from one seed, the seed of divinity. In the same manner, in this huge body of yours, there is an infinitesimally small seed called the aspect of *Atma*. If you take this seed which is in you, give it nourishment, and let it grow and prosper, then it will show the divine form of the universe. But where should we put this seed, how do we protect it and promote it to grow into a big tree? Can we put this seed in our palm and pour water on it? Will it become a tree? A seed will become a tree only if it is put in the soil and watered suitably. Even in that soil, if you put the seed too deep or too shallow, it will not become a tree.

In the same manner, in the soil of our heart, if we can put the seed of God's name, and if we can water it with the water of *prema*, it will sprout into a good tree. It is in this context that a divine vision of *Vishwavirat* has been described as one consisting of thousands of heads, legs, and hands. Wherefrom has this *Vishwavirat* vision come? It is simply the magnified version of what is within ourselves. When I open my eyes, I see so many thousands of heads; but when the eyes are closed, I do not see even one head. When the eyes are open, I not only see these thousands of heads, but I also see this wall, this window, all the photos, and everything around me. If I go outside and see with open eyes, one sees the mountains, the sky, the rivers, and the distant land; but, at that instant, if one closes one's eyes, why is it that one does not see even a small ant in this entire creation?

If the eyes are open, we see the entire creation; and if the eyes are closed, we do not see anything of the creation. Thus, we conclude that this entire creation has come from our own vision. If there is vision, there is creation; and if there is no vision, there is no creation. Just as with extrovert vision we are able to see the external creation, so also with the help of inward vision, we can see the inner self. This is what Krishna taught Arjuna. It was with a view to help Arjuna develop this inner vision, that the Lord had given him so many directions.

What does not flow is not water, what does not burn is not fire, and as in these analogies, a person who does not have inward vision cannot be called a human being. Capacity to burn is natural to fire. Water has the natural capacity to flow. Similarly man should have the natural capacity of inner vision. An animal has only external vision.

The *Vedas* have told us that what we see is only a reflection of what exists internally. That which we see inside or outside is essentially one, and the same thing is what has been taught to us in this aspect of *Vishwavirat darshan* of Narayana. There is only one thing and that one thing is perceived in many ways. This is what has been demonstrated in this vision and is described as *Ekoham bahusyam* (I am one. I shall become many).

You go to sleep in the night, and you dream that you are a part of the summer camp. You see so many other companions sitting along with you. In your dream you also see Swami speaking. You see the congregation and other parts of the house. You should ask who has brought all that there in front of you in your dream. No one has brought them, your own mind has created the form of Swami and this mansion, your companions and all. All that is the creation of your own mind.

Man's mind alone is responsible for man's bondage and his freedom. Krishna taught Arjuna, in the very first instance, that the most important thing is the control of one's mind. Thus, the first thing to do is to control your mind. The very first thing that we must do is to try and burn away the desires that come to our mind. The desires that are in your mind, may be known to others or may not be known to others, but are bound to come out some day or the other. You may pretend as if there are no desires in your mind, but the desires will never allow you to hide them. They will always come out. These desires are like fire. If you take fire and try to hide it in a cloth, the desires will burn the cloth and come out. The desires and thoughts of yours are bound to come out and show themselves.

Krishna taught Arjuna that it was better to throw out the desires than to keep them hidden. Arjuna was told in the very first instance that neither he nor the Pandavas are the persons who were going to kill the Kauravas. Neither to Arjuna, nor to the Pandavas, nor to even Krishna was there birth or death. There is neither birth nor death to the essential in us, namely the *Atma*. Therefore it is not right to subordinate ourselves to this body which is like a leather bag, forgetting the indestructible *Atma* that is within us.

So long as we are human beings, it is difficult to comprehend the difficult divine aspect taught by Krishna to Arjuna. This is the reason why Krishna came in human form, created a bodily relationship with Arjuna and others, and pretended as if he was the brother-inlaw of Arjuna and vice versa. In the ordinary daily matters, Krishna was always leading a sacred life. What we see in the *Mahabharatha* or the *Bhagavatha* or what we see in the cinema do not constitute a true picture of the life of Krishna. What we see today is created artificially; but if we go fully into the conduct of Krishna, we will understand that he was pure, steadfast, and sincere. He was always supporting truth and practising it. That is the reason why Arjuna was always addressing Krishna as the embodiment of truth rather than as his brother-in-law.

When the battle was over, Krishna went to Dwaraka and went to the place where his father, Vasudeva, was living. Vasudeva asked him, "You have always spoken the truth; and I would like to know from you, as the protector of truth, what are the true changes that came about in the Kauravas and the Pandavas." Even if a son is always speaking the truth, no father will come forward and say that his son speaks the truth and protects the truth. In this context, we should really try and understand the deep significance of the father addressing the son and telling him that he had always spoken the truth, and protected the truth.

But unfortunately, in the books that we read and the cinemas that we see, Krishna is depicted as a cunning and tricky person. The picture of Krishna formed in this manner is not correct. This is not what is contained in the *Mahabharatha*. People write such stories in order to make money and make their stories more attractive.

That our own countrymen do this and distort the truth for the sake of acquiring money is deplorable. It is not that Krishna alone was speaking the truth and protecting truth. The Pandavas were also great adherents of truth. The great protectors of truth, Krishna and the Pandavas, gave this country the sacred text of *Mahabharatha*. The forbearance and the great breadth of vision which the Pandavas exhibited, as well as the strength of character and determination which they exhibited in their conduct, cannot be seen in any other citizens of this country. Because the Pandavas had always obeyed Krishna, they directly imbibed from Krishna the sacred qualities of truth and forbearance. When Ashwatthama, who killed the *Upapandavas*, (Pandava children) was brought before Droupadi, in spite of her great grief at the loss of her children, she moved forward and touched his feet and paid respects to him. It is such great qualities of truth and forbearance that we should observe in the Pandavas and respect them for such qualities.

If the mothers of today were in such a state of suffering as *Droupadi* was, they would have pounced on Ashwatthama and strangled him to death, even if they did not have the strength to do that. But Droupadi had such sterling character that in her great suffering she only asked, "These *Upapandavas* who were killed by you did not come to you in any emotion or excitement. They did not have any weapons in their hands. How did you bring yourself to cut their throats and kill them when they were sleeping?" In spite of the fact that all her sons were killed by Ashwatthama, she was telling him with great forbearance and equanimity of mind, "My husbands were the disciples of your father, Dronacharya. They learnt all aspects of weaponry from him; and you, who are the son of Dronacharya, killed my sons who should be like your disciples." This was the way in which she was pleading with Ashwatthama. Bheema was unable to bear such sorrow; and because of this, he was in great emotion which drove him to the point of exhibiting his physical prowess to the world. In fact, he was looking at this quality of forbearance of Droupadi as a laughing matter.

Bheema was greatly surprised at the peaceful attitude of Droupadi. He thought that the suffering of having lost all her children had driven her to insanity, for, otherwise he was not able to understand how a true mother could show such forbearance when the person who had killed all her children was standing before her.

He said, "If you do not kill Ashwatthama, I will kill him with my fists."

Droupadi was a great woman with exemplary character. If only the women of today take her as an example and follow her qualities of forbearance and calmness, our country will improve very much. When Bheema, the strong person, was preparing to kill Ashwatthama with his fists, would it be possible for a weakling like Droupadi to go and stop Bheema? It was only the purity of her thought that was her strength. She had no physical strength. Then she tells Bheema, "It is not right for you to kill a person who is afraid, who comes to you asking for shelter, a person who is asleep, or a person who is drunk and has forgotten himself. It is not right to kill such helpless people."

Droupadi was such a great woman that in order to protect right conduct, she would even oppose her husbands. She was not a woman who would bring disrepute, by any of her acts, either to her husbands, or to her father, or to her sons. She did not want anyone to get hurt by her acts.

When Pandavas were preparing to go to the forest, Dharmaraja sent for Droupadi and asked her to sit by his side. Dharmaraja told her, "Owing to certain personal differences between the Pandavas and the Kauravas, a situation has come about by which we will have to go to the forest." He told Droupadi that these troubles and tribulations were something which they could not avoid, and that it was a very hard thing to be living in a forest for twelve years and follow it up with one year in which they had to remain incognito. Dharmaraja told her that the men will somehow bear the difficulties and that it was not an occasion for women to go into the forest, and he advised her to remain back and take care of the old Dhritharashtra and Gandhari. The Pandavas had asked Droupadi to take care of Dhritharashtra and Gandhari, the two main people who were cruel and responsible for their having to go to the forest. This is a very great quality in the Pandavas, and we must learn a lesson from this conduct. If the Pandavas really hated the Kauravas, is there any meaning in this act; and can we justify the fact that the Pandavas asked Droupadi to stay back and serve the Kauravas? The moral of this is that whatever has to happen in one's life will happen, but to take such inevitable events and use them to promote hatred is not the correct thing to do, and it is not a good human character.

The pain which we have to experience, the misfortunes which come to us and the troubles which we have, are not things which arise externally, nor are they God given. They are simply things which are the result of our own actions. It is only as a result of one's own weakness, that man blames someone else for the troubles and misfortunes that he gets. This is not a right attitude. Mahabharatha teaches us that it is not right to blame others for our troubles.

You want to eat food and fruit which is very good and tasty, but in order to get such fruit, you cannot use seeds which will give poisonous plants. The kind of fruits that you get on a tree that you plant will depend on the kind of seeds that you put in. If you put in seeds of poisonous plants and expect tasty fruits, how can you get them? The troubles that you have or the good that you have now will depend upon the kind of actions you have done in your previous birth. Not to recognise this and blame others is not correct.

The *Mahabharatha* has taught us a lesson that we should regard our actions as being responsible for our sorrows or joys. But as a human being, you should perform whatever actions you have to perform. The capacities that have been given to you under the name of *Purusharthas* must be fully utilised. Do not think that you will achieve this or that, and do not think that you will be able to do great things without the grace of God. Do not get tired out in that process. The kind of seeds which you have put in, which have brought you to the position in which you are today, will determine the results that you will get later on. If the seed belongs to one kind of plant, how can you aspire to get a different kind of fruit? Therefore, the kind of seed which you use will determine the kind of fruit that you will get, and you will have to accept that fruit. You may be very intelligent and clever. All your intelligence and cleverness will not enable you to get over your own *Karma*. Brahma, the creator, prepares a garland of all the good and the bad that you have done, without making any change, and will put it round your neck and will send it along with you into this world when you are born.

It is necessary for us to recognise this causal relationship. We are responsible for the good that we do and for the bad that we do, and the desires that we get are merely consequences of this. The *Mahabharatha* has been teaching us this lesson. While this is as it may be, Droupadi, to maintain the reputations for her husbands, her parents, and parents-in-law, is talking about this code of right conduct.

She said, "I was born to the great king Droupadi, I have become the daughterin-law of the world famous king Pandu, I have married the great Pandavas who are proud of themselves, I have given birth to sons who are heroes. How can I be a servant?" These words of Droupadi will move one's heart. She wanted her parents to be proud of her, she wanted her children to feel that they are the children of a great mother, she wanted her husbands to feel that they were married to a great woman, she wanted her parents-in-law to be proud of her, and she wanted to please them. The *Mahabharatha* is a text of great events and Droupadi herself was always behaving in a manner in which she maintained the reputation of her great family and her country.

Truly Bharath can be regarded as a true reflection of the qualities of the Pandavas and Krishna. It is customary for us to regard The *Mahabharatha* as a story of a group of people who are warmongers and who have no respect for peace, sanctity, and security of mankind. One can say that Krishna is the *Paramatma* and has taken the five Pandavas as the five elemental substances which are the basis of creation and Droupadi as the *jiva,* and has created the text of *Mahabharatha* for us.

The first thing we should try and recognise in *Mahabharatha* is that Krishna took the form of a human being, and we should examine in what manner he gave us the lessons of code of conduct for other human beings. Whatever part of *Mahabharatha* we may be studying, if we regard Krishna as God, we will never be able to understand the inner significance of that particular portion of *Mahabharatha*. It is only when we regard and pay attention to the human aspect of Krishna and look at the whole story from the angle of Krishna in the human form, that we will understand his greatness.

All your ideas and thoughts have to be transferred to the time when Krishna lived, into the time when the story of *Mahabharatha* took place. Only then will you understand their true significance. If you are remaining mentally in the position in which you are now existing, it will not be possible for you to understand and appreciate the true context of the story of *Mahabharatha* which took place 5000 years ago.

As was told to you yesterday, worship a picture as God; but do not worship God as a picture. Do not bring him down to the level of a tumbler or a table or a piece of cloth. If you want to understand Krishna, take yourself to the position where Krishna lived and worked; but do not bring him to your position. If you want to rise high and go to a high place, it will be possible only if you read good stories and understand them. Therefore, students, boys and girls, with the help of your sacred hearts, understand the ideal lives that were portrayed in *Mahabharatha* and put them into practice in your own lives and follow the paths indicated in *Mahabharatha*. In the hope that you will be able to do this, I am bringing this discourse to a close.

BE GOOD, DO GOOD, AND SEE GOOD

That is the Way to God

Do you know why you have been given ears? Is it for hearing all the sounds that are uttered near you? No, the ears have been given to you so that you may listen to songs relating to the glory of God.

Divya Atma Swarupas,

All the creation that you see emanates from the Lord. That the great variety that we see around us is coming only as a result of the change in our own qualities is a truth that is asserted by the sacred texts. Man is sometimes very happy, sometimes he is afraid, and at other times he is courageous. These changes come about in quick succession and in a casual way. Let us examine the main reason for all these changes. The main reason for all these changes is the change that comes in our own mental attitude. These are manifestations of one's own qualities. Man has three distinct *gunas* or qualities. They are called *sathwa*, *thamo*, and *rajo gunas*. If these three qualities are mixed in a balanced manner, there will be no drastic change in one's nature. Sunlight is composed of seven different colours. When these colours are mixed in appropriate proportions, there will be no change, and the sun will be shining in its natural colour. On the other hand, if there is an imbalance in the manner in which these colours are mixed, then you will find that some special colours show themselves. In the same manner, if the *sathwa, rajo*, and *thamo gunas* are mixed in balanced proportions, there will be no big change in what we see around us; but if there is an imbalance, and if one of the qualities has gained the upper hand, then you will find that there are drastic changes.

These *gunas* have certain natural qualities. The quality of *sathwic* nature appears to us as if it is the very essence of peace. The *rajasic* quality appears to us as a mild *jyothi* (light). The *thamasic* quality appears also as a *jyothi* but covered by smoke. In these qualities, on some occasions, depending on how they are mixed, we find that there are some changes. When a mouse for 152 *Summer Roses on the Blue Mountains, 1976* example, has been saved by a lion from the trouble in which it has found itself, we find later on that the mouse expresses its gratitude to the lion when the lion is in distress.

When Sugreeva found that his own brother took away his kingdom, turned him away into the forest, and took away his wife, he wanted to take revenge and sought the help of Rama. This is a manifestation of his *gunas*. Not only this, many attitudes such as equanimity come out of these *gunas*.

If we add sour buttermilk to sweet milk, we can get tasty butter and curds out of the milk. In the same manner, sometimes bad people join good people and become good in the company of the good people. Men who have good qualities sometimes transmit their good qualities to the bad people who join them. The good people in the world cause good to the bad people in the world also.

The analogy for this is found in the case of an axe, which is a bad one, when used to cut a sandalwood tree. In this case, the fragrance of the sandalwood tree comes to the axe as well. When we mix cold water with warm water, we will have neither cold water nor warm water but we will get a middle temperature. So also, when we mix two qualities, the extremes disappear and we get an intermediate mixture.

It is in this context that we can conclude that the good or the bad, the joy or sorrow, calmness or excitement come to man as a result of the *gunas* in him. For man, it is very essential to see that his qualities are protected. Man should promote an appropriate admixture of his *gunas* for the practice of *sadhana*.

The life of Krishna is not an exhibition for man but it is an ideal example. His life is to be followed by men as a worthy example. His life was intended to be an ideal example to be put before every human being. Krishna told these words to Dhritharashtra on several occasions during the peace negotiations. Not only this, when Uddhava came to conduct the negotiations, it was demonstrated that justice is something which is natural to man. Thus he argued that everyone, when he wants to do his duty, has a right to insist that he should be allowed to perform his duty. In order that man may claim what is rightfully and justly his, he has the right to protect his own responsibilities and to insist on rightfully performing his duty.

The Pandavas never wanted to get anything which they did not deserve and which they did not have the right to ask for, and the Pandavas never tolerated injustice. Krishna told the Kauravas in very clear terms that the Pandavas were always insisting on their right to both responsibilities and duties. Sometimes we misinterpret it, and we think that he was promoting war. What Krishna did was not warmongering. Krishna was an ideal example, and he always insisted on one's rights and responsibilities.

There is an incident which brings out that he clearly demonstrated and demarcated one's rights and claims. There was always a close and intimate relationship between Krishna and Arjuna. In this context of close friendship and taking advantage of such close friendship, Arjuna went close to Krishna on one night and tried to get answers for some of his doubts. Arjuna asked Krishna, "Have I got the right to get a sacred text like the *Gita* taught by you, especially when I know that I am suffering from ego and when I know that I do not have any superior knowledge? There is the allknowing Bhishma, who is very wise, and in his presence, I am like a small lamp in the presence of a huge light. Under such circumstances, have I the right to learn the *Gita* from you? What is the meaning of picking me up and teaching me the *Gita*? Perhaps Bhishma was not suitable because he was on the side of the Kauravas, but we have Dharmaraja who is the embodiment of *dharma,* and on all counts, he deserves to be taught the *Gita*, and why is it that he was ignored? There is also my elder brother Bheema who was bypassed? While these superior persons Bhishma, Dharmaraja, and Bheema were there, why is it that they have been ignored and I, who am immersed in seeking material benefits all the time, have been chosen for this; and do I have the right to be chosen like this?" Then Krishna drew Arjuna close to him affectionately and said, "You are thinking that I, in my divine compassion, am doing you some favour. This is not true. You are not able to recognise the great human qualities, and you think I am doing you a favour. This is not correct. As you said, Bhishma is a very learned man; but in spite of his wisdom and in spite of his recognising that the Pandavas are the embodiment of truth and they follow *dharma* and his accepting that the Kauravas follow *adharma,* he has gone and joined the side of Kauravas. What is the meaning of this? I do not like this riding two horses at the same time. I do not agree to this. You people have been regarding Bhishma as a great man. I do not agree with this attitude of yours. A Mahatma is one in whom the thought, word, and deed harmonise completely. A person in whom the thought is one, word is another, and deed is yet another cannot be called a great man. He will be called a *duratma* (an evil person). He is unable to recognise the meaning and the significance of his action when, on the one hand, he says that the Pandavas are good people and that victory is going to be on the side of good people and yet leads the army of the Kauravas, whom he acknowledges as bad people.

Now, we will come to the aspect of Dharmaraja. He is one who has no forethought, and he will always repent after his action. Repentance is a very natural quality. So, what is exceptionally great in him? Repentance is a common quality seen in many people and it is seen in him also. He always talks of justice and righteousness. These do engage his attention always. He is not recognising the duty at the right point of time. An individual, who does not recognise his immanent duty, has no right to listen to such a sacred text as the *Gita*.

As regards your brother Bheema, he only has animal or physical strength; but he does not possess the intellectual or the mental strength. You are characterised by forethought, more than repentance. As a forethought, you have already asked me how you could kill your kith and kin; and even if the kingdom is won after so much bloodshed, how you could enjoy it. You said that it is better to beg and eat rather than get a kingdom by killing your relatives. Thus, you have forethought. You are not the person who runs after the kingdom. You have no such desire to rule over a kingdom. You have recognised your duty. What is troubling you till now is the aspect of your right. To some extent you are thinking about what is just and what is not just. Man's duty is to be able to pursue justice and sacrifice everything in order to behave in a just manner. Man who recognises his sacred duty has the right to listen to this sacred text of the *Gita*."

Today, the biggest drawback in human beings is that men are not recognising what is just, and men are not recognising their right and the duty which they have to perform. Man is always hankering after something which is not his own and which is not rightfully his. Man is struggling to acquire various things in an unjust manner. Man is pushing away his real duty and is simply thinking of his present convenience.

Krishna's example and ideal is to make you recognise your duty. His second ideal is to show people that for the sake of justice, they should be willing to sacrifice everything, even life. (For the sake of justice, even life must be sacrificed.) In this context, it is necessary for us to understand the inner meaning of the conversation between Arjuna and Krishna. When Krishna was conducting negotiations for peace, Arjuna was very apprehensive and he asked Krishna, "The Kauravas are not going to accept peace in any way, so why are you conducting these negotiations and spending so much time in negotiating for peace which is not going to come about anyway?"

Krishna explained that an individual who stands by and watches *dharma* being overcome by *adharma* and truth being destroyed by falsehood is better dead than alive. One should not remain passive when injustice pushes aside justice. To that Arjuna asked, "Is it possible to get *Amritha,* the immortal liquid, from poison? Is it possible to put flowers in a raging fire? What is the use of talking of peace in these impossible conditions? The Kauravas have such a narrow vision; are they going to come and accept our peace offers? It is better that you stop here. Is it possible to bring the north pole and the south pole together? This is an impossible task, and we should undertake the war as everything is ready for the war."

When we listen to these words of Arjuna and contemplate on how Arjuna regarded peace as an impossible achievement, we can understand how much Krishna had done and to what lengths he went in order to negotiate for peace. But many writers and citizens of India have characterised Krishna as one who never cared for peace, not recognising the efforts that he made for peace. They thought that he was wanting to promote war. This is not right. Arjuna, who regarded peace as impossible said just before the battle began, "How am I going to kill so many people who are my relatives! This is impossible. My head is reeling, let us abandon the battlefield and go home." Here Krishna took the contrary view, and admonished Arjuna, "You have come into the battlefield like a hero and now you talk like a coward. Battle is not something which has come suddenly at this moment. There is a long background for this and the preparations have been going on for a whole week. You have all taken out your rusty weapons, cleaned them, and made them ready.

All the arrows, which gathered cobwebs, have been cleaned. You have asked for the help of all your relations in the battle. Having made all these preparations, what is the meaning of all this talk of going back home without fighting? If you had told me this earlier, I would not have taken all this trouble. This is disgraceful. You are turning into a coward. You must fulfil your duty and not become a coward."

Here Krishna taught Arjuna how he should be prepared to fulfil his duty. Here we see a conflict. Till then Krishna was trying to negotiate peace and avoid war; but at that critical juncture, the same Krishna, who wanted to avoid war, is telling Arjuna that he must take part in war.

We must understand the inner meaning of this. In the first instance, Krishna wanted to establish peace and as a result of that he wanted no loss of life in the world. Thus he wanted to give prosperity to the world. This was Krishna's first attempt. Later as time went on, he was insisting on justice and right and was telling the Pandavas that, in the context of one's justice and right, one should fulfil one's duty. Thus, in the performance of one's own duty and acceptance of one's right, we see an ideal example in Krishna's life. It is very necessary for young students like you to understand the inner significance of Krishna's using words like "duty", "justice" and "right".

Today students read a large number of books which are totally unnecessary. They read a large amount of useless literature which does not give them any ideals. Instead of pursuing true education which gives you knowledge and *Vidya* (wisdom), you are simply pursuing material information and becoming *vithyarthis*. A few minutes ago, talking about education, one of our speakers gave you the essence of what true education should be and gave some good examples of it. Truly, if we look around the country, we will get a doubt whether there is any education which can be called true education at all and whether any individual can be called a teacher in the true sense of the word.

I will give an example of what really happened in one of our universities. Today's teachers are such that they are not willing to go into a class which they are to teach. This particular teacher put the tape recorder on, and he himself went to the staff room and was sleeping. On that day, as the lesson was given on a tape recorder, the students took down notes and they went home. On the second day again, the teacher brought the tape recorder, started the tape and left the classroom. Some of the students also brought their tape recorders, and they left their tape recorders to record what the teacher was saying through the tape, and they also left the class. By some good fortune, the principal happened to walk into the class that day and, to his surprise, found only tape recorders on all the tables; and there were no students at all. There was neither the teacher nor the student. If the education is like that, can we call it education at all?

Therefore, in order that you may develop yourselves into ideal citizens, it is essential for you to understand

and comprehend the basic aspects of our civilisation. In the first instance, it is very necessary for you to understand the qualities which enable you to be called human beings. Morality, truth, and sacredness of your heart and pursuit of self are the qualities which you should have; and these are the things which will entitle you to be called a man. We can assert, without any fear of contradiction, that the man who has lost fear of sin and love of God is only a man in form; and at the core, he is not a human being.

God's *leelas* and actions are very surprising, and an ordinary man cannot easily understand them. In that context, when God himself comes down in the form of an *Avatar* and preaches the essentials, many people who do not understand, begin to misinterpret his words and actions, and the true meaning completely disappears from the minds of everyone. *Avatars* come to propagate truth, to proclaim truth, and to make you practise truth. There is an incident in the *Mahabharatha* to illustrate this. In the open assembly, the Kauravas, who were very evil-intentioned people, wanted to put Droupadi to shame. Her powerful and heroic husbands were sitting on one side.

When Droupadi was being humiliated, she realised that her husbands could not rescue her and she was asking and praying for help from Krishna. However much and however intensely she prayed to Krishna, he was not to be seen at all. In many ways, she was describing Krishna and his greatness. She addressed him as one who lives in Dwaraka, as one who lives in Mathurapuri and so on, but there was no response. In utter disgust and as a last resort, she addressed Krishna as *Hrudayavasi*, i.e., one who lives in one's own heart. In the very next moment, Krishna appeared on the scene and protected her in the required manner and saved her honour.

After all the trouble was over, when they were sitting and talking like brother and sister, she asked Krishna why he had not responded to her many prayers when she was being humiliated in the Kauravas assembly. Krishna asked her in what manner she had addressed him. She replied that she had addressed him as one who resided in Dwaraka. Then Krishna said, "Oh, sister, what a mistake it was. How far was Dwaraka and how could I respond to your call especially because your call had to go so far and I had to come from there. You also say that you addressed me as Mathurapurivasi. Even Mathurapuri was very far and it would have taken a long time for me to respond to your call. You were in Hastinapura and you wanted to call me from Mathurapuri. How is that possible? Then you had also addressed me as Gokulavasi. Even Gokula was very far away and it would have taken time for me to respond. But when you addressed me as *Hrudayavasi*, as the dweller in your heart, I readily responded and came to your rescue."

If you write a letter to Puttaparthi, it will go to Puttaparthi, but not to Bangalore, where I will be staying sometimes. In the same way, if Krishna was addressed as *Dwarakavasi* when he was really a *Hrudayavasi*, he will not receive the prayer. In order to show the devotees true faith and determination, God sometimes does such things. So, at no time is a camp address more important than the permanent address. Then Krishna said, "I will now give you the correct address, listen to it. Where my devotees sing my glory, there I am permanently installed and that is my correct address." The *Mahabharatha* contains such beautiful stories as if it were written in jasmine flowers.

It is not right to keep such sacred meanings aside and go after some misinterpretations given by misinformed people. The ideals which we have to follow, the rights that we should claim, and the duties that we have to perform are all contained in the *Mahabharatha* and are good examples. Sometimes God's *leelas* are quite surprising. As a result of such surprise actions, many doubts arise in the minds of men. There is one small example for this. On one occasion, the battle of *Mahabharatha* was very fierce and was taking place in all the corners of the battlefield.

In one direction, Aswatthama had prepared the *Padmavyuha*. On another side Bhishma was preparing for a terrific fight. On the other side, there were other warriors preparing for war. Karna was standing ready for a fight. On the side of the Pandavas, some of the brothers undertook to fight Karna. Dharmaraja and Sahadeva took the other direction and were preparing to give battle. Arjuna was preparing to fight with other heroes. In this way, the battle became fierce in all the four directions. At home, in the camp, was young Abhimanyu. Dronacharya sent a message to Abhimanyu that *Padmavyuha* was ready and that it must be fought against. When a message is sent inviting one to come and fight in a battle, it is not right to refuse the challenge.

If he had refused to answer the challenge, he would bring disrepute to his father; and in order that such disrepute does not come to his father, he readily accepted the challenge.

Abhimanyu thought that if he refrained from going to war because he was a young lad and because he did not have his father's permission, his father might be annoyed with him and say that he had brought disrepute to the family by not accepting the challenge. In this conflict of ideas in his own mind, he came to the conclusion that whatever may happen, he was going to safeguard the reputation of his father; and he went to the

Padmavyuha and lost his life. Of course, Krishna knew that Abhimanyu went into the battle and lost his life.

Arjuna and Krishna came back together and even as they approached the camp, Arjuna felt uneasy and saw bad omens. Arjuna was feeling that Abhimanyu, who usually would come to receive him, had not come that day. There were bad omens and Arjuna felt that there was something wrong. Even from there, Krishna started preaching *Vedanta*. He said, "The body is impermanent, it is made of the five material elements; and the body is sure to fall one day or the other; and the permanent aspect is the *Atma*." He also preached about all the relationships and said that a wife is not even known to the husband before marriage, and a son is not related except by marriage. We should never give any regard to such bodily relationships; and any moment, death may occur. One must be prepared to shed one's body at any time.

While teaching such *Vedantic* truths to Arjuna, Krishna asked him whether these were true or not; and on this Arjuna replied that it was the truth and, in fact, one does not know when one is going to die; and he accepted this as truth. Krishna even asked him if he was saying that these were the truths from the bottom of his heart, believing in them, or whether he was saying that they were the truths simply because Krishna was saying so. Neither Krishna nor Arjuna were people who would simply speak without conviction. Arjuna was not the kind of person who would support what Krishna said unless he felt from the depths of his heart that it was true. Krishna then said, "If you accept all this as truth from the depth of your heart as your own conviction, suppose you now get the news that your son Abhimanyu is dead, are you going to weep or accept it in line with the *Vedanta* that you have now accepted as the truth?" Arjuna was thrown into confusion and he asked Krishna if Abhimanyu was safe or not. Then Krishna said, "Arjuna, your son Abhimanyu has attained the heaven where heroes of the war go."

As soon as Arjuna heard this, he never waited for a moment and immediately accused Krishna of having destroyed a whole family. He said, "O, Krishna! what have you done to the Pandavas who had great faith in you and surrendered to you? A situation has come where there is no continuation for the dynasty of the Pandavas? He was thus accusing Krishna all the way till they reached Hastinapura. The situation at that time was such that whatever reply Krishna gave and whatever philosophical truth he may have communicated, it would have had no effect on Arjuna. So, Krishna simply listened to all the abuses that were being showered on him. While Arjuna was accusing him in many ways, Krishna realised that it was not an opportune moment for him to retort; and he was silent all the way. Whatever questions one may ask and whatever doubts may be expressed, in order that an appropriate answer may be given, a suitable time should come. *Avatars* will never reply unless such suitable time comes. In an *Avatar,* there will never be a situation in which you can find fault with Him. The individual who accuses an *Avatar* will be hurting himself in his eyes with his own finger. God is always a non-interfering witness. He will simply look at things which take their own course. That is the reason why God is always described as one who has no qualities and attributes in an ordinary human manner. After reaching home, they found that all the relations were very sad and were weeping because Abhimanyu had died. But neither sorrow nor pleasure can ever be permanent.

Sorrow cannot remain all the time and happiness cannot remain for all the time. After sorrow, happiness must come. Pain and pleasure always come together and it is not possible for anyone to separate them from each other. Pleasure alone, isolated from pain can never be seen. When pain fructifies, such pain will be called pleasure. Therefore, between pain and pleasure, we talk of some pleasure and some sorrow. As time went on, Subhadra was feeling very sad. At that time, Uttara was in the family way and was approaching the time of her delivery. But the son, who was born to Uttara, was almost lifeless. The situation at that time was such that Droupadi had become old and Subhadra also was approaching old age. The only way in which the dynasty of the Pandavas could be propagated was by the birth of a son to Uttara. The Pandavas were anxiously waiting for the news concerning the delivery of Uttara's baby. Only if a son was born, would it be good news for the Pandavas.

Such grief-stricken Pandavas were sitting anxiously and Droupadi brought a practically lifeless son to the Pandavas, and she also broke down in tears. The day on which Aswatthama and Arjuna fought with each other they used weapons of great power and potency, which were responsible for the damage to the pregnancy of Uttara. Today when we use an atom bomb, it is reported that pregnancy is destroyed in the wombs of mothers. This is not something which has been recently found out. It was known even in those days. Today, all the power is only that of a machine. If we let loose a bomb, there is no way in which it can be retracted. The damage is permanently caused; but in those days, it was more the power of the *manthras*. When once this *manthra* has been used, it could also be retracted if so desired. But today, if a bomb is used there is no way of retracting. When the Pandavas looked at the sight of a lifeless son, they were greatly stricken, and they did not know what to do.

Dharmaraja immediately sent Arjuna to bring Krishna to the place. Krishna came there and found the Pandavas in great sorrow. As a cat enjoys the situation when it is a matter of life and death for the mouse, Krishna was smiling when the Pandavas were literally steeped in misery. He was talking in a very light manner and asked Dharmaraja and Arjuna why they were so sorry and glum. At this, Droupadi brought the cradle in which the lifeless baby was kept and placed it before Krishna and asked him why he had done this tragic thing to their family. Krishna took the cradle into his hand, and he started looking at the baby and describing it in nice terms by comparing the nose to that of Abhimanyu and the face to that of Arjuna.

Dharmaraja took up the cue and said, "Yes, even his breath is like that of Abhimanyu." Then Krishna exclaimed, "Why, is there no life in the baby?" and he started to shake the baby vigorously, and the baby started to cry. At that instant, the pleasure and joy of the Pandavas knew no bounds and Arjuna exclaimed, "Oh, Krishna, the protector of our family!" They praised him in that manner.

Krishna smiled and came to Arjuna and said, "Be aware of whatever you are saying. Now, you say that I am responsible for the continuance of your family. That day you described me as one who completely destroyed your family, and today you are praising me as one who is a protector of your family. Was that the truth or is this the truth?" Although Arjuna had forgotten what he had said, Krishna did not forget, and he reminded Arjuna about the old incident. "All that we do, either good or bad, knowingly or unknowingly, will always produce a result. So it is necessary for us to do good so that the consequences will also be good. When one is born out of a mother's womb, one does not come with a garland. You do not have, even as a specimen, a chain of gold around your neck. There is only one chain around your neck. All the *karma* that you have done in your previous births constitute the only gold chain round your neck. But that necklace is something which is not visible. In order that we do not have a chain of bad actions around our neck when we are born, it is necessary for us to recognise, as a primary lesson of the *Mahabharatha,* that we should do good deeds in our daily lives. It is in this context that it is said, *"Do good, Be good, and See good."* That alone will take you to Madhava!"

Man should Not, at Any Time, Behave Like an Animal

Do you know why you have been given a human body? Is it to take it to all the corners of the world? No, that is not the purpose. You have been given this body so that you may demonstrate, with its help, the truth of the statement that the body is intended for doing good to other human beings.

Divya Atma Swarupas!

It is for us to recognise that the compassion that all the living beings deserve from us forms the essence of our being able to get a vision of the *Atma.* The greatest thapas is the bringing together of the compassion that is present in all beings. The sacredness of life that has been given to a human being is at a very high level. The life of a cow, of a horse, and of an elephant are at a lower level. These lower forms are being looked after by the human being who is at a higher level. Sometimes these forms are also being worshipped by the human beings. The reason for this is that they live a life which is *sathwic.*

When we look at the other categories of animals like lions and tigers, we see that man hates them and even tries to kill them. It is essential for us to understand the inner meaning and significance of our trying to kill some animals while we respect and adore another class of animals. The *sathwic* qualities of a group of animals represented by the cow, and the *rajasic* qualities of a group of animals represented by the tiger, are responsible for this difference of approach.

We know that of all the animals in this world, to take birth as a human being, is a very difficult matter. Having attained this difficult human birth, we should not behave, at any time, like an animal. We should think and take note of this aspect. The reason for this is mainly the kind of food that we take. The kind of food that we take determines the kind of behaviour that we develop. If a tiger enters a herd of cows, then the cows cannot survive and live.

So also, as in that analogy, in the heart of man there are good and *sathwic* qualities comparable to the qualities of a cow. If into that group of good qualities, we send in food represented by the *rajasic* qualities of the tiger, it is impossible for the good to survive any longer. If you put seeds in a land which is not fertile, the seeds are not going to sprout. So also in a man who has *rajasic* qualities in his heart, the kind of *sathwic* qualities like *puja* or compassion cannot thrive. It, therefore, becomes necessary for man to do such things by which the field of his heart can be purified and cleansed. Therefore, man in this life must take courage and move forward in his journey of life.

Krishna has taught in the *Gita* that the purity of *karma* is extremely important. The kind of work we engage in will determine the kind of fruits that we get. The kind of food that we eat will determine the smell of the belch that follows. The quality of bread that we will be able to prepare depends on the kind of flour we use.

God never does things which do not have a good reason behind them. God never utters words which have no meaning. Whatever He does, sees, and says carries with it an inner deeper spiritual meaning.

There is a small example for this. The two armies of the Kauravas and of the Pandavas were standing on either side. On the side of the Pandavas, there were seven units of armies. On the side of the Kauravas, there were eleven units of armies. It is not as if Arjuna was ignorant of the number of units on the Kauravas side and the number of units on the Pandava side.

Knowing this fully well, Arjuna requested Krishna to take his chariot and put it right in the middle of the two armies. When Krishna asked him for the reason for his behaviour, he replied that he wanted to determine with whom he should really fight, if he should fight at all. When we examine this in the context in which he made this statement, we realise that he made this statement after he had gone with the intention of fighting. Krishna prepared the chariot and Arjuna prepared all his weapons including the Gandiva, and they were all set for the battle. After reaching the battlefield, why did he change his mind? Was it his weakness or did he become despondent? He began asking the question as to who will benefit from the battle and who will get prosperity from the battle. He realised that the very people for whose sake he was fighting the battle will probably be killed, and so he felt that the battle had no purpose. The kings want to rule over people and build up the prosperity of the people and the kingdom. If the people are going to be killed in a battle, where is the question of prosperity and a kingdom? After the entire family and group of people are wiped out, for whose sake was he going to establish a kingdom and rule over it? Some people have described this as *moha* or attachment to his kith and kin, and they named the chapter *Vishada Yoga*. This cannot be described as a period of internal controversy or discussion within himself. He has entered this argument within himself to decide between truth and untruth, between propriety and impropriety. He discussed within himself the aspect that the Kauravas have been ruling unjustly, and the fact that they have been having untruth and impropriety on their side, and did not, himself, want to undertake the same impropriety and untruth. There were certain distinctive features and distinctive qualities on the side of the Pandavas, therefore, God was also on their side.

Here it becomes clear to us that Krishna was on the side of the Pandavas because of their good qualities. If we look at this situation in a somewhat superficial manner, then we will see that because Arjuna was thrown into this despondent and confusing situation, an opportunity had risen for Krishna to preach the sacred text of the *Bhagavad Gita*. If Arjuna did not fall into an introspective and despondent situation like that, Krishna would not have had an opportunity to preach the sacred Bhagavad Gita.

Just as we know that pleasure is an interval between two pains, so also in the interval between two situations, sometimes good comes about. Krishna here plays the part of a typical human being, and by making Arjuna behave as a typical human being, Krishna created a situation whereby the *Gita* could be expounded. Man's life is transient. It is momentary, and in this context Arjuna had a chance to recognise the permanent truth. The Pandavas were held up as an example by which the sacredness of the heart of a devotee could be understood. Sometimes, as a result of difficulties, the devotees have their hearts merged in sorrow. This results in their ego and other bad qualities in their hearts, coming to the surface and troubling them. To get such ego, jealousy, and bad qualities out of the heart of devotees, God sometimes undertakes certain programmes.

On one occasion, Arjuna performed the *Aswamedha Yagna* and let loose the horse. According to the rules of that *Aswamedha Yagna*, if a horse was let out and someone else captured that horse, then the owner had to fight with the person who had captured the horse; and if he lost the fight, he had to forfeit his kingdom to the victor. The Mayuradhwaja Raja caught the horse, and he was fully aware of the then code of conduct regarding the horse. Krishna and Arjuna went in search of the horse, and they found that the horse was captured by the Mayuradhwaja Raja. Krishna and Arjuna were contemplating whether to undertake a fight with Mayuradhwaja. Krishna told Arjuna that Mayuradhwaja was no ordinary man and that he was a great devotee of his, and it is not easy for Arjuna to fight with him. Arjuna stated that according to the code of conduct he had to fight with the person who captured the horse.

Then Krishna commanded Arjuna to fight the battle. Arjuna fought with Mayuradhwaja in many ways; but it was not possible for him to defeat his opponent and even his principal weapon, the Gandiva, was damaged in the process. As Arjuna was asking Krishna for help, he too was preparing for the fight. Mayuradhwaja was no doubt aware of Krishna's greatness, but the code of conduct required that Mayuradhwaja engage in battle, and so Mayuradhwaja took out each one of his weapons and sent them at Krishna after uttering the sacred name of Krishna. The arrows were so hard and so powerful that Krishna started running hither and thither. Arjuna started shouting to Krishna that he should use his sacred *chakra*; but Krishna replied that against Mayuradhwaja, neither Arjuna's Gandiva nor Krishna's *chakra* will have any effect. Arjuna did not take this matter seriously. He thought that Krishna was only joking and that Krishna was really not intent on fighting. Arjuna thought that if Mayuradhwaja was really a devotee of Krishna, would he undertake to fight against Krishna? He thought that Mayuradhwaja was not a true devotee.

Krishna wanted to demonstrate to Arjuna that Mayuradhwaja was indeed a very ardent devotee. So Krishna and Arjuna disguised themselves as two brahmins and came to Mayuradhwaja's house. According to the tradition, it was the duty of the householder to receive the guests and honour them, and in this aspect there was none better than Mayuradhwaja. As soon as Mayuradhwaja saw the two brahmins coming, he himself threw away the King's garb and wore clothes typical of the Brahmins. He brought water and washed the feet of his guests and honoured them suitably. Mayuradhwaja requested them to be his guests.

With a view to making Arjuna realise the depth of the devotion of Mayuradhwaja, Krishna had been planning this meeting for quite some time. When Mayuradhwaja asked Krishna and Arjuna to accept his hospitality and be his guests for food, Krishna replied, "We do not have the time to accept your hospitality. We have come here with a specific problem and require your help. While coming to your house, my son has been swallowed by a tiger and, at this time, only half the body of my son has been swallowed and the other half is outside. A formless voice said that if the body of my son was to be freed, I will have to get half the body of King Mayuradhwaja as a meal for the tiger and then, I was told, my son would be set free."

As soon as Mayuradhwaja heard of this, he saw an opportunity to be of some service to his guest. He knew very well that immortality comes out of sacrifice, and he was prepared to sacrifice his body. He knew very well that the human body was given to him so that he might be able to help others. He knew that the human body would drop off some day or the other, and so he was prepared to sacrifice his body to satisfy others. He called his wife and son and asked them to cut his body into two halves with a sword. His wife and son thought that Mayuradhwaja was preparing to fulfil a sacred task and so they also prepared to cut the body into two halves. Arjuna and Krishna were watching this situation without even batting their eyelids once.

As they were watching intently, they found that the left eye of Mayuradhwaja was shedding a tear. Finding that the situation was developing, Krishna wanted to test him even further and said, "What is the value of the gift which is given with sorrow and tears in one's eyes? I do not want such a gift. A gift must be given freely and willingly." Mayuradhwaja, who was undisturbed and sitting peacefully with closed eyes, opened his eyes and said that he had no sorrow in giving his body. If, at all, he had any sorrow, both eyes should shed tears. Why is it that only one eye is shedding tears? You must consider and understand why tears are coming from only one eye. It is not as if Krishna did not know the truth behind this. He only wanted to show Arjuna the depth of the devotion of Mayuradhwaja.

Mayuradhwaja replied and said, "Oh, Lord, this body is going to be cut into two parts and the right part is going to be gifted to you for a sacred purpose. The left part is crying and shedding tears because it will then be thrown away and simply become food for the crows. It is crying because it is going to be thrown away in such an unsacred manner." As soon as Arjuna listened to these words, he started to repent and realised that this was a lesson taught to him and that there were more ardent devotees of Krishna than himself.

The world is full of devotees of varying types. If it was in the aspect of devotion, Mayuradhwaja would place at the feet of the Lord everything that he possessed. If we look at it from the angle of a householder, we have seen that he will honour any guest that came to his house by giving him anything. If we look at it from the point of view of the proper code of conduct of a ruler, Mayuradhwaja was one who would observe this fully. He was fully prepared to fight and establish the code of conduct. Mayuradhwaja was thus one who was always prepared in any sphere of activity whether it was worldly, material, or spiritual, and was ever ready to sacrifice and do anything. In order to proclaim this aspect of performing one's duty in different spheres, Krishna brought this example to the world and to Arjuna.

Having passed through a period of slavery for several centuries and having attained our independence by our own struggle, if we become unmindful of our traditions which are 5000 years old, and if we are not able to understand the sanctity of the ideals that were established by the examples shown by Krishna, there is no wonder that we are in such an unfortunate situation as we are in today. Krishna was one who taught that one should be prepared to sacrifice everything for the sake of justice. Krishna taught this in the form of *Vedanta*. Krishna's teachings and ideals were not such that while teaching that if you get a slap on one of your cheeks, you should be so considerate as to show the other cheek, yet you go ahead and produce an atom bomb in practice for the destruction of the world. This irreconcilable situation between preaching and practice did not belong to Krishna. Holding an atom bomb in one's hand, people keep on shouting for peace. The kind of peace which they want cannot be attained, even if they go to the moon. All the time preparing for war and heading for agitation and revolution, we just talk of peace in the world. This is not the kind of philosophy which Krishna stood for or taught.

Krishna was one who undertook to bring under one rule, the eighteen different kings and kingdoms that were existing at that time. That was the ideal which Krishna stood for. Who was the king under whom Krishna brought all the different kingdoms? It was Dharmaraja. Krishna did not want to become the king himself. If we really pay heed to the ideals of Krishna or what Krishna did, we will not be in the unfortunate situation today when the country is divided into many parts.

Boys and Girls

Recognise the ideals of this country and *Dharmarajya* that it stands for. Use all your physical and mental strength to get back this sacred *Dharmarajya.* I hope and bless you that this should be possible.

The Human Body is Like a Water Bubble on the Surface of Water

It is easy to talk of principles and codes of conduct but it is a very difficult matter to put them into practice. Whether it be for the young people or whether it be to the grandfathers, it is the same. This is the truth and the simple truth that I am giving you.

Students, Boys and Girls!

The results of your examinations as announced today are indeed happy news; but so long as the education that you get is such that it promotes only ignorance and does not give you the needed strength to promote the prosperity of our nation and traditions, then the education is useless. Of all the branches of education, spiritual education is the real education. When we compare this with the other branches of education, we can see that the spiritual education is like the ocean while the other branches of education are like the rivers.

When the rivers go and merge in the ocean, they acquire the depth and glory of the unfathomable ocean. In a similar manner, when all other forms of education go and merge with the spiritual education, they acquire the form and grandeur of the spiritual education. It is only when your education is combined with *thapas* that there is a possibility of the blossoming of your heart and the ennobling of your ideas.

Thapas does not mean that you should give up everything and go to the forest and stand there with your head on the ground. *Thapas* is one, with the help of which, you can make your thought, word, and deed harmonise with each other. It is only when such a sacred type of education is given along with proper culture, that there is a chance of the great ideas blossoming properly in you. It is only then that the noble and good ideas that are inside you can be exhibited properly. Education cannot be entirely and wholly related to worldly matters. Education should promote your character.

It is necessary for the students of today to acquire such sacred education and that alone will give us the good results. If today we really want to understand the history and culture of ourselves, then it becomes necessary for us to learn and study the *Sruthi* and *Ithihasas*, the components of our *Vedanta*. When we read such texts, we should take great care to see that our own ideas, concepts, and prejudices are not injected into what we read. We should try to understand the original content as far as possible. In the centuries that have gone by since the creation of such texts, several aspects have undergone a great deal of transformation. As a result of the passage of time, we find that the continents on the earth, the seas, and the very sources of the rivers have undergone great changes. A river which may have flowed in a particular direction some centuries ago will be flowing in a different direction now. That river may have changed its course. We will find that there is a very marked difference between the course taken by a river some centuries ago and the course taken by the same river at the present time. But when the man of today looks at the course taken by the river today, he transfers it to what is in his concept; and he thinks that the river took the same course some centuries ago also. This is not right.

There is a small example for this. We ask ourselves the question, is the land which we now call Lanka the same as the one which existed in the *Thretha Yuga* as the land ruled by Ravana at the time of *Ramarajya*? No, this is not so. At that time, Lanka was hundreds of miles away from the tip of India and at that time, it was at the equator. As time went on, and as we moved from the *Thretha Yuga* to the *Kali Yuga*, this particular island, which was on the equator, drifted hundreds of miles northwards. When we look at this island, which we now call Lanka, we find that it has shifted to the north of the equator.

It was recorded in the Greek history that this island, which we now call Lanka, was completely submerged under water when the oceanic catastrophe called the Atlantis occurred. The Greeks were no ordinary people. They were very advanced in sciences and were very knowledgeable in many fields. They were describing the fact that Lanka was submerged in the ocean and drifted away and this phenomenon was being accepted by them. At that time, these people were so advanced that they had travelled to the moon and designed several types of air transport and were such that they had mastered the science of flying.

As we know, today the entire world regards the standard of time as the Greenwich standard time. In World History, it is known that the astrologers of that time were taking the longitude passing through Lanka and when the sun rose on this longitude they took it as the standard time for the calculation. It is on the basis of this standard of time that our people decided on the time of the birth of Krishna, the time at which Krishna gave up his mortal body, and the dates of the *Mahabharatha* battle, and so on. When the Pandavas lived, the time scales were determined on the basis of this longitude which passes through Lanka. When we take this as the basis, we come to the conclusion that the period which we now call *Kali Yuga* started in the year named Pramadi, in the month named Sravana, and in the fortnight named Bahula and on the day called Ashtami.

According to the English calendar, this will be described as February 20, 3102 years before the advent of Christ. In order to bring out this aspect of the commencement of a new *Yuga* on February 20, 3102 B.C., our ancestors have been calling that day as Ugadi, or the day of the beginning of a new era. As this was the commencing day of a new *Yuga*, it was called the Ugadi.

When looked at from this angle, we should also learn a different aspect, although it is not very pleasant. This particular day called the Ugadi is also the day on which Krishna gave up his mortal body in a sacred place of pilgrimage called Prabata near Dwaraka. There is a proverb, according to which we think of all kinds of extraordinary and unusual ideas when we near our end.

The Yadavas, the community in which Krishna was living, had some such strange ideas then; and they brought about their end themselves. Although Krishna was preaching the acceptance of only *sathwic* food, the Yadavas violated this sacred injunction on a holy day. When they were performing a religious ceremony, they used articles which should not have been used and prepared food containing meat.

They also partook of alcoholic drinks and consumed these articles. On account of such food and drink, they became intoxicated and lost their balance. They began to beat each other and they reached a stage when they prepared to kill each other. In this manner, they extinguished the entire Yadava clan. It is in this context, bearing in mind the ideals which Krishna had promulgated, that Gandhi also wanted to forbid meat eating and alcoholic drinks; but unfortunately he did not succeed.

The Yadava community, which was then subjected to this distress, lost their lives. In this battle even Vasudeva was killed. However, many Yadava women, who were not there, survived. Balarama also was killed in this battle. Within a short time, Vidura came to that place. When Vidura looked at that place, it struck him as a place of terror.

Uddhava also reached the place at that time. When Uddhava looked at that situation, he was afraid that his close friend Krishna may also have given up his mortal body, and he was looking for Krishna's body. Arjuna also helped Uddhava in this quest.

They were looking everywhere for the body of their dear friend. In that gruesome fight, they were told that the body of Krishna was cut and dismembered and parts thrown at different places. Arjuna and Vidura thought that they could not identify Krishna's body. In that situation Vidura and Arjuna thought that it was no use for them to live in a world in which Krishna was not living, and they prepared to drown themselves in the Yamuna river. It was a time of great disaster, and as a consequence, all the air and surrounding waters became greatly polluted and that was polluting the whole atmosphere.

While both Vidura and Arjuna were looking at the river, they found a blue cloth fluttering at some distance and heard a sound from that place. Vidura was greatly surprised and wanting to know what it was, he ran towards the sound. Under a tree, he found Krishna sitting in a very peaceful manner. It looked as if Krishna was also preparing to give up his body, but Krishna did not think it proper to give up his body when his friends and relatives were so near. With a view to sending Uddhava away, he taught him the *Bhagavatha* and asked him to go and bring Arjuna. Uddhava appeared to be happy and wanted to share the news of Krishna's safety with Arjuna, and he ran towards Arjuna.

Observing that Uddhava was now far away, Krishna gave up his mortal life. When Uddhava and Arjuna came near the tree, they found that the body was no longer there. They watched this situation for two to three days. They felt that Krishna had decided that the purpose of his human existence was over and he had given up his mortal body at that time. They then came back to Dwaraka. Sathyabhama, Rukmini, and the *gopikas* were in great sorrow as they had lost everything in their lives, and Arjuna and Uddhava were unable to look at their suffering. Arjuna thought that it was not good to leave the women alone at that place. So he took his Gandiva and proceeded to take them to Hastinapura.

On the way, the forest tribes attacked them and wanted to take away the women from the group. Since

Arjuna was leading them, Sathyabhama, Rukmini, and the other *gopikas* were shouting for his help and requested him to save them from this situation. Earlier, Arjuna took part and was victorious in several battles. He had showed great strength in the battle of the Mahabharatha and in the battle of Khandavavana. Arjuna had shown great courage and strength on many occasions.

On this particular occasion, he could not even lift his Gandiva and take aim. Then Arjuna thought, "All that strength shown was because of Krishna; and when Krishna is not there, I am not even able to lift the Gandiva." He felt that although his hand had been holding the Gandiva all these years, it was the strength of Krishna that was using it, and he felt very helpless at that time. As Krishna was his *Antaryami* (inner motivator) all those years, he had felt strong; but now that Krishna was no longer in him, he felt like a bag of leather.

The inner meaning of this is that, so long as Arjuna felt that Krishna was there in an ordinary human manner, he had all the strength; but as soon as he felt that He was no longer there, he had lost all the strength and the will to fight.

Just because Krishna's gross body had left, Arjuna thought that Krishna had left him. Because he was under the illusion of identifying Krishna's gross body with Krishna himself, he lost all his strength. To think that one is full of weakness is not correct. The correct attitude is to regard God as formless, without attributes. We should take it that God is present in us. That should be the right attitude. So long as one has a form, it is quite natural that he thinks of that form; but since that form has to be forgotten some day or the other, it is good to concentrate on the formless supreme and give up attachment to a form.

Our *Vedanta* has taught us the philosophy of *vairagya,* or detachment, to help in this process of concentrating on the formless supreme power which is behind every form. It is inevitable that the *jiva* should leave the body; if the *jiva* does not leave the body, then the body has to leave the *jiva.*

This body is like a water bubble on the surface of water. This water bubble is born out of water, lives on water, and survives on water, and finally it gets dissolved in water. It is only when we develop a correct attitude to the formless supreme power that we will be able to have permanent happiness.

If we take a ball and hit it on a hard ground, it will rebound to the extent determined by how hard we hit the ball on the ground. If we hit this ball on a soft muddy ground instead of hard ground, it will not be able to recoil, and in fact it will even get entangled in the muddy ground. In a similar manner, if the pure aspect of divinity goes and hits a sacred heart, it will rebound. If, on the other hand, we have a muddy and impure heart, when divinity impinges on such a heart it will get stuck and entangled.

Therefore, purity of one's mind, and an exemplary life are essential. Truth and honesty are to be regarded as two eyes for us. For these two eyes, we have a disease of selfishness; and because our eyes are inflicted by this disease, we are not able to have a pure and clean heart. Young people should have purity of mind. They should take great care to protect truth and honesty. This was the ideal taught and demonstrated by Krishna.

Krishna and his aspect of Love are known to the citizens of Bharath. He is one who has eternal youth. We should understand the significance of saying that he is eternally young. By saying that he is eternally young, we should not imply that he has a young and youthful body forever. This should convey to us the meaning that he has no anxiety and that he has a smiling disposition always. This kind of bliss and happiness also gives happiness to one's body and bodily health.

It is in this context, that it has been said that happiness is union with God. Either for the decay of the body or for the ageing of the body, our own conduct is responsible; and for our conduct, our desires are responsible. For the sake of desires which are connected with the world, we should not use this body. Pain and pleasure are like clouds which move away from our heart. So, all these desires should be regarded as clouds. It is in this context that the *Vedas* have compared our minds to the moon and our eyes to the sun.

The *Vedas* have also taught us that our heart is like a sky; and in this sky of our heart, our mind is like the moon in the sky, and our eyes and intelligence are like the sun. In this sky of our heart, our thoughts must be treated like passing clouds. Thus, in the sky of our heart, there are millions of names of the Lord shining like the stars; and on the sky, if we have our mind shining like the moon, that will be a correct situation. This moon, which we have compared with our mind, must be given the status of the full moon. When the mind has been trained to get the form of a full moon, there will be an opportunity to correct and set right our hearts. This sacred text of *Mahabharatha* has given us so many lessons which will help us make our heart comparable to a full moon. Krishna's ideals wanted that you should all make your minds pure and accept truth and honesty as the basic things on which our life should be based.

Basing on this, it is also correct for us to decide the day on which he was born. That day on which Krishna was born, according to these calculations, will come to be the 20th of July, 3228 years before the Advent of Christ. If this has to be put in our calendar, it will be in the year Srimukha, month by the name Sravana, fortnight by the name Bahula, and the day of Ashtami.

The star will be Rohini and the time will be 3:00 a.m. after midnight. If we count backwards from today, the day on which Krishna gave up his mortal body will work out at 5078 years. If we want to check this, we see that 3102 B.C. and 1976 add up to 5078 years. Thus, since the *Kali Yuga* has started, we have now gone through 5078 years.

That is also the time when Krishna gave up his life, and that is also the day when the *Kali* age commenced. This day is also the first day of the *Kali Yuga* and we call it Ugadi. But the *Kali Yuga* started in the year Pramadi and so it appears that this *Yuga* is full of danger and harm.

Truly, instead of calling this *Yuga* as the *Kali Yuga*, it is right and appropriate to call it the *Kalaha Yuga*, or the age of quarrels. Whether you go to a house, a village, or a country, we see quarrels. Young people of today should do such things by which this name of *Kalaha Yuga*, or age of quarrels, is changed to an age of prosperity by living up to the ideals of Krishna.

It is necessary that in this world there should be two categories of people. Without knowing pain, pleasure will not be enjoyed. Pleasure comes as an interval between two pains. Without sorrow, you can never understand the meaning of happiness. Although two aspects are always present, we should try and promote good, happiness, and pleasure. In our own body while good blood is flowing on one side, we find that simultaneously impure blood is also flowing. Even in our homes, we see that while good and pure drinking water is brought from a pipe from one side, the ugly and bad drainage water is sent away by another pipe.

They are both present in the same home. In a village or a city, while the drinking water is brought through certain pipes, alongside this will also be pipes which carry the drainage, and both will look similar and clean externally. In the same manner, in our mind there are always two streams going. One will be a stream of good ideas and the other a stream of bad ideas, both flowing together. But, you must make an attempt to accept the good and reject the bad.

In the world there are agitations, there are revolutions, and these are common. In the midst of such revolutions in the world, man must make an attempt to distinguish the right from wrong and separate truth from untruth. People who are young have to make a long journey in this train which we call a society.

The older people in this train are such that they will drop out on wayside stations. In this train of society, you are the people who have to travel a long distance, and you should be prepared to take the necessary steps to rectify the defects in that train. You are to set right the faults in this country, and you should imprint the good ideas in your mind. Today, if you think that a particular thing your elders are doing is not right, you should not yourselves do the same thing when you grow up. When you become older you should be prepared to put into action what you now think are the good actions of your elders.

No one amongst us wants to have the consequences of a bad act, but yet we are prepared to continually do bad things. We only do not want to accept the consequences of such bad acts. We all want to have the consequences of good things, but we are not prepared to do good things. If you believe that in order to get good consequences, you must do a good act, then the very first thing that you must accept is to do good things. What you regard as sin should be kept away and you should never participate in such actions.

The harmony of the word that you utter, the deed that you do, and the thought that you get has been referred to as thapas. Krishna told Arjuna that this coordination between thought, word, and deed is the real meaning of thapas and that thapas cannot be interpreted as standing on one leg. In fact, Krishna described standing on one leg as a mere physical exercise. The ideals that were handed over to us in the *Mahabharatha*, the ideal and exemplary life which Krishna led are important to us. I am hoping that the youth will put them into practice in their lives.

BIBLIOGRAPHY

Adas, Michael: *Machines as the Measure of Men: Science, Technology, and Ideologies of Western Dominance*, Ithaca, Cornell University Press, 1989.

Ahmad, Imtiaz: *State and Foreign Policy: India's Role in South Asia*, New Delhi, Vikas, 1993.

Ali, Tariq: *An Indian Dynasty: The Story of the Nehru-Gandhi Family*, New York, Putnam, 1985.

Austin, Granville: *The Indian Constitution: Cornerstone of a Nation*, Oxford, Clarendon Press, 1966.

Baird, Robert: *Religion in Modern India*, New Delhi, Manohar, 1981.

Baker, Christopher J.: *An Indian Rural Economy: The Tamiland Countryside*, Oxford, Clarendon Press, 1984.

Basham, A.L.: *A Cultural History of India*, Oxford, Clarendon Press, 1975.

Basham, A.L.: *The Origin and Development of Classical Hinduism*, New York, Oxford University Press, 1989.

Basham, A.L.: *The Wonder That Was India, 1: A Survey of the History and Culture of the Indian Sub-Continent Before the Coming of the Muslims*, London, Sidgwick and Jackson, 1967.

Bayly, C.A.: *Rulers, Townsmen, and Bazaars: North Indian Society in the Age of British Expansion, 1770-1870*, Cambridge, Cambridge University Press, 1983.

Bayly, C.A.: *The New Cambridge History of India : Indian Society and the Making of the British Empire*, Cambridge, Cambridge University Press, 1987.

Beach, Milo Cleveland: *The New Cambridge History of India: Mughal and Rajput Painting*, Cambridge, Cambridge University Press, 1992.

Brown, Judith M.: *Modern India: The Origins of an Asian Democracy*, New Delhi, Oxford University Press, 1985.

Chandra, Bipan: *Modern India*, New Delhi, National Council of Educational Research and Training, 1971.

Datta, V.N.: *Sati: Widow Burning in India*, New Delhi, Manohar, 1990.

Derrett, J. Duncan. *Religion, Law, and the State in India*. London: Faber, 1968.

Dikshit, D.P.: *Political History of the Chalukyas of Badami*, New Delhi, Abhinav, 1980.

Eaton, Richard M.: *The Rise of Islam and the Bengal Frontier, 1204-1760*, Berkeley, University of California Press, 1993.

Fairservis, Walter A.: *The Roots of Ancient India: The Archaeology of Early Indian Civilization*, New York, Macmillan, 1971.

Gandhi, Mahatma: *Non-Violent Resistance*, New York, Schocken, 1951.

Goalen, Paul: *India: From Mughal Empire to British Raj*, Cambridge, Cambridge University Press, 1993.

Hamilton, J.R.: *Alexander the Great*, Oxford, Clarendon Press, 1965.

Heinsath, Charles: *Indian Nationalism and Hindu Social Reform*, Princeton, Princeton University Press, 1964.

Jeffrey, Robin: *People, Princes, and Paramount Power: Society and Politics in Indian Princely States*, New Delhi, Oxford University Press, 1978.

Jones, Kenneth W.: *Arya Dharm: Hindu Consciousness in 19th Century Punjab*, Berkeley, University of California Press, 1976.

Kapur, Rajiv: *Sikh Separatism: The Politics of Faith*, New Delhi, Vikas, 1987.

Keay, John: *Democracy and Discontent: India's Growing Crisis of Governability*, Cambridge, Cambridge University Press, 1992.

Kopf, David: *The Brahmo Samaj and the Shaping of the Modern Indian Mind*, Princeton, Princeton University Press, 1979.

Mahalingam, T.V.: *Administration and Social Life under Vijayanagar*, Madras, University of Madras, 1969-75.

McLane, John R.: *Indian Nationalism and the Early Congress*, Princeton, Princeton University Press, 1977.

Minakshi, C.: *Administration and Social Life under the Pallavas*, Madras, University of Madras, 1977.

Noble, Allen G., and Ashok K. Dutt: *India: Cultural Patterns and Processes*, Boulder, Colorado, Westview Press, 1982.

Possehl, Gregory L.: *The Harappan Civilization*, London, Aris and Phillips, 1982.

Rudner, David W.: *Caste and Colonialism in Colonial India: The Nattukkottai Chettiars*, Berkeley, University of California Press, 1994.

Sharma, Kususm: *Ambedkar and Indian Constitution*, New Delhi, Ashish, 1992.

Singh, Harbans: *The Heritage of the Sikhs*, Columbia, Missouri, South Asia Books, 1983.

Thapar, Romila: *Ashoka and the Decline of the Mauryas*, London, Oxford University Press, 1961.

INDEX

G

H

I

J

K

L

M

N

O

P

R

□□□